Practical Development Environments

Other resources from O'Reilly

Practical Development Environments

Matthew B. Doar

O'REILLY®

Beijing • Cambridge • Farnham • Köln • Paris • Sebastopol • Taipei • Tokyo

Practical Development Environments
by Matthew B. Doar

Copyright © 2005 O'Reilly Media, Inc.
All rights reserved.
Printed in the United States of America.

Published by O'Reilly Media, Inc.
1005 Gravenstein Highway North
Sebastopol, CA 95472.

O'Reilly books may be purchased for educational, business, or sales promotional use. Online editions are also available for most titles (*safari.oreilly.com*). For more information, contact our corporate/institutional sales department: (800) 998-9938 or *corporate@oreilly.com*.

Editors:	Andrew Odewahn and Mary T. O'Brien
Production Editor:	A. J. Fox
Cover Designer:	MendeDesign
Interior Designer:	Marcia Friedman
Creative Director:	Michele Wetherbee
Printing History:	September 2005: First Edition.

RepKover™ This book uses RepKover™, a durable and flexible lay-flat binding.

ISBN: 0-596-00796-5

[M]

To all the toolsmiths who haven't yet
found a name for what they do

TABLE OF CONTENTS

LIST OF FIGURES

LIST OF TABLES

LIST OF EXAMPLES

Preface

A GOOD TECHNICAL ENVIRONMENT FOR DEVELOPING YOUR SOFTWARE can make or break a project, or even a company. What goes into a good technical development environment? This book contains helpful answers to that question and describes some of the current tools that can help provide a good software development environment. Areas covered include: version control, build tools, testing tools, bug tracking systems, documentation, release, and maintenance.

What This Book Is About

A *development environment* is the whole collection of tools that people use to create software, not just a few tools that are specific to a particular programming language. Examples of these tools are version control tools such as CVS, build tools such as *make*, and bug tracking tools such as Bugzilla. *Practical development environments* are the environments that are really used by successful projects, and are consequently reused for many different projects. Just as there is a wide range of productivity for different programmers, there is a wide range of productivity for different projects, and that's often due to differences in development environments.

This book is a guide—a collection of advice about real development environments. Each of the core chapters considers a different kind of tool: tools for tracking versions of files, build tools, testing tools, bug tracking tools, and tools for creating documentation. Each chapter discusses what you should look for in each kind of tool and what to avoid, and also describes some good ideas, bad ideas, and annoyances for each development activity. Specific instances of each type of tool are described in detail so that you can decide which ones you want to investigate further.

The tools described in this book are mostly intended for small to medium-sized projects, up to around 200 developers. However, the concepts and concerns described in each chapter are equally valid for large projects. One of the key ideas throughout this book is to automate wherever possible, and this becomes even more important as a project grows.

Finally, this book recognizes that some progress is better than none, and encourages you to take even the smallest steps to improve your own development environment.

What This Book Is Not About

This book is *not* about a set of abstract concepts, patterns, or a single way of doing things. It is a collection of practical, commonsense advice—the kind of ideas that you wish you had thought of before the project began. These ideas and concerns are valid for whatever programming methodology or programming language you use.

This book doesn't tell you how to write faster code, how to write code with fewer memory leaks, or even how to debug code. It does tell you how to compile your product faster, how to keep track of all the code you write, and how to track the bugs in your code. You will need to refer to other places for all the specific information about each tool. For example, this book doesn't provide detailed steps on how to set up a Subversion server.

One topic that is not covered in this book is IDEs (integrated development environments), which are editing tools (often for specific languages) with integrated access to tools such as the ones that are described throughout this book. The subject of editors and IDEs deserves an entire book to itself.

Although this book does describe many different tools, it's not simply an encyclopedia of tools. That kind of book or web site is useful for comparisons, but what is often more useful is information about what other projects are using, and how their tools are used. There are also many suggestions throughout the book about where to look for related tools, including Appendix B.

Nor is this book about developing hardware, though plenty of the advice and tools are applicable to hardware development environments.

Finally, this is not a book that uses words such as *paradigm* and *ontology*. In this book, companies and projects release products; they don't "optimize passions for agile solutions." And bugs are called bugs.

Who Should Read This Book

Much of this book is about choosing and using different tools to provide a satisfying software development environment. The people who do this are acting as *toolsmiths* for their software projects, whatever their official role is within the project. Sometimes the toolsmiths are developers; sometimes they are testers, managers, or technical leaders; sometimes they work in an IT group. Sometimes their main role is as an actual toolsmith for the project. The role of a toolsmith, whether by accident or design, is discussed further in Chapter 12.

As someone interested in this book, you probably fall into one of the following categories:

Tools, build, and release teams
> The toolsmiths who implement the software development environments for projects. You have probably come across many of the issues discussed in the book, but some are new.

Developers and testers
> The people who use the development environment but who want to write code, not maintain makefiles. Many developers and testers contribute to project environments, often through frustration with their current environment. This book should give you ideas for new tools and directions for your development environment.

Technical writers
> Again, people who use a development environment but who want to write words, not maintain templates. Likewise, this book should give you ideas for new tools and directions for your development environment.

Managers
> People who often first see long-term productivity problems with the current environment. Such longer-term issues are described in the book, as are many ideas for different tools.

System administrators/IT staff
> You provide the machines for all of the above groups but often don't have the time to maintain lots of different tools for other people. Still, you have to know what project members need and want in their environments. Many of the tools described in this book can also be used for your own IT environments.

What's Inside

Chapter 1, *Introduction*
> Describes the different activities involved in producing a piece of software; open and closed software development; and some classic situations that arise when developing software products.

Chapter 2, *Project Basics*

Describes the different areas of software development: SCM (software configuration management), building software, testing, tracking bugs, writing documentation, releasing products, and maintenance.

Chapter 3, *Project Concepts*

Discusses the concepts such as integration and automation that are used throughout a development environment. Preconstructed development environments such as SourceForge are also discussed in this chapter.

Chapter 4, *Software Configuration Management*

Discusses how to use SCM tools to keep track of different versions of files.

Chapter 5, *Building Software*

Discusses tools for building software from source files.

Chapter 6, *Testing Software*

Discusses testing software.

Chapter 7, *Tracking Bugs*

Describes different bug tracking tools, what to look for in them, and what to avoid.

Chapter 8, *Documentation Environments*

Describes some of the more common documentation tools and how they are used.

Chapter 9, *Releasing Products*

Discusses the process of releasing software.

Chapter 10, *Maintenance*

Discusses the problems of maintaining your environment, and also how development environments can help with the maintenance of older software products.

Chapter 11, *Project Communication*

Discusses ways to improve communication within your project.

Chapter 12, *Politics and People*

Offers a standalone collection of observations about what a toolsmith does for a development environment, and some other decidedly nontechnical aspects of software development environments.

Appendix A, *How Tools Scale*

Discusses how tools scale as a project grows.

Appendix B, *Resources*

Lists sources of information about software tools and development environments.

Note that prices where quoted are in U.S. dollars as of 2005 and should be used for guidance only. Please contact the vendor directly for an accurate price. The URLs in this book are correct as of August 2005.

Style Conventions

Items appearing in the book are sometimes given a special appearance to set them apart from the regular text. Here's how they look:

Italic

> Used for book titles, email addresses, URLs, filenames, and Unix tools such as *gdb*. Also used to emphasize text and to introduce new terms.

`Constant width`

> Used for literals, functions, labels related to builds (e.g., branch names), excerpts of code and command-line interaction, and XML/HTML markup.

`Constant width italic`

> Used for replaceable parameters and variables.

`Constant width bold`

> Used within command-line excerpts to highlight text typed by the user.

Using Code Examples

This book is here to help you get your job done. In general, you may use the code in this book in your programs and documentation. You do not need to contact us for permission unless you're reproducing a significant portion of the code. For example, writing a program that uses several chunks of code from this book does not require permission. Selling or distributing a CD-ROM of examples from O'Reilly books *does* require permission. Answering a question by citing this book and quoting example code does not require permission. Incorporating a significant amount of example code from this book into your product's documentation *does* require permission.

We appreciate, but do not require, attribution. An attribution usually includes the title, author, publisher, and ISBN. For example: "*Practical Development Environments* by Matthew B. Doar. Copyright 2005 O'Reilly Media, Inc., 0-596-00796-5."

If you feel your use of code examples falls outside fair use or the permission given above, feel free to contact us at *permissions@oreilly.com*.

Safari Enabled

 When you see a Safari® Enabled icon on the cover of your favorite technology book, that means the book is available online through the O'Reilly Network Safari Bookshelf.

Safari offers a solution that's better than e-books. It's a virtual library that lets you easily search thousands of top tech books, cut and paste code samples, download chapters, and find quick answers when you need the most accurate, current information. Try it for free at *http://safari.oreilly.com*.

Comments and Questions

We have tested and verified the information in this book to the best of our ability, but you may find that features have changed (or even that we have made mistakes!). Please let us know about any errors you find, as well as your suggestions for future editions, by writing to:

O'Reilly Media, Inc.
1005 Gravenstein Highway North
Sebastopol, CA 95472
(800) 998-9938 (in the United States or Canada)
(707) 829-0515 (international or local)
(707) 829-0104 (fax)

We have a web page for this book, where we list errata, examples, or any additional information. You can access this page at:

http://www.oreilly.com/catalog/practicalde

To remark on or ask technical questions about this book, send email to:

bookquestions@oreilly.com

You can sign up for one or more of our mailing lists at:

http://elists.oreilly.com

For more information about our books, conferences, software, Resource Centers, and the O'Reilly Network, see our web site at:

http://www.oreilly.com

Acknowledgments

I have a wonderful family—my beloved wife, Katherine, and my dear children, Lizzie, Jacob, and Luke—who all supported me in writing this book and then left me alone, except when they didn't. My mother, Susan, is all I could ask for, and much more. May the love of God rest and remain with you always, and thank you.

I have also enjoyed numerous conversations with insightful colleagues and friends, especially Bill Willcox, Steve Colyvas, and the brothers Josh and Alex Siegel. My father-in-law, Joe Baginski, had an amazing 42 years of relevant development experience with IBM, and I don't think there's much in this book that will catch him unawares. I particularly appreciated two years of carpooling with Tim Kolar, Lol Grant, and Derek Godfrey. They finally convinced me that not everything has to have an analogy, and I believe this book feels better for that, metaphorically speaking. I also want to thank my colleagues at Trapeze Networks and Venturi Wireless for their understanding when I was sometimes mentally absent while writing this book.

At O'Reilly, I am grateful to Mike Hendrickson for taking on this unexpected book, and to my editor Andrew Odewahn, who has opened my eyes to the wonder that is professional editing. My thanks to Andrew Savikas for describing the O'Reilly documentation environment, and to Mary O'Brien, Rob Romano, and Abby Fox for all their work in making this book what it is.

My thanks to Hugh Doar, Marie Godfrey, Jeff Jahr, Karl Klashinsky, Peter Miller, and Dan Shahin for their helpful comments on different parts of the book. Thanks to Steve Reinheimer too for his help with the reviews. I'm particularly grateful to Mark Baushke, Steven Knight, and Steve Loughran for their extensive comments, which covered the whole book. Any errors that remain are, of course, solely mine.

As I was researching this book, I was struck by the differences between 2005 and the early 1990s when I was researching material for my PhD thesis. There were a few specialized research sites available then, but not very many. Then! Yahoo! arrived! closely followed by Gooooogle. While by no means all-seeing, Google certainly found plenty of opinions about everything in this book, so thanks to the people who created and maintain it.

For the necessary stimulants to keep me going when writing the book was hard, I'd like to thank the Coca-Cola Company for its caffeine, the plantations of Arturo Fuente for their nicotine, and the Laphroaig distillery for its alcohol.

> Writing a book is an adventure. To begin with, it is a toy and an amusement. Then it becomes a mistress, then it becomes a master, then it becomes a tyrant. The last phase is that just as you are about to be reconciled to your servitude, you kill the monster and fling him to the public.
>
> —*Winston Churchill*

## CHAPTER ONE

Introduction

Projects have Environments in which People produce Products.

"PITHY, BUT PAINFUL," WAS A FRIEND'S WRY REPLY** when I asked his opinion of the above epigraph as a summary for this book. At a very high level, it really does describe the creation of software. The key word is *environments*, which in this book refers to all the tools used to produce software and how they are used, but not the details of how the software is written, or even what language the software is written in. For this book, an environment includes the software configuration management (SCM) tools, build tools, testing and bug tracking tools, and the release and maintenance processes. All these areas are covered in subsequent chapters of this book.

This chapter begins with an overview of how a software product is typically created. If you are involved in this process from day to day, you will probably be familiar with most of the steps. The amount of work in each step is different for different projects, groups of people, or companies, but all the steps appear in some guise. This chapter also briefly describes the difference between open and closed software.

The chapter then continues with some uncomfortable software development mistakes that most developers have stumbled across; avoiding these costly mistakes justifies reading the rest of this book.

Developing Software Products

Figure 1-1 shows the different activities that are generally involved in creating a software product, though it's only a loose description of what really happens when developing software. The activities probably don't occur in the same order in your experience, and each one is often repeated many times as a product is developed and maintained. You can probably also add some other arrows from experience with different projects that you've worked on. Some projects may not even have had all their activities connected, which is one of the things that a good development environment can help you with.

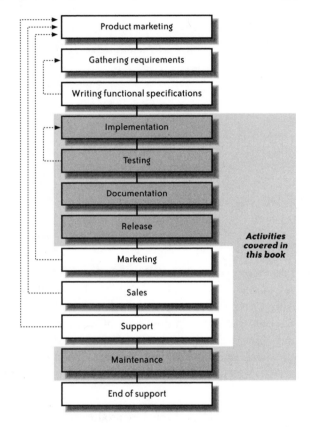

FIGURE 1-1. Typical activities involved in creating software products

Large or small, formal or more relaxed, open or closed (see "Open and Closed Software Development," later in this chapter), all software projects have activities that resemble those shown in Figure 1-1. A short description of each activity follows:

Product marketing

This goes by many names, but whatever it is called, it always involves creating the ideas for the product. A subtle blend of technical knowledge about what has been done and what might be possible is combined with some imaginative flair for what might actually be wanted by potential customers. This is different from general marketing, which is described below.

Gathering requirements

The process of collecting information to clearly communicate to everyone in the project exactly what the product is supposed to do. Some different ways that this information can be described include documents, prototypes, and examples of how the product would be used.

Writing functional specifications

Functional specifications describe how the product can be created to fulfill the requirements.

Implementation

The gritty edge, where the product is actually created. A surprisingly small amount of the total time to develop a product is usually spent here.

Testing

This is where the implementation is compared with the requirements. A surprisingly large amount of the total time to develop a product is usually spent here, and yet this is commonly the first thing removed from busy schedules.

Documentation

Documentation describes how to use the product. Internal documentation may also describe how to maintain the product for future developers. Often written by a group called something like Technical Publications.

Release

The process of shipping the product to customers and making sure that the product will work properly outside the environment in which it was developed.

Marketing

Creating and controlling the market for the product. It also involves changing the product to suit the market, which connects back to the product marketing stage.

Sales

Persuading customers to use the product, often with the expectation that they will pay money for it.

Support

Helps the customers use the product when the documentation doesn't answer their questions. Support also provides a contact point for any licenses needed to use the product, and may cover training as well.

Maintenance

If the product is commercial or is widely used, then as the world around it changes, the product will need work to keep it functioning properly and hence producing more revenue and happy customers.

End of support

Eventually no one wants to buy or use the product, not even the developers. Customers need to be told when product support will end, and the whole development environment and source files need to be carefully archived.

Some projects have particularly small or nonexistent activities, or the different activities may be connected very differently. For instance, the requirements document in a small startup company can often be the result of a late-evening "wouldn't it be cool if..." session. A large project with hundreds of developers may have rigid requirements, with regular quarterly meetings to discuss changes to the design documents. Some activities not mentioned above include those performed by management, IT staff, and the legal department—all necessary overhead.

Open and Closed Software Development

Traditionally, software development is *closed*. This means that whether or not users are charged for the actual product, the source files that are used to create the product are confidential. Sometimes you can purchase the source, but that's extra.

Open software development refers to a number of different ideas about software development. The best known one is that the source files for the product are openly and freely available, so customers can change the source files and then rebuild the product themselves, at least in theory. The source files may also be free, as in costing nothing. Many open source projects also allow anyone to redistribute the source files, subject to the requirement that if you make changes, you must make those changes publicly available. If you continue to distribute the changes you make to a product, then you may have produced a *fork* of the project, and the product will have become two different products. Forks are an accepted part of open software development.

Examples of some well-known open source software products are shown in Table 1-1.

TABLE 1-1. Major open software projects

Software	URL	Description
Apache	*http://www.apache.org*	Most of the world's web sites run on the Apache web server.
GCC	*http://gcc.gnu.org*	The most widely used compiler for C and other languages.
GNU/Linux[1]	*http://www.linux.org*	The best-known open source Unix-based operating system.
Mozilla	*http://www.mozilla.org*	The Firefox web browser and many other Mozilla projects that grew out of the original Netscape browser.
Perl	*http://www.perl.org*	Powerful scripting languages, also known as *dynamic* languages.
Python	*http://www.python.org*	
Tcl	*http://tcl.sourceforge.net*	

[1] The term *GNU/Linux* is generally used instead of *Linux* throughout this book, since almost every Linux distribution is shipped with GNU tools.

The idea of open source development was pioneered by the Free Software Foundation, or FSF (*http://www.fsf.org*), founded by Richard Stallman in 1984; it has produced hundreds of open source products under the banner of the GNU Project (*http://www.gnu.org*). The FSF prefers to use the term *free* rather than *open* for this kind of software.

The Open Source Initiative, or OSI (*http://www.opensource.org*), was founded in 1998 and describes itself as a marketing program for free software. The OSI tends to distance itself from some of the philosophical positions of the FSF. As might be inferred from the name, the OSI uses the term *open* for this kind of software. Eric Raymond is one of the best-known people associated with the OSI.

> **NOTE**
>
> You may also come across the compromise acronym F/OSS for "free/open source software," or the terms *gratis* for "free as in beer" (no cost) and *libre* for "free as in freedom."

There are a confusing number of different licenses for open source software. The best-known one is the GNU General Public License (GPL) from the FSF. The most common confusion about the GPL seems to be whether using source files that were distributed under the GPL means that the rest of a product's source files must be made publicly available. It all seems to depend on how the GPL-licensed source files are used by the proprietary part of the product. I am not a lawyer, but there's a useful book on this subject by someone who is: *Understanding Open Source and Free Software Licensing,* by Andrew M. St. Laurent (O'Reilly).

Regardless of whether a project is open or closed, each of the activities listed earlier in "Developing Software Products" is present. Customers for closed software are people and companies who have paid money to use the product. Customers for open software are people and companies who use the product, and they may well pay for support. Both kinds of software have to track the different legal licenses used for different parts of the product. Development environments for closed and open software projects often differ only in how much money will be spent on tools.

Although this book contains many references to open source projects and open source tools, creating a good development environment is about choosing the most appropriate tools. Both closed and open source tools are discussed in this book.

Dirty Secrets of Software Projects

Software projects can fail for many reasons, and one of them is a bad development environment. Here is an informal list of some frustrations and embarrassing mistakes commonly made in producing software. None of these have anything to do with failures caused by things like missing specifications, specifications changing over time (the dreaded "feature creep"), poor estimates of how long a project will take, or even whether the problem being solved is a really difficult one. Each of these problems is due to the tools or processes of the environment in which the software was produced:

- We can't rebuild the same product that we shipped to the customer, so we'll ship her the latest version, just to be safe.

- Building from scratch (also known as a *clean build*) each time is often the only way to get the product to build reliably. This takes so long that the developer goes off and does something else. Consequently, every developer thinks that his build tool is too slow.

- Testers, technical writers, and managers can't build the latest version of the product. Even if it has already been built for them by someone else, it's unclear where to find the latest version.

- Fixes for known bugs are not released, because it's too hard to properly test the required changes and they may break other parts of the product.

- Everyone finds the bug tracking tool awkward to use.

- The environment used by developers and the one in which the product is used by customers are different in some important ways, so the developers never actually see problems the same way that a customer does.

- Getting a product ready to release takes so long that any late-arriving changes don't get tested or documented.

- The wrong set of bits gets shipped to the customer. This one should make anyone involved in developing software wince, but it does happen.

- Nobody knows when to remove a feature from a product, because no one knows whether the feature is actually being used.

- Communication between groups happens by reading printouts left at the printer nearest to the coffee machine.

Sadly, the list could go on and on. Its contents are obviously subjective, but each entry has happened in real projects. The good news is that none of these Dirty Secrets are inevitable and they can all be eliminated with careful attention to the development environment. The promise of this book is that you can stop these kinds of embarrassments from happening to your project.

What Does "Practical" Mean?

What makes something practical? The title of this book strongly suggests that its contents are about practical solutions to common problems in development environments. Here is what *practical* means for the tools used in development environments:

- Available (whether open or closed source)

- Appropriately priced (for open software, this often means no cost)

- Usable—installation and configuration to match the local development process is possible, the tool doesn't crash regularly, there aren't too many bugs, and documentation is adequate

- Can eventually produce software for the platforms used by the customer

On the other hand, impractical tools for development environments are those that are:

- Dead—no longer sold or supported

- Too expensive to even consider spending any time evaluating

- Tortuous to get working or configured as needed, or impossible to maintain and upgrade

Abstract frameworks, conceptual models, and design patterns are all useful for categorizing solutions to problems encountered in development environments, but the aim of this book is to provide ideas that are more practical. The basic areas of projects that are summarized in the next chapter are ideas that are applicable to all software projects, whatever the product's purpose is and whoever the customers are.

A Personal Tools Quiz

To make the ideas in this book seem more personal, try answering the following questions (honestly):

- Name the biggest mistake that you, personally, made in each of your last three projects. Program design doesn't count; tools and processes do.

- Name the biggest mistake you think *someone else* made in your last three projects.

- Imagine that you could totally replace just one software tool that you use daily. Which one would it be, and why?

- Which tool is so good that you would have to be seriously bribed to be persuaded to stop using it?

- Which part of producing software just seems to take much longer than it should? Do you feel that you really understand what goes on in that part?

Your answers should give you some good ideas about which parts of this book will particularly interest you. It was questions like these, and a lack of written guidance on addressing the issues raised by their answers, that made me want to write this book in the first place.

## CHAPTER TWO

Project Basics

THIS CHAPTER BRIEFLY DESCRIBES THE DIFFERENT PARTS OF A PROJECT and then introduces the main activities invoved in software development and the corresponding tools that make up a development environment. The activities are software configuration management (SCM), building software, testing software, tracking bugs, writing documentation, releasing products, and maintenance. This chapter ends with some personal recommendations of tools for three different types of development environments.

Whether you are starting a project from scratch or looking to improve an existing development environment, my opinion is that *you should consider the different parts of the environment in the same order used in this chapter* and in this book. That is, SCM is the most important part of an environment; next in importance are the build tools, then testing and bug tracking, and so on. This is because your choice of SCM tool is likely to have the largest impact on your environment. This is not to say that any of the parts are unimportant, just that improving how your SCM tool and build tool are used will probably improve your environment more than improving the bug tracking tool or release process. Similarly, if you are creating a new project, an SCM tool should be chosen before a bug tracking tool.

The Parts of a Project

Figure 2-1 shows the different parts of a single project. This project has source files that become products, and those products have customers who use the products. The project has project members (developers, testers, technical writers, toolsmiths, managers, and product marketing staff), who are also customers for their own products. The development environment for this project is made up of both the tools and the local processes and policies for using those tools.

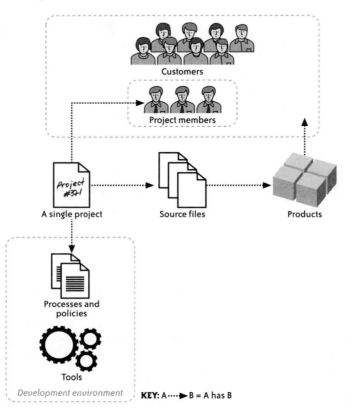

FIGURE 2-1. Different parts of a project

If there are many projects within an organization, then each project will have some areas that overlap and some that don't. For instance, two projects may have different policies about how to use the same bug tracking tool. The processes and tools are chosen to work with the source files but need to be able to operate even when the same source files are used by different projects with different policies.

Software Configuration Management

SCM, the subject of Chapter 4, is the ability to keep track of different versions of the source files that are used to create software products. Even when just one person is changing these source files, it's very useful to be able to see how a file evolved over time or even to undo some changes that in hindsight you regret making. As projects grow in size and complexity, effective SCM tools become vital. To put it another way, projects that don't use an SCM tool won't grow successfully.

SCM tools also provide a good way to share your work with other people in a controlled manner. Rather than just using a common location such as a directory to exchange files with other people, with an SCM tool you can make sure that interdependent files are changed together and you can control who is allowed to make changes. SCM tools also allow you to save messages about what changed in the source files, and also why the files were changed, which can be used to work out which releases a particular bug was fixed in.

Many SCM tools provide ways to support one or more existing releases of a product, while still allowing the team to develop the next release using different versions of the same source files. For instance, after a product is released, all the source files for that release can be marked (or even *branched*) to allow future bug fixes for that release, while the next release is developed independently.

Chapter 4 describes all of the above in more detail and examines seven of the most commonly used or promising SCM tools: CVS, Subversion, Arch, Perforce, BitKeeper, ClearCase, and Visual SourceSafe.

Building Software

Software products are built from their source files, also known as *source code*, which is often the collection of files stored in an SCM tool. A build tool uses the source files and follows some specified build rules to run other tools such as compilers to create the product from the source files. These build rules are usually specified in configuration files known as *build files*, which are part of the source files for a product.

Build tools have to be aware of which products can be built from a given set of source files and other files such as libraries. They also have to know which parts of the product depend on which other parts, so that if one source file is changed by a developer, then all the other affected parts will also be rebuilt. Build tools should be able to execute the correct commands for building the same product on different platforms, while hiding the idiosyncrasies of each platform from the product's developers as much as possible. Build tools are also used to generate executables that run on platforms other than the platform that the build tool is actually run on; this is known as *cross-compiling*.

Chapter 5 describes what to look for in a build tool and examines some commonly used build tools such as *make*, Ant, Jam, and SCons in more detail.

Testing Software

Testing a product spans the range from individual developers writing unit tests that check small parts of an application, to system tests that use the whole application, to customers giving feedback about how they really want the product to work. Chapter 6 focuses on testing environments for unit tests and system tests.

One of the cornerstones of the XP (extreme programming) methodology is the importance of extensive unit tests, written even before the functionality that they test has been written. No matter what your methodology or style of programming is, a healthy test suite is good for reassuring yourself that your latest changes haven't broken some other distant part of the product.

Of course, running all those different tests and interpreting their results quickly becomes tedious; if testing is not automated, it is often postponed and then finally abandoned. So it's important when developing and maintaining a product to have a test environment where tests can be added easily and run easily, and where the test results can be clearly understood.

Tracking Bugs

Testing a product provides information about which parts of it are working and which are not. This information needs to be made available to developers, other testers, managers, the people that decide when a product is ready for release, and also to those who support a product. Bug tracking tools are commonly used to do this. Bugs are sometimes referred to as *issues*, because they are often requests for changes or some other category; some other terms, particularly *defect* and *incident*, can have legal implications and are best avoided if possible. The term *bug* is used colloquially throughout this book to refer to all these categories.

Bug tracking tools often store information about bugs in a database and then provide convenient GUIs and command-line interfaces (CLIs) for adding information about bugs to the database, changing the information recorded about bugs, and creating reports about different kinds of bugs. At a minimum, a recorded bug has a description of the bug (what happened, what should have happened) and an identifier that is unique for each different bug. Other information that is frequently recorded with each bug includes who found it, the steps to reproduce it, who is working on it now, which releases the bug exists in, and which releases it has been fixed in.

Many bug tracking systems define a number of states and allow each bug to be in just one state at a time. This is intended to help guide the workflow of the team when they are working on different bugs. For instance, a new bug may be in the Open state, then move to an Accepted state, then to a Fixed state, and then to a Closed state. This is part of applying a *change management* process (see "What SCM Is and Is Not" in Chapter 4) to how you want bugs to be fixed.

Tracking bugs is a lot more than just not forgetting what still needs fixing in a product. For good and bad, it becomes a way to measure development and testing progress toward the next version. Observing the numbers of bugs in different states over time can play a part in deciding when a product is stable enough to ship. It is also a rather simplistic way to measure how busy individuals are—for instance, by the number of bugs they have assigned to them. As such, bug totals often take on a meaning far beyond a simple record of the problems in a project. Bug tracking tools can even become a way to avoid communicating directly with other project members, as described in "Twisted Communications" in Chapter 12.

Chapter 7 discusses many more aspects of bug tracking and examines some of the more commonly used bug tracking systems: spreadsheets, Bugzilla, GNATS, FogBugz, JIRA, and TestTrack.

Writing Documentation

An ideal product is so transparent that it needs (almost) no documentation. Software products that are as well-designed and well-implemented as this Platonic ideal are rare indeed, so documentation is an expected part of all products. Whether the documentation is a simple *README* file, a large manual that ships with the product, or interactive help available when the product is used, the contents still have to be written by somebody, usually a technical writer.

Chapter 8 takes the viewpoint that the documentation is part of the product and that there are plenty of similarities between writing software and writing documentation. For instance, large documents are made up of smaller ones; different parts of a document depend on other parts of the document; and both source code and natural-language documents can benefit from tools, whether they are compiler warning flags or spellcheckers.

Another similarity between software and documentation is that both are transformed from one file format into other file formats as part of being released. A source file is compiled to an executable. A document is often written in one source file format (such as Microsoft Word or FrameMaker) and then converted to another release format (such as HTML or PDF, Adobe's Portable Document Format) for use by the customer. Some commonly used documentation formats are discussed in "File Formats for Documentation" in Chapter 8 (HTML, PostScript, and PDF) and "More File Formats" in Chapter 8 (TeX, Texinfo, *troff,* and POD).

A different aspect of documentation is when it is intended for use by a project itself. An example of this is when the APIs (application programming interfaces) of different parts of a product are documented to help other developers use them. There are a number of tools, such as Javadoc, to help with this, and these are also examined in "Internal Project Documentation" in Chapter 8.

Chapter 8 also examines in more detail a variety of file formats and their related documentation environments, including raw text, FrameMaker, XML in DocBook and OpenOffice, and Microsoft Word.

Releasing Products

Once a product has been developed, tested, and documented, it eventually becomes ready to release. You want to release the software according to some predetermined plan. Too often, however, products just escape into the hands of customers because no one considered issues such as release numbers and license keys before releasing the product. Chapter 9 describes all of this.

With the increase in malicious software, assuring customers that the files they download are actually the same as the ones that you released is becoming an essential part of releasing software products. The use of digital signatures and checksums to help with this is discussed further in "Securing Your Releases" in Chapter 9.

Since installing a product is often a customer's first experience of the software, and first impressions count, the installation process is important. Chapter 9 also examines the most common packaging formats and installation tools for a variety of platforms, as well as some common irritations with installation tools and the installers that they produce.

Maintenance

Maintenance of a product after it has been released takes up a large part of a product's life span. Chapter 10 describes some typical product maintenance activities and how the tools in a development environment can help you with them.

How to maintain a development environment is also discussed, including what kinds of things stop working as an environment ages and how to know when to throw tools and files away.

Recommended Tools

This section contains my personal recommendations for tools for development environments. The recommendations are intended for projects with less than 1 million lines of source code and under 200 people involved in developing, testing, documenting, and releasing the product. The annual budget for tools probably ranges from zero to $100,000. These choices are purely personal ones made from the tools available in 2005, with no undue influences from any individual companies or projects.

> ### NOTE
>
> If you use a tool that you feel is much better than one of the tools I've recommended, feel free to send me email about it via *bookquestions@oreilly.com*. My own contact details are available at *http://www.pobox.com/~doar*.
>
> IDE recommendations are also welcome, but rants about editors (the programs, not the people) are generally unproductive—use one that does the job for you, and learn it well.

If these recommendations are enough for you to make progress with a development environment, that's great! Reading the sections about each tool later in the book is still a good idea to get some more background, especially "Choosing New Tools" in Chapter 3.

However, a development environment is more than just its tools. The discussions of the best practices and annoyances of each area in the chapters that follow will help you use each of these tools in a more productive manner.

Modern Environments

This list of tools is for environments that can afford the effort of using tools that are still themselves being developed. Some reading of mailing lists and weblogs, and possibly some local development of the tools by a toolsmith, may be necessary.

SCM tool
> Subversion ("Subversion" in Chapter 4) with FishEye (*http://www.cenqua.com/fisheye*)

Build tool
> Ant ("Ant" in Chapter 5) for projects using Java™; SCons ("SCons" in Chapter 5) for most projects and other languages

Test environment
> xUnit ("xUnit" in Chapter 6)

Bug tracker
> JIRA ("JIRA" in Chapter 7)

Documentation
> Anything that uses an XML source file format with an open DTD or schema; examples include OpenOffice and DocBook ("XML: DocBook and OpenOffice" in Chapter 8)

Classic Environments

This list of tools is for environments that want to use tools that have been stable for a number of releases and have an extensive support network. These are the tools that you can buy more than one book about.

SCM tool
> CVS ("CVS" in Chapter 4) with FishEye (*http://www.cenqua.com*); alternatively, Perforce ("Perforce" in Chapter 4)

Build tool
> Ant ("Ant" in Chapter 5) for projects using Java; otherwise, *make* ("make" in Chapter 5)

Test environment
> xUnit ("xUnit" in Chapter 6)

Bug tracker
> FogBugz ("FogBugz" in Chapter 7), but only if the preconfigured settings work for you; otherwise, TestTrack ("TestTrack" in Chapter 7)

Documentation
> FrameMaker ("FrameMaker" in Chapter 8)

Future Environments

This is a list of how I foresee development environment tools changing in the next five years. Most of these tools don't exist yet, though the foundations for them certainly do. An important question for future development environments will be how well each of the tools is integrated with the other tools—SCM with bug tracking is one example—and how much of the process of using them can be automated.

SCM tool

BitKeeper ("BitKeeper" in Chapter 4) or Arch ("Arch" in Chapter 4), but with better integration with bug tracking systems and a clearer view of recent changes.

Build tool

SCons ("SCons" in Chapter 5), with mappings from other languages so that you can write Perl or Java build files as well as Python build files. Support for parallel builds on multiple machines as well.

Test environment

More extensions to the xUnit architecture ("xUnit" in Chapter 6) to support system tests and historical reports of test results.

Bug tracker

A bug tracking system based on an SCM tool, so that every single change to the whole system is recorded. Better built-in support for a bug that appears in multiple releases of a product is also long overdue. Better integration with build tools, so that it's easier to know which bugs were fixed in which releases. Support for changing bugs while disconnected from a network could also be useful.

Documentation

I would hope that a real typesetting tool such as T$_E$X and all the concepts of literate programming will come back into style one day. Until then, anything that uses an XML source file format with an open DTD or schema.

Release

Better automatic deployment of software products, along with any other pieces of required software. Doing this both atomically and efficiently. Better integration of installation tools with build processes.

As an imaginative finale, with the increased importance of licensing for software, one useful option for a compiler might be the ability to understand various common licenses in source files. Functions from each source code file could then be identified by their license type, and only fully license-compatible libraries and executables would be created. In fact, there are already companies such as Black Duck Software (*http://blackducksoftware.com*) and Palamida (*http://palamida.com*) that provide tools to enforce what is referred to as "software compliance management."

## CHAPTER THREE

Project Concepts

THIS CHAPTER DESCRIBES IDEAS THAT ARE PART OF A DEVELOPMENT ENVIRONMENT but are not specific to any particular kind of tool. Examples of such ideas are the following:

- Preconstructed environments, where all the tools for a development environment are provided "out of the box" for you

- Integration of tools to make them work better together

- Automation of the different parts of software creation

- Naming schemes

- Internationalization of products and tools for use in other countries

Preconstructed Development Environments

Preconstructed development environments (PDEs) are what I have chosen to call software development environments that are provided as a single set of software applications. (Whether or not they are *practical* development environments, as in the title of this book, is a separate issue for each PDE.) Another name sometimes used for them is *collaborative development environments,* but it seems to me that development environments are always collaborative, and what sets these environments apart is that they come ready-made, prefabricated—in short, preconstructed.

If you are setting up a development environment and one of these environments works for you, maybe you won't have to choose every tool to use in your environment. Still, the other chapters in this book contain much more than just which tool to choose, so read on.

One well-known example of a PDE is SourceForge (*http://www.sourceforge.net*), which uses the term "software development website" to describe itself. A typical PDE provides an SCM tool, a bug tracking tool, a project home page, and somewhere to download released files from. Some PDEs also provide online discussion forums, weblogs, and "farms" of different machines for developing ports of the project to multiple platforms and for running tests. Some even provide databases ready for use by the different projects. Still others have usage statistics for each project and places to post requests for help or jobs. The various parts of the PDE should all work together and, as much as possible, already be configured to make hosting your project quick and easy.

PDEs are rather like preconstructed houses. They are quick to set up and start living in, but they can be harder to change later on. One benefit is that once you have used a particular PDE for one project, it becomes easy to find your way around other projects that are using the same PDE. Once you have found the statistics for one SourceForge project, you know where to look for the statistics for every other SourceForge project.

Another analogy is to writing a document. You can choose to either use a text editor to create the document locally on your own machine exactly as you want it, or enter the text on a remote machine (as with weblogs and *Wiki* entries), leaving the effort of formatting and publishing the document to someone else. (Wikis are web sites that can be modified by anyone.)

Some of the potential benefits of PDEs are:

Ease of integration and use
> All the necessary parts of the environment should work together in a standard, straightforward way, which should make them easier to use.

Lower administrative costs
> If the environment is a remote one, then the environment provider may be able to spread the costs of toolsmiths (or whoever supports the necessary applications) over multiple projects. If the environment is installed locally, then having fewer knobs to twiddle may mean that there is less custom work to be done by toolsmiths.

However, the benefits of preconstructed environments should be tempered with the following potential problems:

Customization
> Many software development teams are used to being able to tweak their development environment. Part of this may be due to the Unix philosophy of using lots of smaller tools rather than one big tool. Preconstructed environments are often not really designed to be modified beyond some carefully exposed portions of the existing APIs of their underlying tools.

Register Your O'Reilly Book!
oreilly.com/go/register

Register your books to receive important updates, upgrade offers and our catalog. Go to *oreilly.com/go/register*, or complete and return this postage paid card.

Name

Company/Organization

Address

City   State   Zip/Postal Code   Country

Email address   Telephone

Book Title   ISBN #

Book Title   ISBN #

Book Title   ISBN #

Security

If an open source remote environment is used, the project's source files and data may become publicly available. If an environment that supports closed projects is used, one where the source files and data are not public, then separate projects have to be very carefully insulated from each other. This is possible (for instance, by using virtual machines), but it does require careful configuration and monitoring to be truly secure.

Backups

Many environments will regularly provide each project with a collection of files suitable for backups, but it is still up to some project member to make sure that the backups actually occur. Testing the recovery of backups is also hard to do in some preconstructed environments.

Portability

One concern that is also related to backups is how to extract a project's source files along with all its history, bugs, mailing list archives, and documentation from a particular environment. For instance, what happens if the environment provider goes out of business, or changes its terms of usage? It generally helps if the backups are in a standard, open format that can be imported by other tools. Just as with office software suites, it's usually much easier to import projects into PDEs than to export projects from them.

OUTSOURCING YOUR ENVIRONMENT

The idea of outsourced development environments, which is akin to the idea of an application service provider, seems to have grown up with the Internet in the late 1990s. Perhaps part of the reason is that various services such as search engines are provided remotely, but there is also great interest in how the same development environments can be provided for use within companies. After all, if a company can outsource its IT department or developers, it may also make sense to outsource the creation and maintenance of the tools used to develop the software.

Before you outsource your development environment, make sure that you have good answers about how much you can customize the environment, how secure it is, how backups are performed and tested, and how you would extract your project from the environment to move it somewhere else.

The differences between many PDEs are whether the source code that integrates the various parts of the PDE is open or closed source, and which tools are supported. If you want an exhaustive comparison of various open source PDEs, see the thorough "Comparison of Free/Open Source Project Hosting Sites," by Haggen So (*http://www.ibiblio.org/fosphost*). For now, I'll focus on the most popular PDEs: SourceForge, GForge, CollabNet, Savane, and BerliOS. These five PDEs are compared briefly in Table 3-1. The values for the number of projects and number of users are taken from each PDE's web site in August 2005. A plus sign (+) indicates a strength and a minus sign (–) indicates a relative weakness, either in features or usability.

TABLE 3-1. Comparison of PDEs

Feature	SourceForge	GForge	CollabNet	Savane	BerliOS
Location	*sourceforge.net*	Various	*tigris.org*	*savannah.gnu.org*	*developer.berlios.de*
Number of projects	100,000	5,000	500	2,200	2,200
Number of users	1,000,000	130,000	Thousands	32,000	11,000
SCM tools	CVS, ViewCVS	CVS, ViewCVS, Subversion	CVS, ViewCVS, Subversion	CVS, ViewCVS	CVS, Subversion
Bug tracking	–	+	+	–	–
Other tools	Databases, compile farm, donations, and more	Time tracking, themes	Better searching	Overall site statistics	Multiple languages supported
PDE source open/closed	Closed	Open	Closed	Open	Open
Cost	$0; $40/year for better searching and support; or $2,750 for the commercial version	$0	$0; or $2,400 for the commercial version	$0	$0

SourceForge

SourceForge (*http://www.sourceforge.net*) is the original PDE, dating back to early 2000. The software to run the web site was originally open source but was then closed when the SourceForge web site was announced. As of 2005, it remains the largest PDE, both by number of registered projects (over 100,000) and users (over 1 million), though many of the projects are inactive. SourceForge is designed for open source projects and has mechanisms for donating to projects. Each project has access to a wide range of (mostly standalone) tools linked by a central project home page. There is also an option to subscribe to Source-Forge for around $40/year, which gives you better searching abilities over all the projects, higher-priority technical support, and direct downloading of files. The bug tracking system is fairly basic. For example, you can add categories for your project's bugs but can't remove old categories.

There is also a commercial version of SourceForge, SourceForge Enterprise Edition, which is available from *http://www.vasoftware.com* for around $2,750 per user. Some advantages of the commercial product are that it was designed for integrating with a wider range of different applications; security and access control is better supported; and it has a greater ability to search the project's source files and documentation.

GForge

GForge (*http://www.gforge.com*) is an open source PDE, though the GForge Group calls it a "collaborative development environment." The source code for GForge is a fork of the last open source version of SourceForge's source code. Numerous changes, including support for Subversion, have been made since then. Commercial support and even "plug and play" machines with GForge preinstalled are provided by the GForge Group, which includes some of the core GForge developers. The GForge Group itself does not provide any public project space using GForge, but it estimates that there are around 5,000 projects and 130,000 users of GForge. GForge 4.0 was released in October 2004.

While GForge is open source, there are compelling arguments for using a preconfigured server or commercial support if GForge is being used in a corporate environment. For one, GForge has many different software components to be installed and configured. Customization of GForge in such a way that future upgrades will be possible is always going to be easier if the core developers do it.

CollabNet

CollabNet Enterprise Edition (formerly SourceCast) from CollabNet (*http://www.collab.net*) is a commercial "collaborative software development environment." CollabNet was founded in 1999 by Brian Behelendorf and O'Reilly & Associates. As of 2005, the product costs around $2,400 per developer per year. Unlike the commercial PDEs from GForge or SourceForge, CollabNet maintains its system as a managed service for its customers. The development of CollabNet is itself distributed around the world and coordinated using CollabNet. The open source NetBeans IDE project (*http://www.netbeans.org*) is a good example of CollabNet in action, as is Sun's Java community at *http://java.net*.

Tigris (*http://www.tigris.org*) is a free web site run by CollabNet to encourage the development of better open source software tools for collaborative software development. There are hundreds of relatively active projects hosted at Tigris, and the projects are carefully chosen to match the goals of the Tigris community. One of the best-known Tigris projects is Subversion, the SCM tool intended as a replacement for CVS (see "CVS" and "Subversion" in Chapter 4). CollabNet offers Subversion as one option for its SCM tool. CollabNet also provides hosting and the development environment for the SCM tool CVS at *http://www.cvshome.org*.

Savane

Savane (*https://gna.org/projects/savane*) is the open source software package used to run GNU's Savannah PDE, which is where GNU software is developed (*http://savannah.gnu.org*). It also runs *http://savannah.nongnu.org* for other non-GNU free software development. Savane is also used to run the GNA! PDE at *https://gna.org*. The source code for Savane is a fork of the last open source version of SourceForge's source code. As of 2005, there are over 2,000 projects and nearly 30,000 registered users. Support for Savane is informal, but enthusiastic.

BerliOS

BerliOS is a service funded by the German government and industry to encourage the development and use of open source software. Services are available in German, English, and Spanish. As of 2005, around 2,200 projects with just over 10,000 users are active at BerliOS Developer (*http://developer.berlios.de*), the PDE provided by Berlios. BerliOS also provides DocsWell, a database for open source–related documentation; SourceWell, a news service for open source projects; SourceLines, a best-practice database for successful open source projects; SourceBiz, a list of open source companies; DevCounter, a database of open source developer profiles; and OpenFacts, a Wiki-based open source knowledge database.

Just like Savane and GForge, BerliOS Developer is based on early SourceForge source code and is still open source. Installation documentation for BerliOS Developer is rather scarce, probably since it is similar to SourceForge installation.

Improving PDEs

It's one thing to use a remote preconstructed environment such as SourceForge, where you're depending upon a remote group of toolsmiths to develop and maintain your development environment for you. It's quite another to expect to be able to run a single installation command and have a working SCM tool, a bug tracking tool, a web server, and so on. No PDE that I'm aware of is there yet, but I think that this is where PDEs should be heading. The alternative is to have a consulting company such as the aforementioned GForge Group do it all for you.

Another area where PDEs could be improved is in the integration of their different parts—for instance, having SCM commits for a bug automatically add links in the bug entry to web pages that show the changes in the appropriate files. One approach taken by many large integration tools is to use a common data format for exchanging data between different parts of the application. This makes adding different SCM and bug tracking tools easier in the future, at the cost of having to add another access layer to every tool. This idea can be taken a step further: imagine a common data format to describe the services such as the SCM tool and bug tracking system that a project is using. Such a format would make it easier to import and export projects from different PDEs.

Something to watch for in the future will be PDEs that come complete with automation environments, which are tools that perform lots of different automated tasks for you (see "Automation Environments," later in this chapter). Automation environments that regularly check out your source code and then build and test the product can really help to bring a project together. Expect to see this appear as part of PDEs in the near future.

Why Integration Is Helpful

Regardless of which tools are used in a development environment, integration of all the different kinds of tools is part of what creates an environment that is satisfying to work in. Manually copying information from one tool in order to do something with another tool is an inefficient use of time and is also prone to error. Tools that work well with each other are one mark of a good development environment.

There is another side to the idea of integration, though. Just as with most machines and hardware, the connections in software are often the most fragile part of a system. Upgrading tools can break integration schemes, and unexpected inputs from one tool can break another tool in unusual and hard-to-debug ways.

There is also the problem of how to handle one tool being unavailable for a period of time. For instance, if your SCM tool usually updates your bugs with information about the file changes related to each bug, what should the SCM tool do when the bug tracking tool is unavailable? Stopping work for the whole environment means that any one tool in an environment becomes a single point of failure. However, simply ignoring the bug tracking system means that the information there becomes "best effort" and cannot be relied on to be complete. A reliable distributed environment is a hard thing to achieve. The key question to consider when integrating tools is what the developers most want to know. Effort is often spent on uncommon scenarios just as an intellectual challenge, to see if something could be done.

Two of the simplest ways of integrating existing tools in development environments are through URLs and email. A web server can be a useful place for gathering project information from multiple tools.

Imagine that you want to make emails about changes to source files that are sent from the SCM tool more helpful than just a list of the names of the changed files. You could have the SCM tool insert the details of the changes in the email or send them as an attached file. But that's a lot of text that may hide other information. Adding URLs into the email that in turn point to a web server with the files' differences makes the changes easily available from most mail clients. Another advantage of URLs is that they are relatively easy to generate, since they are just short text strings. The mail doesn't even have to be sent as HTML for this to work with some mail clients.

Email is another common way to integrate different tools in an environment. Many tools can be configured to send email when changes occur, and the content of the email is usually in a standard format. A simple program can be started periodically, read any waiting email, and use the command-line interface for some other tool to make changes. For instance, integrating a bug tracking system and a customer support system could be done using email generated when a bug is changed. Email also has the advantage of being queued up for delivery, so even if one of the tools is not working, the information will be saved until the tool is ready again.

URLs and email are the simplest ways to integrate tools in a development environment. They work well for relatively low volumes of data and when the integration can take minutes to occur—that is, it doesn't have to work in real time. More complex forms of integration include the use of COM, which is one way that Microsoft tools such as Visual Studio are able to add tools from other vendors to their menus, and broadcasting "events" to sockets that are being listened to by many other tools.

Full-scale, reliable, and robust integration of different systems in an environment generally requires much more complex solutions. This is the land of *middleware* and business process management (BPM). Middleware is technology such as CORBA ORBs or Web Services that is used to send structured information from one system to another, and BPM is what to do with the information. This level of integration is beyond the scope of this book, since development environments (as opposed to bank transfers and trading floors) rarely require such robust and tightly coupled integration schemes.

Why Automation Is Vital

There is no separate chapter on automation in this book, because I believe that automation is vital in all aspects of a development environment. If you do something nontrivial twice, then at least document the steps that you followed. If you have to do it again, consider automating it. If a task has two or more steps and is manual, then someday someone will either perform the two steps out of order or forget one of them.

THREE STRIKES AND YOU AUTOMATE

- The first time you do something, you just do it manually.

- The second time you do something similar, you wince at the repetition, but you do it anyway.

- The third time you do something similar, you automate.

(Martin Fowler, *Refactoring: Improving the Design of Existing Code*, Addison-Wesley, 1999)

Automation by reducing the repeated parts of a task to a single command is one good idea. Improving tools and other parts of your environment will relieve the short-term points of pain, but automation will raise the whole level of productivity of your project one notch.

While it is easiest to automate an environment when it is first created, automation can be gradually introduced to an existing environment. First choose an automation environment (see the next section, "Automation Environments") and then begin by automating how source code is obtained from your SCM tool. Then automate running a build using that source code. Then work out how to run unit tests and capture their results automatically. Finally, make sure you can automatically update bugs with details of the build, create change logs and a list of bugs fixed in each build, tag the source files, and deploy the results of the build and tests to a suitable location for the rest of the project members to use. Once all of these steps have been automated, you won't have to do any of this manually. Each of these steps is discussed in the relevant chapters. The point is that you can add automation one piece at a time.

However, automation does have some consequences:

- Debugging a process once it has been automated is somewhat harder than debugging the manual version of the same process. This is because there are usually more logfiles, configurations, and other levels of indirection to understand.

- If a task doesn't clean up all of its temporary files, logfiles, and other output, then some disk or other will eventually fill up. If you can't change the task to clean up after itself, then establish a policy about how many days' output should be kept, do some calculations to see whether the available disk space matches the policy, and then make sure that the older files are removed, preferably by another automated task.

- Even if storage space is not an issue, programs should always clean up after themselves, if only to save people from having to ask what a file is for and where it came from. Left-over files tend to be created faster by automated tasks because they are easier to run without thinking about side effects than are manual tasks.

- Other resources such as CPU cycles, network bandwidth, and other server loads should be monitored to make sure that the automated task is not stopping other people from working. If you know what your task is doing to others, then you can fine-tune when it runs. If you don't know, then automated tasks are easy targets for blame if everything starts to run too slowly.

- How do you know when an automated task is broken? Sometimes, as with builds, this is obvious: there's no new build. Other tasks' effects are more subtle. For example, cleaning up old builds and their entries in a bug tracking system will require more than just checking that there is now more free disk space available. There are numerous monitoring applications available, mostly customizable, that work well if you put the effort into defining their tests. Mailing the daily state of an automated task to yourself (or even better, to an appropriate email alias) as a "heartbeat" will give you examples of what a task is supposed to do, which is very useful when something changes unexpectedly later on.

- There is the dismay when something breaks in an automated task and you have to reconstruct how the task was supposed to work when it was run manually. This is where the documentation of the manual task becomes very useful, even more so if it has been kept up-to-date.

The places where tasks are automated are also good places to document the details of the task. Whether done simply as comments in a shell script or a build file, or set up to provide helpful hints during an installation process, the documentation will remind you later why something was automated in a particular way.

Automated long-term monitoring of an environment is also an excellent way to gather statistical information that can be used to plan for investment in a development environment. For instance, hard data showing how the performance of a particular server has changed over a year is the first step in deciding when to upgrade it, or to answer vague comments from developers about how "everything seems slower recently."

Automation is one mark of people who are thinking about what they are doing as they write software. If you find yourself working in an environment where there are many manual steps, first document them and then automate them for your own use. Once they work well for you, generalize them for others in the project. If you can get someone else such as the project's toolsmith to take over the automation, so much the better.

Finally, the following definition made me smile and nod in agreement:

> Oughttamatic: (*adj*) Programmable in principle, but considered so trivial in practice as to be often performed manually—thus guaranteeing occasional errors. Ex: "Yeah, it's the third time I've created a new passwd entry using cut-and-paste and forgotten to increment the UID; I really oughttamate this." (Karl Fogel, *http://www.red-bean.com/kfogel/glossiary.html*)

Automation Environments

An *automation environment* is a tool that performs a variety of automated tasks for you. An automated task is anything that has been modified so that you can run it, usually from a command line, without any manual interaction. An automated environment makes it easier to run each of these tasks in the correct order and at chosen intervals.

An automation environment is a key part of the XP concept of *continuous integration* (CI), which involves keeping a product integrated and working correctly all the time. For that reason, automation environments are sometimes referred to as "CI frameworks." If you find the phrase "automated environments" too unwieldy, then perhaps EFA for "environments for automation" might do.

Many different tasks are commonly controlled by automation environments. (Exactly what some of these tasks involve is explained in more detail in subsequent chapters.) Some of these tasks are:

- Checking out the latest versions of source files

- Calculating the appropriate build or release number

- Tagging the source files

- Building one or more products from the *virgin* source code (source code that has never been used for any kind of build; see "Build States: Virgin, Up-to-date, Changed, Interrupted, Clean" in Chapter 5)

- Testing the products with both unit tests and system tests

- Moving the generated release packages to a suitable location for other people's use

- Marking certain bugs as having potential fixes available in this release

- Creating change logs and release notes about what changed in this release

- Notifying people when a release becomes available, and also notifying the responsible individuals when a build or test fails (see "Automated Releases" in Chapter 9)

- Publishing test reports and build logs to a web site (see "A Project Web Site" in Chapter 11)

- Collecting project data and running static analyzers on the source code (see "Static Code Analyzers" in Chapter 6)

- Regenerating the dynamic parts of a project web site (see "Dynamic Web Pages" in Chapter 11)

This list of tasks is quite extensive and varies widely in practice. A good automation environment is able to integrate with all of the tools in your development environment, whether by CLI, email, or custom scripts (see "Why Integration Is Helpful," earlier in this chapter). Some of your individual tools may be able perform one or more of the tasks listed above by themselves, without the need for an automation environment. For instance, a build tool may be able to create release packages for your product, or you may want to describe your project's structure using a tool such as Maven (see "Ant" in Chapter 5). Great! Call those tools from the automation environment and have them do the work for you. Some automation environments will allow you to define quite complex dependencies between projects; for instance, so that project X will build only after projects Y and Z have been successfully built and tested.

How the information in the reports generated by an automation environment is provided to people makes a critical difference in how useful the information is. To avoid annoying everyone in the project, the default policy should be that only the transition from success to failure of build and test results should generate notifications, since developers will quickly ignore repeated emails. A good tool will let you specify the notification policy for different products and cases. Notification should be as rapid as possible, and the tool should support sending notifications by as many methods as possible. Email messages are still the most common kind of notification, but pagers, SMS messages, RSS feeds, and even X10 connections to control red and green lava lamps have their time and place.

For each series of builds, the generated reports should include a short name for the builds (e.g., "the Windows server build"), a build label (see "Labeling Builds," later in this chapter), and platform details such as processor type, operating system, and version. The reports should be available in multiple formats, including summaries and text-based versions. One common format for reports is a "waterfall," which has columns of builds with the most recent builds at the top, as shown in Figure 3-1. Build and test failures need to be shown in ways that help people identify their causes, so links to errors in logs and source files are good to have. Reports can also list all recent changes to the source code and who made the changes; this is sometimes known as the *blame list*. Displaying estimates of how much time each build will take, also called the ETA (estimated time of arrival), is a nice touch.

Another measure of how easy a particular automation environment is to use is how easy it is to extend. Your project might decide to use a different SCM tool or want to use *make* instead of Ant, so your automation environment should either support a wide range of tools already or have a clear and openly available API for adding support for new tools.

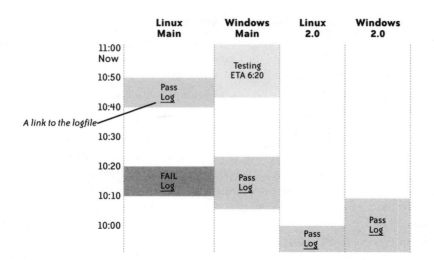

FIGURE 3-1. An automated build report

Most automation environments store information about past tasks; sometimes this is in files and sometimes in a database. Either way, automated environments are also useful for monitoring the general historical health of your development environment. Other pieces of information that are useful to keep track of are:

Slow SCM tools
A graph that is worth generating occasionally is how long it takes to check out a brand-new, virgin set of files with your SCM tool at different times of the day. If there are long delays at certain times, this will frustrate project members.

Long builds
How long automatic builds take can be measured by the automation environment or extracted from the build logs. Unexplained spikes in a graph of how long a virgin build takes should be examined carefully, since they may indicate errors in changes to the project's build files.

Build sizes
Historical information about the size of a project and the size of the released packages is useful for avoiding "code bloat."

Some useful tools for monitoring the health of a development environment include Orca (*http://www.orcaware.com*) and Argus (*http://argus.tcp4me.com*). Both of these tools can generate informative web pages, and Argus can be configured to send alerts about problems as they are detected. MRTG (*http://people.ee.ethz.ch/~oetiker/webtools/mrtg*) is another commonly used tool for monitoring the status of networks.

The rest of this section examines four automation environments. Two of these environments were inspired by Ant (the Java-based build tool discussed in "Ant" in Chapter 5) and are still most commonly used for building products written in Java. There are a number of other automation environments with future promise that are not discussed here, including

WHEN TO BUILD?

A common question is how to schedule builds. One guideline is that most testers rarely want more than one new release to test every day, though if a critical bug is fixed, they will often want a new release as soon as possible. Another guideline is that developers want to know as soon as possible after they commit changes to the source code whether they have caused a problem, since the sooner they know, the easier it is to identify the change that caused the problem. You may also need to be able to suspend builds at certain times (for example, when machines are being backed up).

On change (whenever something changes)

This has an appealing logic to it: if nothing changed, why do a build? This does assume that everything about the build is tracked in your SCM tool and also that you know that a given change is part of a series of changes that will eventually stop. Simple rules such as "wait a random time up to five minutes after any commit and reset the timer if another commit occurs" work well enough. If commits with your SCM tool are atomic, then you can impose a limit on the number of postponements.

Some SCM tools such as CVS can take a long time to discover whether anything has changed recently in a large project. One way to work around this is to arrange for all commits to change the timestamp of a single file that can then be tracked.

Scheduled (once every hour, day, or week)

Creating builds on a scheduled basis is good because it becomes a pulse for the project. If people know when the builds will occur, they know how long they have to wait to see fresh results. If your product takes less than 30 minutes to build, hourly builds are reasonable; otherwise, noon and nightly builds work well. If your builds take longer than one day, "Slow Builds" in Chapter 5 has some ideas that may help speed them up.

One common approach is to run just a subset of the tests regularly or to do only incremental builds when something changes, and then perform full builds and run all the tests less regularly (for example, every night).

Continuous (when the last build finishes)

This is the truly continuous approach to builds, which can be seen in action at Mozilla's Tinderbox web page of recent builds (*http://tinderbox.mozilla.org/showbuilds.cgi*). This minimizes the time before problematic changes are tested, but comes at the expense of increasing the load on your machines' disks. (My experience is that the filesystems on automated build machines have more problems than machines belonging to individuals or other kinds of servers, even when they have non-RAID partitions for the build files.)

DamageControl, Gump from the Apache Project, and BuildBot, a Python-based tool with good support for cross-platform builds. For a more extensive comparison of different automation environments, see the large but only partially complete comparison table at *http://docs.codehaus.org/display/DAMAGECONTROL/Continuous+Integration+Server+Feature+Matrix*.

Shell Scripts and Batch Files

The simplest way to automate a number of tasks is to execute them from within shell scripts or batch files. Such scripts can be fast to develop and they can be scheduled to be run regularly by the Unix tool *cron* or the Windows at command. However, there are good reasons to avoid using them as your entire automation environment. "Shell Scripts and Batch Files" in Chapter 5 lists some of the disadvantages of shell scripts as build tools, and "Shell Scripts and Batch Files" in Chapter 6 discusses the drawbacks of using them as test environments. Many of those problems apply to automation environments as well. Things that are awkward with shell scripts or batch files include:

Debugging
  Tracing the execution of tasks when errors occur or when the tasks interfere with each other can be difficult.

Portability
  Running the tasks on multiple machines and different platforms can be awkward.

Watchdog timers
  Checking whether a task is deadlocked and has to be terminated can be complex.

Report generation
  Creating HTML reports with scripts is tedious and prone to error.

Script development
  Saving even a minor change to a shell script can cause odd errors to occur if the script is already running.

Running tasks regularly is easy to do using *cron* or the Windows at command (though how to make at run a task more than once a day is nonobvious). The biggest problem with both of these tools is when some scheduled tasks start to make other tasks take longer. For instance, a build that used to take 40 minutes may sometimes take 65 minutes due to other scheduled tasks running at the same time. If two builds on the same machine will cause errors, then this problem may occur intermittently, appearing to break builds at random. Of course, one way to avoid this is to check at the start of a build whether another build is already running and, if so, to stop the current build.

If you do use *cron* to execute lots of tasks, one useful thing to do is to track how long each task takes so that you can see where tasks are overlapping. The *crontab* file shown in Example 3-1 does this.

EXAMPLE 3-1. Measuring the duration of cron tasks

```
# The logfile where the durations will be recorded
DURATION_LOG=/tmp/crontab_task_durations.log

# Set the format for the output from the 'time' command
TIME="start:4 duration:%E name:myprogram"
# This task is run at four minutes past every hour
4 * * * * /usr/bin/time -a -o $DURATION_LOG myprogram
```

EXAMPLE 3-1. Measuring the duration of cron tasks (continued)

```
# Change the format for the output from time to show
# when the second task started
TIME="start:8 duration:%E name:myprogram2"
# This task is run at eight minutes past every hour
8 * * * * /usr/bin/time -a -o $DURATION_LOG myprogram2
```

Tinderbox

One of the oldest public automation environments is the open source Tinderbox tool from the Mozilla organization (*http://www.mozilla.org/tinderbox.html*). Like other tools from Mozilla such as Bugzilla (see "Bugzilla" in Chapter 7) and Bonsai, Tinderbox is written entirely in Perl, still contains some Mozilla-specific functionality, and is generally complicated to install.

Tinderbox is not available as a single package for download. Instead, you check the source code out from CVS by typing:

```
cvs -d :pserver:anonymous@cvs-mirror.mozilla.org:/cvsroot login
```

Use the password anonymous when prompted and then type:

```
cvs -d :pserver:anonymous@cvs-mirror.mozilla.org:/cvsroot co mozilla/webtools/tinderbox2
```

There have been no recent updates to Tinderbox. You can also browse the source code, which is reasonably well documented, at *http://lxr.mozilla.org/mozilla/source/webtools/ tinderbox2*. Tinderbox2 is the current working version of Tinderbox.

Tinderbox uses formatted email messages from scripts running on the different build machines to update a central collection of HTML reports. You write the scripts to perform the particular task and schedule them as you wish, and then the scripts email the results to Tinderbox. In general, if you can configure the contents of email messages that are sent from a tool, then you can integrate that tool by using Tinderbox directly. Tinderbox comes with a small set of states such as *building, testing,* and *build_failed* to describe your builds but allows you to add more states, change their names, or change the color used for each state in the HTML reports.

Tinderbox integrates well with the other Mozilla tools, and you can arrange for build summaries to have URLs linking to browser-based views of your repository and change logs. Logfiles from builds are automatically parsed by Tinderbox, and links to errors are added to the reports. Since it uses scripts to execute tasks, Tinderbox can run *make* as easily as it can run Ant, and Tinderbox is suitable for large non-Java projects.

Anthill

Anthill (*http://www.urbancode.com/projects/anthill*) is a "build and release management tool" that runs as a Java servlet inside an application server such as Tomcat. An open source version is available at no cost, but there is also a commercial version named AnthillPro with more features that is available for $2,499 per year.

One of the strengths of Anthill is that it can be administered using a web-based interface, though the underlying configuration files are all in XML and so can also be edited with any other text editor. A wide range of SCM tools are supported by Anthill, including ClearCase, CVS, Perforce, Subversion, and Visual SourceSafe. The underlying build tool is usually Ant, but *make* is also supported. Multiple projects are supported, and multiple builds can occur at the same time.

CruiseControl

CruiseControl (*http://cruisecontrol.sourceforge.net*) is an open source "framework for a continuous build process." It was inspired directly by the XP concept of continuous integration and, being a Java-based tool, will run on most platforms.

As of CruiseControl 2.0, multiple projects are supported. The different SCM tools supported by CruiseControl include ClearCase, CVS, Perforce, Subversion, and Visual SourceSafe. The underlying build tool is usually Ant, though the Ant exec task can be used to run other tools indirectly. There is also a project named CruiseControl.NET, which is a port of CruiseControl to the .NET platform.

Information about using CruiseControl is widely available. The best how-to document currently available about installing and configuring it is at *http://www.javaranch.com/journal/200409/DrivingOnCruiseControl_Part1.html*. There is also a book about project automation that uses CruiseControl as its core: *Pragmatic Project Automation*, by Mike Clark (Pragmatic Bookshelf). There are also two Wikis about CruiseControl, one at *http://confluence.public.thoughtworks.org/display/CC/Home* and another, more general one at *http://c2.com/cgi/wiki?CruiseControl*.

Labeling Builds

There are numerous places in a development environment where having a standard way of describing a build is useful. If you don't define a standard way, then the SCM tags for a build will be formatted one way, the build will appear in the bug tracking system in a different way, and the release names will be defined in yet a third way.

What information should be in a build label? My suggestions are:

Build type
    Was this build for internal testing (QA) or release (REL)?

Version
    The major, minor, and patch numbers; for example, 1_3_0. "Release Numbering" in Chapter 9 has more details about different versioning schemes.

Build number
    A number that uniquely identifies each build. "Build Numbers" in Chapter 9 has more details about using build numbers.

Date

The year, month, and day when the build was started, in that order so that builds can be sorted on this field. If you plan to do more than one build per day, then the hour and minute from a standard time zone are useful too.

Special

If the build is otherwise significant, add an optional field at the end. An example is BETA for a beta release. Put this at the end of the label so that alphanumeric sorting of the label is not overly affected by it.

Each of these fields should be separated from the next with a character such as #, -, or _ so that the label can be parsed by shell scripts and other programs. If the # character is used with the above label format, then the label for internal build 129 of Version 1.3.0 of a product on July 9, 2005 would look like:

```
QA#1_3_0#129#2005_07_09
```

Another requirement for a build label is that it should not contain characters that are illegal in any of the contexts that the label will be used in—that is, SCM labels, file and directory names, field values in your bug tracking system, web pages, and documentation. Characters to avoid include $, <, >, |, /, \, spaces, and tabs. Underscores don't show up in underlined links on web pages. Some SCM tools have their own restrictions as well.

Build labels don't need to have a branch name in them, since the version number and build number can tell you whether a branch was used for the source code. Embedding the name of a branch point in a build label also seems like overkill, since this can be recorded elsewhere, along with rest of the information about the purpose of the branch.

Once a build label format has been chosen and agreed on, document it and post it in a public place. Consider very carefully any requests to change it, since its details will have been embedded in numerous tools and filenames.

Naming Projects and Machines

This section contains ideas for choosing names for projects and names for computers. Planning all these things in advance may seem excessively controlling to some people, but in my experience, deciding on this information once, before things are done differently by each person, will help project members communicate clearly.

Choosing Project Names

Project names are usually chosen by engineering groups, with one name for each significantly different version of the products that they are working on. There should be no need to change a project's name once it has been chosen. Product names, on the other hand, are the names that customers see, and these names are usually chosen to help a product sell or to become popular. Product names can change at the whim of a market research poll or a new VP of Sales.

Some general guidelines for choosing names for projects are:

Keep it short
> Since project names may appear in filenames or source code, shorter project names are preferable; four to six characters is common. Longer names will only be abbreviated anyway, and usually in two different ways.

Use distinctive sounds
> Project names should sound different from each other when spoken aloud by people whose native language is not the one used by the rest of the group. Even if everyone speaks English, having two projects named "ctest" and "seebest" is too close for comfort.

Use low-frequency letters
> It's much easier to be confident that all references to a project name can be found if the name contains characters that are less common in the local language. This is a good argument for choosing project names that use unusual characters, such as the letters *q* and *z* for English.
>
> A few years ago there was a project named IDS that apparently had a function named IDSConnect. Then the project was renamed DIS and all its functions were renamed accordingly, which led to their function for creating connections being renamed to DISConnect. The letters *d*, *i*, and *s* are too common in English to simply reuse them in such an anagram.

Make it unmarketable
> Sometimes a project name will be reused as a product name, but not if it is already trademarked, or if you make it odd or crude enough!

Project names don't have to have a theme, though that can be fun. They don't even have to be meaningful, just memorable with an obvious way of pronouncing the word. You can choose a number of suitable names once and then let people decide which one they want to use next. Names of stars, types of sushi, rare diseases, and characters from comic books are some ideas to start with for project names.

Choosing Machine Names

What you call different machines might seem to be of little consequence until you remember that you'll type the names of frequently used machines many, many times. Choosing a different theme for firewalls, servers, testbed machines, printers, and people's individual machines will make it easier to identify machines from their names. Google Sets can help you find groups of names. The most appropriate names that I have seen used were for two printers: *chainsaw* and *clearcut*, which describe what printers do to forests quite well! Among the worst names I have seen were for two servers: *left* and *right*, for their locations in the original server room. You can guess where they ended up when the server room was rearranged later on.

There are actually two official RFCs on this subject ("Requests for Comments" or RFCs are the oddly named standards for how the Internet works; see *http://www.rfc-editor.org*). "Choosing a

Name for Your Computer" (RFC 1178) has plenty of good advice. A few of my favorite suggestions from it are excerpted here (with my comments in square brackets):

Don't overload other terms already in common use

…One machine was named "up", as it was the only one that accepted updates. Conversations would sound like this: "Is up down?" and "Boot the machine up" followed by "Which machine?"…

Don't use your own name

…It is especially tempting to name your first computer after yourself, but think about it. Do you name any of your other possessions after yourself? No. Your dog has its own name, as do your children. If you are one of those who feel so inclined to name your car and other objects, you certainly don't reuse your own name. Otherwise you would have a great deal of trouble distinguishing between them in speech.…

[I would add: unless you can be absolutely sure that when the machine is reassigned, its name will be changed.]

Don't use long names

…Experience has shown that names longer than eight characters simply annoy people.…

Don't use digits at the beginning of the name

Many programs accept a numerical Internet address as well as a name. Unfortunately, some programs do not correctly distinguish between the two and may be fooled, for example, by a string beginning with a decimal digit.

Names consisting entirely of hexadecimal digits, such as "beef", are also problematic, since they can be interpreted entirely as hexadecimal numbers as well as alphabetic strings. [Though I've never seen a real problem due to this.]

Don't expect case to be preserved

…Convention dictates that computer names appear all lowercase.…

The other RFC on this subject is "The Naming of Hosts" (RFC 2100), an amusing variation on T. S. Eliot's "The Naming of Cats."

Choosing New Tools

Whether you are choosing a tool for a new project or looking for a tool to replace one already in use, there are a number of helpful places to start.

First, other members of the project are likely to have suggestions for different tools. Send out a request for information, making sure it has an obvious deadline for replies. Specify what the tool *must* do and what you would merely like it to do. If there is a tool in current use, be very clear about what you believe the problems are with it. Be sure to ask people about whether they have actually used their recommended tool, not just evaluated it. Make sure you ask them whether they have administered the tool since using and administering tools can be very different experiences. (ClearCase is the classic example of this phenomenon.)

Other places to search for more information include:

Open Directory Project
> The Open Directory Project (*http://dmoz.org*) claims that it's the largest human-edited directory of the Web. You won't find every tool in each category, but you'll probably find most of them.

Newsgroups
> Don't use Google or some other search engine to search only web sites. Search the newsgroups as well—for example, by using the Google Groups link. Company web sites' search forms may also turn up information that is not available from other search engines.

Discussion web sites
> Slashdot (*http://slashdot.org*) and other opinionated forums are sure to reflect a diversity of thoughts about the tools. Some of these opinions may be based on experience, but many are surely not. *Caveat lector*, or "let the reader beware."

A number of web sites, magazines, books, and other resources for choosing tools are listed in Appendix B.

Steps When Changing Tools

When you have decided that a tool must be changed and you have some ideas about what to replace it with, there are a number of steps to follow:

1. It is helpful to start with a clear and broadly agreed-on understanding of what the tool must do and not do, and what features would be useful but are not essential. These requirements will probably change as you investigate the available options, but they're a good place from which to start.

2. Create a document that summarizes the different choices and their perceived advantages and disadvantages, or rate them in a number of different areas. Make sure you know which requirements are mandatory and which are merely desirable. Propose some tentative schedules for how the tool could be introduced.

3. Evaluate the two or three leading choices, ideally by installing them locally on a development machine and using them with your own data or files. Record all the key information about installing, configuring, and using a new tool while you are doing it and it is fresh in your mind. Other ways of evaluating an open source tool are reading the source code and looking at the number of bugs, the number of messages on mailing lists, the amount of recent SCM activity, and the download statistics, if available.

4. Talk with senior developers on your project about their impressions of each tool. Ask the tool's vendor or project administrators for names of people who already use the tool that you can talk to. Add all these comments to the document, but keep them separate from each other, since they come from different perspectives.

5. Discuss the document with the senior members of the group and come to a decision. It helps if you can make a business case for the cost of each tool and the expected return on investment. Add people's names and a date, and save this document for revisiting in the future when people ask why a particular tool was chosen.

6. Document how you expect the new tool to be used and send this out to the whole project. Offer to describe it in person if your numbers and locations permit.

7. If at all possible, bring up the new tool in parallel with an existing tool and migrate people to the new tool gradually. If a switchover date is necessary, publicize it well in advance and make sure that extra support is available for the tool when it goes live.

8. Archive and move the old tool aside so that it isn't used by mistake or ingrained habit. It may still occasionally need to be used in the future—it may still be required for generating patches for older releases. If the tool is installed on peoples' individual machines, send detailed instructions about how to migrate safely from the old tool to the new one.

9. Update the documents about the development environment, especially the documents for new developers.

Some tools will need to have their data exported and then imported into the new tool. Bug tracking systems are one example of this; SCM tools are another. While you are migrating this data, it's worthwhile to consider how you will export the data from the new tool into yet another tool a few years from now. This is one area where file formats that are openly available and well documented will make your life much easier.

Finally, no matter how easy the transition to the new tool is, expect some level of complaint—it's the cosmic background radiation of software projects.

Internationalization and Localization

Two other aspects of both environments and the products that are created with them are *internationalization* (i18n) and *localization* (L10n). i18n is designing and implementing a product so that it can be localized, and it is notoriously difficult to do so after a product has grown. L10n is the work of creating a version of the product for a particular locale. Among other changes, L10n can involve translations; changes in the sort order for strings; different keyboard shortcuts; changes to date, number, and currency formats; and changes to the layout of UIs.

i18n and L10n of products and their installers is widespread. English is just another language; it will be the first one localized for only if it is the common language of the project. However, fully localized software development environments still seem quite uncommon outside Japan and France. This would require that the operating system and all other tools (such as the file editors, compilers, build tools, and bug tracking systems) use the local language and formats.

A number of non-English-speaking developers choose their tools by what the tools can do; whether the tools support their particular language is a secondary consideration. The basic free translation services that are provided by Google and Babel Fish (*http://world.altavista.com*) can help with the occasional message from a tool that they find confusing. To be precise, you can translate the words in the message, but messages from some tools are notoriously hard to understand even for fluent speakers of the original language of the message.

If you expect your environment to be used by people who are not comfortable with English, then the development tools should be carefully chosen to support this need. Open source tools from projects with lots of contributors and tools from large companies usually support the largest number of localized versions. If a tool discussed in this book has been internationalized, then this is mentioned. If a number of localized versions of the tool are available for the current release, then this is also noted.

Authentication, Authorization, and Accounting

AAA is a convenient acronym for authentication (proving who someone is), authorization (deciding who is permitted to do what), and accounting (keeping a record of what happened). AAA is important for all of the tools in this book, but perhaps SCM tools and bug tracking systems depend on it the most. Effective AAA depends on a good understanding of security issues and often uses cryptographic techniques and tools to enforce the chosen policies.

For some environments, strong AAA is a crucial requirement. In the same way that laboratory notebooks can be used as evidence, the output from some SCM tools has become evidence in cases such as the SCO debacle and other corporate patent wranglings. Accounting data for the U.S. Sarbanes-Oxley Act may be related to the information stored by an environment's tools. The FAA (Federal Aviation Authority) requires storage of the software used in its systems for at least 25 years.

Even the smallest companies and projects want to be confident that no one has added a "back door" to their product, either to get around paying for licenses or for other, more malicious purposes, such as spreading computer viruses and other malware. To avoid this, changes to a project should be made only by the people who have been both authenticated and authorized to make them. Finally, the changes themselves need to be auditable.

## CHAPTER FOUR

Software Configuration Management

THE FIRST HALF OF THIS CHAPTER DESCRIBES WHY KEEPING TRACK OF HOW YOUR SOFTWARE CHANGES, a process more formally known as *software configuration management* (SCM), is vital for any project. This chapter covers exactly what is meant by SCM, and how it differs from *change management* or *configuration management* (CM). Seven of the most commonly used or promising SCM tools are examined: CVS, Subversion, Arch, Perforce, BitKeeper, ClearCase, and Visual SourceSafe.

The second half of this chapter discusses some of the most common annoyances encountered when using SCM tools and describes some of the ways you can avoid them.

WARNING

The acronym SCM has been reverse-engineered over the years to stand for "source configuration management" and "source code management." The original, most widely used meaning is "software configuration management." SCM is also known colloquially as "version control" and "revision control." Since the number of TLAs (three-letter acronyms) is limited, reuse is inevitable; thus SCM also refers to "supply chain management" and "software compliance management," luckily in slightly different contexts.

Why Do I Need SCM?

The source code of all projects changes over time as the projects grow. Most of the time, the people working on the project add new parts to it and fix the broken ones. Occasionally, large reorganizations of the source code can occur, sometimes as part of cleaning up the code (also known as *refactoring*).

The simplest and most unwise way to work on a project is for a group of people to work on the project's files in a shared directory. Each developer has to be very careful not to change any file unless he can be sure that he is the only one changing it.

Being well aware of the woefully short life span of most hard disks, if the group is wise it makes regular nightly backups off site, keeping the last three copies available locally for convenience. If an individual is going to make a large change, she can make her own copy of the affected files locally, just in case something goes horribly wrong while she's making the change. When the time comes for a release, the current versions of all the files are copied to "somewhere safe."

This simple way of working on projects is how an estimated 40% of software projects are developed.* I don't know about you, but that figure is hard for me to believe. Sure, it's just an average, and on *average* every human being has one ovary and one testicle, but if the 40% value really is true, then stunned contemplation is my first reaction. Surely all those people must have heard that there are software tools to help with this kind of thing? The Capability Maturity Model (CMM; see *http://www.sei.cmu.edu/cmm*) certainly has. For your project to be anything but "ad hoc, and occasionally even chaotic," it says you need SCM.

The rest of this chapter can serve as an introduction to some of the major problems that such an environment will almost inevitably get tangled up in, and some of the ways to avoid those problems. If this is the situation you are in, the next few paragraphs should also help motivate you and your group to introduce an SCM tool. In the too-simple environment described, eventually the following situations or questions will occur:

- More than one person wants to work on the same file at the same time, but it's too hard to find everyone and to get them to agree that a file is available, so nobody works on that file. Integrating different people's work becomes very hard to schedule and takes a long time to finish.

- "All this code used to work! What changed since yesterday?"

- "When was this line of code changed? There's a bug in it and we need to know how many versions of the product are affected."

---

* Three different references that suggest this value are:

Soumitra Dutta and Luk N. Van Wassenhove, "An Empirical Study of Adoption Levels of Software Management Practices Within European Firms," *http://elab.insead.edu/publications/journalpapers/esalfull.pdf* (1997).

Alan Zeichick, "Debuggers, Source Control Keys to Quality," *Software Development Times* (March 1, 2002).

Michael Cusumano, Alan MacCormack, Chris F. Kemerer, and William Crandall, "A Global Survey of Software Development Practices," MIT Sloan School of Management Paper 178 (June 2003).

- "Who changed that line?" This question usually means either "For what purpose was that change made?" or "We need to know who would write code like *that!*"

- "Most of those changes were a mistake and they should be removed, but we do want to keep a few of the changes."

- "We need to fix that bug in multiple versions of the product."

- "Hey! Who stomped on that change I made yesterday?"

A good SCM tool can provide solutions to all of the above situations and questions. No software project of any size should be attempted without some form of SCM, and occasional copying of the source directories doesn't count as adequate SCM!

What SCM Is and Is Not

A simple description of SCM is that it's a way to keep track of the different versions (the *configuration* part of SCM) of everything that is necessary for a software project over time. What is tracked is usually files of one kind or another, but could just as well be versions of entries in a database. SCM tools are usually separate applications from the filesystem, though this is by no means always the case.

Sometimes people confuse build tools and SCM tools, but the difference is simple. Keeping track of which files go into a product is the task of build tools. Keeping track of all the versions of those files as they change is the task of SCM tools. Some build tools can use SCM tools to obtain the files they need to build a product, but that doesn't make them SCM tools.

Using an SCM tool, you can recover older versions of files after the files have been changed later on. This is very useful when you make a mistake. One view of SCM is that it gives you the ability to retrieve a snapshot of the project at a moment in time and then allows you to move forward or backward in time from that point. You can often *tag* or label the project at different moments in time and then retrieve the files exactly as they were when the tag was applied.

You can also use an SCM tool to share your changes to files with other people in a controlled manner. Many SCM tools show the differences (or *diffs*) between two versions of a file, as well as who made the changes, when the changes were made, and which other files changed at the same time.

Many SCM tools also support the idea of *branches*, which are versions of files in parallel universes. What that means is that you can have two (or more) different versions of a file, both derived from a common version, and you can work with either version at the same time. Branches let you support an existing product made from one set of files, while you develop the next release based on different versions of those same files. Many SCM tools help you with *merging* changes between branches. Figure 4-4 (in the "Branches and Tags" section, later in this chapter) shows this diagramatically.

SOME SCM WORDS

Tag, label

Tagging or labeling a set of files is when you associate a name such as RELEASE_1_0 with some particular versions of the files. A tag marks a snapshot in time, so you can't change the files that are tagged without moving the tag. The word *tag* was originally used by CVS, but is now used by other SCM tools as well.

Branch

A branch is a parallel copy of a set of files, with a name. You can make changes to files that are on branches and still keep track of the changes using SCM. You can also tag files that are on branches—for instance, to mark when releases are made using the branched files.

Merging

Merging is when you copy changes that were made in one branch to another branch. Since the files on different branches may be very different, sometimes it's hard to merge the changes.

Diffs

Diffs are the changes between two versions of a file.

Changeset

A changeset is a group of related changes to a set of files; the changes are applied all together or not at all.

Change log

A change log is a list of all the changes in the files, usually ordered by time.

SCM tools can be divided into two different kinds: *centralized* and *distributed*. Centralized tools store the different versions of the files in a central location, usually on a single server. Distributed tools store the different versions on multiple machines. The difference is somewhat blurred, since distributed tools can choose to use a single location (just like centralized tools), and some centralized tools support distributing their files to multiple servers. There are also SCM tools that support *replication,* where for performance reasons their files can be read from many different servers but are written to only one server. The difference sometimes simply comes down to how the tool was originally designed.

Another way in which SCM tools can differ is whether they expect each file to be changed by more than one person at a time. Some SCM tools stop other people from changing a file while you are editing it; this is known as a *locking* or *serial* model. Other tools expect you to resolve changes that other people may have made while you were all editing the same file; this is the *concurrent* model. All SCM tools have different ways of declaring who can read and write the files that are controlled by the tool. These permissions are often described using a list of permissions, also known as an *access control list* (ACL), for each file.

Some SCM tools use simple text files ("flat text") while others use a database to store their files. This is a sure source of discussion about the merit of each tool. On one hand, simple text files make it somewhat easier to detect corruption, and you can use existing, independent tools to inspect and edit the files. Text files scale well enough for most projects, and you don't have to be a database administrator to use them.

On the other hand, databases have many useful properties such as atomic transactions and faster access times. Also, since flat text files generally don't scale as well as databases do, you might as well use a database right from the start. Databases also let you search more efficiently within the older versions of your files. Subversion (see "Subversion," later in this chapter) allows you to choose either approach. The jury is still out on this choice, perhaps because tools based on the two different approaches are aimed at different-sized projects.

Some modern SCM tools support the concept of *changesets*. A *changeset* is a group of changes to the files controlled by the SCM tool that were made as one logical operation. The advantage of changesets is that they can be applied or later removed as a single operation.

> **NOTE**
> It's worth noting that SCM tools are not the same thing as configuration management (CM) and change management systems (CMS). These systems contain SCM abilities for tracking different versions of files, but also contain and enforce complex procedures which have to be followed to make a change. Such procedures may include scheduled reviews of the change, written approval, and formal tests that the change must pass before being accepted. This is much more than what SCM does. Sometimes people expect SCM tools to magically enforce some change management policy or other, which is really the wrong way around; choosing how to configure an SCM tool is just one part of your chosen process for allowing changes to a project.
>
> Such CM processes are often considered to be too heavyweight for many software projects, though there certainly are instances where they are appropriate; nuclear reactor controls, aviation software, and medical devices are three examples that spring immediately to mind. This chapter is about SCM, not CMS.

Drawbacks of SCM

You might agree that SCM is vital to your project, but at what cost? All tools seem to have some drawbacks associated with them, and SCM tools are no exception. This section mentions a few complications of using SCM tools, but it should be stressed that the benefits of SCM outweigh all these issues. I'm sure that there are trapeze artists who feel that safety nets take away some of the thrills of their act, but you never see them work without a net.

Disk space

Keeping track of the different versions of a large number of files soon begins to take up lots of disk space. Even storing just the source code for a product with a million lines of code can easily take 10MB. Naively keeping complete copies of every file will use up 10MB for each tag. SCM tools usually store only the differences between versions, which are much smaller in most cases. Even with just storing the differences, a total of 250MB would not be unusual for such a product after a year's worth of changes. The price of storage is cheap enough to allow us to ignore this argument.

Performance

Using an SCM tool to obtain a set of files to work with is generally slower than copying the files over from another directory. The SCM tool may keep the files on a remote server across a busy network, and it may have to regenerate in real time the precise versions of the files you requested. You may also have to wait for someone to finish making her changes before you can get the latest set of files. All that work takes a bit more time, but it's usually not much time.

Connectivity

Some SCM tools don't work when they are disconnected from a network—for instance, when you are using your laptop on an airplane. If you are going to do a lot of development disconnected from a network, choose a distributed SCM tool that will work in that mode, or at least one that won't stop you from accessing your files without a connection to its central server.

Complexity

Some minimal training in how to use the SCM tool is likely to be necessary, and any infrequently used commands are quickly forgotten. Complicated activities such as merging different versions of files or merging whole branches of source code together are particularly hard to get right with many SCM tools. This is one reason why the quality of the documentation and support is important to consider when you are choosing an SCM tool.

Cost

If the SCM tool chosen is not free of charge, then the financial cost can become a limiting factor on how the project can grow, especially if a license is needed for each developer who uses the tool. Still, there are plenty of good SCM tools that cost nothing, and my opinion is that you can always find ways to get more money, but you'll never recover time lost to poor SCM practices.

Risk of corruption

Finally, and most disturbingly, if there is a bug in the SCM tool, or bad hardware, or even operating system errors, then your files could gradually become corrupted within the SCM tool itself. This nightmare scenario is thankfully very rare, but is a great reason to use SCM tools with checksums on their files and with tools to validate their files, and to do nightly backups of your SCM tool's files.

A Typical Day's Work with SCM

Each SCM tool has a different name for the collection of files that it tracks. In the rest of this chapter, I'll use the CVS term *repository* for these files, simply because it is familiar to many people. The set of files in which a developer makes changes is named the *working copy* (CVS calls this a *sandbox*). Obtaining a working copy using CVS is known as *checking out* a copy. Publishing the changes to a repository is known as *committing* or *checking in* the changes.

A typical session with an SCM tool involves the following activities:

Checkout

> A developer decides to work on some part of the project. He checks out copies of the necessary files onto his machine. This is his personal working copy. Checking out the files has not changed anything in the repository, and all changes he makes are local to his machine. No one else is affected by his work yet.

Edit

> The developer changes the files in some interesting way, maybe even creating new files, and probably builds a new version of the product using the changed files.

> **WARNING**
>
> Probably the most common mistake people make when they use SCM tools is to forget to add newly created files to the SCM tool. Even though your own builds and tests work just fine, this mistake breaks the build when your changes are committed, leading to self-defensive comments such as "But it works for me!" and "I ran all the tests." Some SCM tools will alert you to the presence of local files that they don't know anything about, but it's still good practice to get used to adding new files to your SCM tool right after you create them, while you still remember that they are new.

Diff

> One common thing to do with an SCM tool is to see what changes have been made in the working copy, compared with the versions of the files in the repository. Another diff-related activity is to see who last changed a particular file and exactly what those changes were.

Update

> While the developer was working on the files in his working copy, someone else may have changed those same files in the repository. The developer has to get the latest versions of those files and make sure that his changes still work correctly with the changes from other people.

Commit

> Finally, the developer has resolved all these changes, added all his new files, tested a version of the product created from his working copy, and is now ready to let other

people in the project see his changes. This happens by committing the changes to the repository. It's helpful if you commit related changes all together, along with a descriptive comment about what the changes were for.

Various tests can be required by the SCM tool before it accepts the changes. For instance, was there a (possibly required) bug associated with these changes? Were the unit tests run and did they behave as expected? Have the changes been reviewed or checked for security or copyright problems?

Last, when the changes are accepted by the SCM tool, some notification (such as an email) is sent to the group, describing the changes and who made them. A *change log* may also be updated. If the files are tagged, then information about the tag should appear in the change log as well.

Figure 4-1 shows a centralized repository being used by three users: Alice, Bert, and Cuthbert. Alice is checking out her own working copy of some of the files in the repository. Bert is updating his working copy, merging in the changes that other people have made to the files in the repository. Cuthbert is committing the changes to the files that he has made in his working copy to the repository, thus making them available to other people.

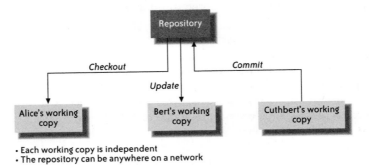

• Each working copy is independent
• The repository can be anywhere on a network

FIGURE 4-1. Using a centralized SCM tool

Using a distributed SCM tool is similar to the process just described, except that there are now many repositories. In addition to the usual checkout, update, and commit operations on a repository, there are equivalents for repositories themselves, at the next level of abstraction. You can:

• Create your repository by copying one of the existing ones, which is similar to checking out a working copy

• Merge in changes from another repository, which is similar to updating a working copy

• Merge your changes to another repository, which is similar to committing changes in a local copy

Figure 4-2 shows distributed repositories being used in the same way as shown in Figure 4-1 for centralized repositories. One way to think about distributed repositories is that each person has her own repository on her machine, and she can commit files to it while disconnected from a network. Then when she is reconnected to a network, she can synchronize her repository with the other repositories.

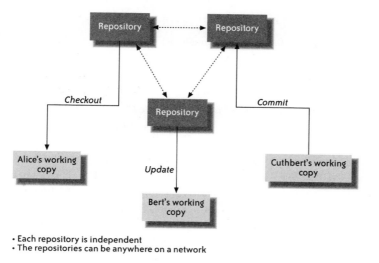

- Each repository is independent
- The repositories can be anywhere on a network

FIGURE 4-2. Using a distributed SCM tool

SCM Annoyances

This section describes some of the common problems that people run into when they use SCM tools with a project. Some problems such as merging are hard work due to the basic nature of the problem, but all the problems can be tamed with a little forethought.

Branches and Tags

To recap, a tag is a name for all the versions of a group of files at one moment in time, just as though you had made a copy of all the files as they were at that moment. A branch does the same thing, but allows SCM-controlled changes to the files later on. Figure 4-3 shows an example of this.

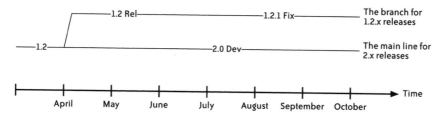

FIGURE 4-3. Changing a file on a branch

Branches are vital because they allow you to make changes to an older version of the product—for example, when you need to fix a bug in a file belonging to the last release of a product. At the same time, you can make changes for the next release to a different version of the same file. If you don't use branches but instead only fix bugs in future releases, this can put pressure on the project to create premature releases.

> **NOTE**
> You should consider how you are going to use branches before you
> release the first version of your product. You should also check that all
> your other SCM-related tools work properly with branches

However, you should try to minimize the number of active branches in your project. Branches make things more complicated because there are now more changes to manage. Imagine three versions of a product: the oldest one is the one that is being maintained, the middle one is the one that is being made available to customers right now, and the newest one is next year's "yup, that bug's fixed in the next release" version. A set of changes to fix some problem has to be created for one of the three versions, tested there, then ported to the other two versions and then tested there too. Even if it is straightforward to port the changes to the other versions, the amount of testing work for one bug has just been tripled. Tracking the same bug in multiple releases is also a hard thing to do well with most bug tracking tools (see "One Bug, Multiple Releases" in Chapter 7).

USING PREPROCESSOR DIRECTIVES INSTEAD OF BRANCHES

In languages such as C that have conditional preprocessor directives (for example, #ifdef VERSION_1), it is possible to use these directives instead of SCM branches. By surrounding the parts of the code that apply to one version or another with ifdefs and using the appropriate #define directives, you can keep branched versions of a file all together in one file. Unfortunately, this idea rapidly leads to unsupportable code. Even with clever editors and tools such as *diff* to show you just the text that the compiler actually sees for each file and combination of directives, the complexity of trying to keep all the possibilities correct soon becomes more complicated than using real SCM branches.

Preprocessor directives can be very convenient when used sparingly, but using them instead of SCM branches is just *not* a good idea. There are some very good reasons why many modern languages such as Java don't support preprocessor directives.

To really see why the number of branches in a product should be minimized, look at Figure 4-4. Each of the source files is named on the vertical axis, and each different version of each source file is a solid circle in the horizontal direction. Every branch that is created is a (logical) copy of all the files into the third axis, the one labeled Branches. Just the copies of File 1 and File 2 are shown, and there have been three changed versions of File 1 on Branch 1. Now this third dimension has an odd characteristic compared with the other two: it's very easy to move in one direction (creating a branch), but it's always much more work to move in the other direction (merging). The more branches of a project that you keep active, the more time you will spend building, testing, and documenting the changes to the project. For the sake of simplicity, I recommend keeping the number of active branches small: two or three at most for a medium-sized commercial product.

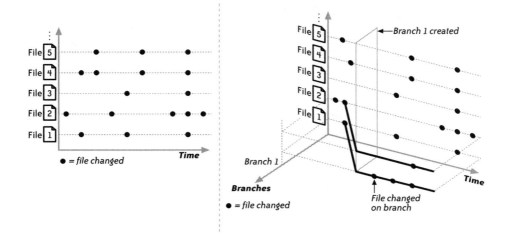

FIGURE 4-4. Branches are in a different dimension

To inexperienced project managers, the concept of branching may seem like an easy answer to many of a project's growing pains. Got a new product? Just put it on a branch. Developing for a new hardware platform? Put it on a branch. Don't like that developer's coding style? Put him on a branch. Some SCM tools even encourage you to think like this. My advice is simple: avoid it! You should use just enough branches for your project and no more. The next section discusses what to do when you do have to create a branch.

When to Branch? When to Tag?

The previous section was pretty emphatic about why you want to minimize the number of active branches in a project. So when is creating a branch appropriate? There are just two common cases:

- A branch for each major release of a product. These long-lasting branches will become inactive when that version of the product is no longer supported.

- Branches for a small number of developers to work on for a short period (days or weeks, usually not months). If the work on the branch is to be useful, it has to be merged back to the main development branch sooner rather than later.

These two cases can be summarized as "branch on incompatible policies." That is, create a branch when the guidelines for committing files are different. For example, the rules about who can commit to a release branch are usually different from the more open nature of the main development branch. Since the two sets of rules are different for the same source files, a branch is probably necessary. A useful article that expands this idea is "High-Level Best Practices in Software Configuration Management," from *http://www.perforce.com/ perforce/bestpractices.html*. (There are other articles that encourage each developer to have his own branch for his work, or even a branch per changeset, but these approaches assume effortless merging abilities from your SCM tool, which is rarely the case in practice.)

> **NOTE**
>
> Before you create a branch, create a *branch point* tag. Then create the branch using that tag. That way, if you branch only a few files but later decide that you want to branch some other files, you can use the tag to branch from the very same point in time. Some SCM tools do this automatically for you.
>
> When you create a branch, always consider when you are going to be able to stop using it, and put as many parts of the project as seems sensible onto the branch. If you branch only a few parts of a project, then it's good to record which parts were and were not branched somewhere. It's also a good idea to record the name of the branch, the branch point, and the intended purpose of the branch somewhere that everyone in the project can find it.

When is it a good idea to tag a project? Good practice is to create a tag whenever anything happens to the project that you might want to reproduce. Examples are creating a release, giving an internal demo, reaching a point in time that you might want to branch from one day, or just getting a build to work again. Since tags are just a way to name a set of particular versions of files, they don't involve the dreaded third dimension of Figure 4-4. Consequently, they require much less effort to work with—there are no merge headaches to deal with later on. However, depending on the SCM tool and the size of the project, tagging may take hours rather than minutes or require locking the repository to stop the files being changed during this time.

Naming Branches and Tags

The naming of branches and tags has surprisingly wide effects on a project. Tag names become associated with builds, test results, and eventually releases, so they appear in many of the related tools such as bug tracking systems. A document with the name of each branch, the branch point tag, and the intended purpose of the branch can help to reduce confusion about how to use different branches. Since there are generally many more tags than branches, it's easier to simply make the tag and branch names meaningful. "Labeling Builds" in Chapter 3 describes the idea of build labels, which are a good basis for tag names.

> **WARNING**
>
> If there is no overall naming scheme for your branches and tags, then ad hoc ones will spring up. Changing the names of branches later on is difficult for some SCM tools such as CVS.

Before you settle on a naming scheme for your branches and tags, note that some SCM tools have nonintuitive quirks about what a name can look like. In CVS, for example, names must start with a letter, not a numeral, so 2_1_release is not permitted. Periods and spaces are also not allowed, so release 2.1 won't work, but hyphens and underscores are permitted (though underscores tend to disappear when the name is used as part of an HTML link). Branch and tag names also have to be unique within a file in CVS; that is, you can't tag two different versions of a file with, say, ALPHA_RELEASE, even if the versions are on different branches. CVS also makes no distinction between tag names and branch names, and working out whether a name is a tag or branch after the fact can be tedious.

Create a document that describes the chosen naming scheme for your project's tags and branches, and try to make sure that the naming scheme follows the release numbering scheme (see "Release Numbering" in Chapter 9) as closely as possible. If you can enforce the chosen naming scheme using the SCM tool itself, so much the better. Restrict who is allowed to create branches, make sure they know what is expected for branch and tag names, and make sure that they have some good sense about when to create a branch. Once you know who can create branches, automate the process as much as possible for them.

A simple naming scheme that has been used successfully with CVS is as follows:

- All branch names end in _branch or _b. Tag names do not.

- Private branches and tags should have _private in their name.

- Tag names that are connected to points where branches occurred should have _bp (for "branch point") in their name. Another idea is to start the names of branch point tags with Root-of.

- Tag names that are connected to points where merges occurred should have _mp (for "merge point") in their name.

Some examples of tags and branch names using this scheme are:

rel_1_1_branch
  The branch for release 1.1 and any of its subsequent patch releases

bob_i18n_private_branch
  A private branch, probably used by Bob for some internationalization work

QA#fugu_139
  A tag for the internal release of build 139 of the project named "fugu"

Root-of#rel_1_1_branch
  The tag that records where the branch rel_1_1_branch originally diverged from the main line

susan_private_branch#main#2_mp
  A tag to record the second merging of the branch susan_private_branch back to the main line

Dates can be troublesome in branch and tag names, especially if the project has people from different countries reading the dates. Some people like to have the name of the tag that was used as the branch point (or *root*) of a branch included in the branch name. This seems to make the branch name overly long, in my opinion, and you should be able to use the SCM tool itself to tell you where the branch came from.

Merge Madness

Merging is taking the changes that were made to files on one branch and making the same changes to another branch. Perhaps the branch was where some experimental changes were developed, and now they're ready for everyone else to use. Perhaps a bug was fixed on a branch for one series of releases, and the same bug needs to be fixed in a different series of releases.

Branching is so tempting, so easy: just copy all those files and make your changes to the copies. Merging is so much harder, and only gets harder as the original and the copies diverge over time. Indeed, there are people who make a whole career out of merging different versions of classical texts back together, word by painful word, but you probably don't want to spend your career merging files. Even with the merge tools that are mentioned next, merges still take time, usually because some human intervention is necessary when the tools can't figure out what to do. Large merges inevitably destabilize the branch they are merged into, so extra testing effort is needed after the merge is complete.

In most SCM tools, automated merging uses the *diff* and *patch* tools in some manner. *diff* uses an algorithmic equivalent of finding the shortest path between two points to create the minimum number of *hunks*, which are groups of lines that could be removed or added to one file to transform it into the other file. *patch* takes these hunks and applies them to one file to create the other file, along with some smart attempts to cope with changes to where the hunks should be applied within the file. Many SCM tools help you only with merges between branched versions of the same file, not between separate files. For more information about *diff* and *patch*, see "Comparing and Merging Files" at *http://www.gnu.org/ software/diffutils/manual*.

So what makes an automated merge fail? Generally, if two files have a common ancestor and both files have had the same lines changed, it is unclear which changes are the correct ones to use. In this case, the changes are *conflicts*, and someone has to resolve them by choosing one or another of the changes. Luckily for SCM and branches, developers tend not to modify the same lines of code at the same time as other developers. You may be pleasantly surprised by how few conflicts there are when merging changes from one branch to another.

Some SCM tools (including CVSNT, Arch, Perforce, and BitKeeper) automatically keep track of when files were merged. If you have a large number of files to merge and they have many conflicts, then graphical merge tools may be useful. Some of the better-known standalone merge tools are the commercial Araxis Merge (Windows only) and Guiffy (all platforms), and the open source WinMerge (Windows only) and *xxdiff* (for Unix).

One good way to organize larger merges is to designate a small number of people as "mergemeisters" and let them perform the merge and resolve as many conflicts as possible. Then have the mergemeisters call in the appropriate people for each group of files that still need to be merged by hand.

Security

Some other important aspects of SCM to consider are those related to security. The source code is the heart of your project, where all your intentions, shortcuts, and errors are plain to see. Several large companies including Microsoft and Cisco have been the targets of successful exploits aimed at acquiring their source code. Even the repository of the source to the CVS tool has itself been cracked.

An SCM tool must make sure that only authorized people can read and change files, and it must keep a record of such actions for audits. It must also be able to protect its own files from accidental or malicious corruption, and it should not be vulnerable to denial-of-service attacks.

Some practical suggestions for securing your SCM tool, and CVS in particular, include:

- Use separate and well-secured machines as SCM servers, which few or no developers can log in to directly. If you have secure server rooms, keep your SCM machines in there. Emergency power is often available in server rooms, which helps keep your filesystem intact, as do redundant disks.

- Use encrypted connections from SCM clients to SCM servers, especially if there is a wireless connection involved anywhere in the network. If people have to have accounts on the SCM server, use a secure shell such as *smrsh* to limit the commands that they are allowed to execute.

- Carefully guard the physical security of your backups of the repository. Destroy the physical media of outdated backups.*

- Track each change in the repository using notifications of commits and inspection of diffs. Train developers to expect to see email when they make changes and to occasionally confirm that the information in the email is also appearing in any change logs.

- The CVS pserver access mode is not designed to be a secure access method; it should be used only inside trusted networks. Use *ssh* and the ext mode for external access, and avoid anonymous access to CVS servers if at all possible.

- Disable the CVS admin command for most people, since this command makes it too easy to change or corrupt a repository in untraceable ways.

An excellent source of further information about this topic is the paper "Software Configuration Management (SCM) Security," by David A. Wheeler, which is available from *http://www.dwheeler.com/essays/scm-security.html*.

---

* Heating any CD or DVD in an ordinary microwave oven for 5 to 10 seconds will both physically destroy the disk and entertain onlookers. My wife and lawyer say, "Don't try this at home!" but my children say, "Again, Daddy, again!"

Access Wars

The development of a software product is often broken up into functional groups, such as networking, GUI developers, testers, technical writers, and toolsmiths. Not surprisingly, the way that a product's source code is stored in an SCM tool tends to reflect how the groups are divided. Disagreements about who gets to make changes ("commit rights") in each group's files is a common source of irritation in a project.

ACCESS WARS: THE BEGINNING

The conversations that lead to long meetings about who should have commit rights typically sound like the following fictional exchange. Luke is a senior member of one group, and Theo is a less-experienced member of a different group.

LUKE: Hi, Theo. I saw the commit email about your changes in some of my files.

THEO: Yes, I just fixed some spelling mistakes.

LUKE: I think I ought to preview changes in code that I have to support. Could you send me the changes and I'll make them myself next time?

THEO: Well, they were only a few spelling changes!

LUKE: Yes, but you also changed the formatting of the code. Our group has different conventions than your group, and we think it helps *us* to understand our code better...

THEO: OK, sure. (*Thinking to himself, "That's the last time I bother to fix his typos!"*)

In many projects, it is considered polite to mention proposed changes in another group's files to that group before you make them; you can also send diffs by email to the group. Otherwise, someone in the affected group always seems to take offense, whether at the changes themselves, or because they were surprised by who made the changes, or because "you might do it again, and it might break something in the future!" There's not much you can do to argue with that, so you might as well coordinate changes in other groups' files with them beforehand: egoless programming only goes so far when it's a whole group's ego.

Even more far-reaching than these seemingly petty territorial conflicts are the effects on a project when different groups start to deny others read access to their files. These aren't the files containing the name of the next CEO of the company or telling where the last project leader was buried. These are cases such as one group of developers allowing only compiled versions of their libraries to be used by other groups, or the Technical Publications group wanting people to use copies of only those documents that they have personally issued. This kind of information restriction hinders effective software development.

Still, looking at the issue from a different angle, preventing your salespeople from promising features in the next release based on a single comment they saw committed to the source code a few weeks ago can actually make software development more coherent. As with all information, it's what you expect the owner to do with it that matters most. The beauty of SCM tools is that if someone else makes changes that you don't like to your group's files, you can not only talk to him but also back out his changes.

Filenames to Avoid

All filesystems have their quirks about what characters are valid in filenames and how long filenames can be. SCM tools have their own set of restrictions on the names of files.

First, a little history. Filenames with spaces in them were most uncommon in older Unix filesystems. Windows 95 began to make them more popular, but Windows also dragged along "8.3" (pronounced "eight dot three") filename restrictions from its DOS ancestry, where the filename could be at most eight characters long, with an extension of up to three characters. Other characters in filenames that have been known to break cross-platform compatibility, or even corrupt the files stored in SCM tools, are /, \, and newline characters. Just to be safe, these characters are all still worth avoiding in filenames.

For example, since CVS was originally developed on Unix, filenames longer than 8.3 were just fine, but support for spaces came later. Unfortunately, the format originally chosen for passing the names of files and their versions to the CVS info scripts, which are part of customizing a CVS server for your site, did not really support spaces in the filenames until more recently, around Version 1.12.6.

Windows filesystems are set up by default to be insensitive to the case of filenames. So three files named *FileWriter.java, Filewriter.java,* and *filewriter.java* (which differ only in the case of one or two characters) would all be treated as the same file in a Windows filesystem. On Unix, and most other operating systems, they would be three different files. This becomes a problem when a Windows user tries to extract these files from a Unix server; it's not clear which file the Windows user will finally see, since the three filenames may be identical in their local filesystem. It should be noted that the same problem occurs with tools such as FTP and with shared filesystems such as NFS. The most obvious solution is to use names that are unique on case-insensitive filesystems.

In general, avoid using the name or abbreviated name of the SCM tool as a filename or directory name. A particularly unpleasant problem can occur if you are working in Unix and are using CVS to store information about CVS—for example, some documents about how you configured CVS for your environment. You won't be permitted to create a subdirectory named *CVS,* because one already exists as part of how CVS works. However, you can create a subdirectory named *cvs,* because *cvs* is a different directory name from *CVS* in the Unix filesystem. Unpleasant surprises are now in store for anyone who tries to check out the subdirectory to a Windows system. The *cvs* directory will interfere with the *CVS* directory that is used by CVS. My suggestion here is to call the subdirectory *scm.*

Some more general advice about the naming of files and directories in a project:

- When naming directories, make sure their names start with different characters. Then completing their names will be easier when using a shell prompt at the command line.

- Use common prefixes for the names of files within the same directory. The extra information can give you more of an idea about where to find the file.

- Don't reuse directory names that are significant in your operating system (e.g., *sys* in Unix and *system* in Windows). It's confusing, and one day some tool will pick up files from the wrong *sys* directory and you may not even realize it.

- Avoid embedding version numbers into the name of a file or directory that's managed using an SCM tool—tracking versions is what the SCM tool is for! Put a version into a filename only if there is an occasion when multiple versions might be used at the same time.

Backups and SCM

SCM tools behave like backups for their users' files, but it is good to remember that unless the SCM tool's own data is properly backed up, the users' files are no better protected than if the users had just copied their files over to another machine. Backups of an SCM tool's data serve at least three purposes:

Disaster recovery
    That is, being prepared for "The SCM server just crashed and it won't come back up!"

Corruption detection
    By comparing the files or database contents in backups

Intrusion detection
    By tracking all the changes that have been made from backup to backup

Standard server backup practices can usually be followed for SCM servers. If necessary, quiesce or shut down the server, export the data from the database or copy the files, compress, encrypt, and uniquely identify the backup files, and archive them off site on permanent media. As with any backup strategy, all this effort is wasted if you don't periodically test that the SCM server can be recreated using a recent backup. Keeping one or more identical SCM servers on standby is useful both for testing recovery of backups and for periodic maintenance. Personally, I like to make my own nightly backups to CD and DVD for all the SCM data that I am responsible for, and then have an IT department also back up the SCM machines. One place to read more about basic backup and recovery best practices is Chapter 11 of *Essential System Administration*, by Æleen Frisch (O'Reilly).

The backup files' size can vary quite erratically due to compression artifacts, but the total size of the files always grows every few days, since version control systems can't discard information if they are to reconstruct the past correctly. Large unexpected changes in the size of consecutive backups can occur and are worth investigating, usually by comparing the contents of the different backups.

What happens in the worst case, if you lose all your SCM data? If you're lucky, someone will have a recent copy of the files on her local machine. You can recreate the recent state of the project by adding these files back into the SCM tool. For this reason, it's a good idea to regularly check out the entire contents of the repository onto at least one machine. Automated builds have to do this regularly anyway.

Backing up CVS

Example 4-1 shows an example script that can be used on a locked repository to create a *gzip*'d tarball of the repository. The backup file should be copied to another machine after it has been created. On a Unix server, this kind of script is typically set up to run nightly, using a *cron* job. Scripts used to back up CVS repositories should expect to encounter filenames with spaces in them.

EXAMPLE 4-1. A shell script for backing up a CVS repository

```
#!/bin/bash
#
# Backup a CVS repository to a gzipped tarball. Also generate output
# describing what has changed since the last backup.
#

# The root of the local CVS repository, the one to be backed up
CVSROOT=/usr/local/cvs

# The uniquely-identified backup filename
backup_home=/backups
backup_file=${backup_home}/cvs_backup_`date +"%m%d%Y.tgz"`

# Record what has changed between each consecutive backup
cd ${CVSROOT}
if [ -f ${backup_home}/du.today ]
then
  mv ${backup_home}/du.today ${backup_home}/du.yesterday
fi
du -k [A-Za-z0-9]* | sort +1 > ${backup_home}/du.today
diff -N ${backup_home}/du.yesterday ${backup_home}/du.today

# Create a list of all the files in the repository.  Note that only
# files whose _full_ name starts with [A-Za-z0-9] are matched.  Make
# sure that empty directories and soft links are handled correctly
# (find -type f loses both of these).
repos_filelist=/tmp/all_files.$$
find [A-Za-z0-9]* -not -type l -print > ${repos_filelist}

# You could also use grep -v here to select portions of the
# repository, and you may want to add this script to the list of files
# that are backed up.
tar --files-from ${repos_filelist} --no-recursion -czf ${backup_file}
chmod ogu-w ${backup_file}

# Clean up
rm -f ${repos_filelist}

# And copy the backup file to another machine ...
```

The source to CVS contains a useful script in the *contrib* directory named *validate_repo.pl*, also known as *check_cvs* in earlier versions. This script can be run nightly to confirm that the repository has not been corrupted in any obvious way.

SCM Tools

The seven different SCM tools examined in this section are a mixture of closed and open source software. There are noticeably more usable SCM tools available than build tools (see "Build Tools" in Chapter 5), and there are certainly more tools available from commercial organizations.

What should you look for in an SCM tool? Beyond the basic saving and retrieving of different versions of files, I suggest, in order of importance:

1. Confidence in the integrity of your data
2. Fast and simple creation of tags, extraction of tagged files, and generation of diffs
3. Good support for branching and merging, ideally with both command-line and graphical interfaces
4. Integration with other existing tools such as bug tracking systems
5. A good web interface to let people browse the different versions of their files and also to search through earlier versions of the files
6. Good support from the tool vendor or the tool's community

"Comparison of SCM Tools," later in this chapter, summarizes the major differences between the tools discussed in this chapter.

CVS

CVS (*http://www.cvshome.org*) is by far the most commonly used open source SCM tool. The CIA project (*http://cia.navi.cx*), which tracks commits from hundreds of open source projects, shows that 70% of their commits come from projects using CVS. Many of the terms used by CVS, such as *commit* and *check out*, have become de facto terms used by other SCM tools. Other SCM tools such as Subversion and Arch are careful to provide a "Migration Guide for CVS Users" document and tools. CVS is licensed under the GPL.

CVS is most commonly used over a network, with a single Unix or Windows-based server providing the repository, though some partial support for distributed servers was added with Version 1.12.10. Developers use CVS clients to check out a *sandbox*, which is their local working copy of the files under control of CVS. Different developers can check out the same files at the same time, since the *C* in CVS stands for *concurrent*. The opposite is true with SCM tools such as Visual SourceSafe, which let only one person at a time work on each file; this becomes a bottleneck even with medium-sized projects. After making changes, the files are *checked in* to the repository, along with some text comments about the changes. The first person to commit her changes forces the other developers to *update* their files before they can commit. CVS doesn't care how long you take between checkout

THE HISTORY OF CVS

CVS, which is usually described as an acronym for Concurrent Versions System, was first released by Dick Grune in 1986 as a series of Unix shell script wrappers around RCS (Revision Control System). RCS is an even older SCM tool designed by Walter Tichy for single-user, single-machine, single-directory development environments. Tichy later went on to design another SCM tool named RCE, which stands for Revision Control Engine. By 1989, Brian Berliner had rewritten CVS in C, and Jeff Polk had made it scale better. CVS was originally intended to run on a single machine; later on, the concept of CVS clients and a CVS server were added by Jim Kingdon. CVS is an SCM tool that has evolved, rather than having an overall design.

CVS has been stable since around the end of the last century, but major releases occur about once per year, with around half a dozen minor releases per year. A number of the early contributors to CVS are now part of the Subversion project.

and commit. CVS *logs* are available for each file, and these logs describe all the checkins for that file. CVS supports branches, tags, and also some basic assistance for merges.

The CVS project uses the GNU Autotools suite (see "GNU Autotools" in Chapter 5) to build executables for DEC Alpha, Cray, HP-UX, Solaris, GNU/Linux, FreeBSD, NetBSD, IRIX, OS/2, Windows, Mac OS X, and VMS, among others (see the file *INSTALL* in the CVS source for the complete list). The CVS source also includes an extensive set of unit tests known as the "sanity checks." CVSNT (*http://www.cvsnt.org*) is a well-established fork of CVS taken in 1999 by Tony Hoyle, originally to add native support for Windows NT to CVS, but the two products still interoperate well. Features that have been added to CVSNT include better support for Unicode, ACLs, and Windows authentication. WinCVS and MacCVS, which are popular GUIs for using CVS on Windows and Macintoshes, respectively, both use CVSNT under the covers.

For many years, the best documentation for CVS was "the Cederqvist," also known formally as "Version Management with CVS" (*https://www.cvshome.org/docs/manual*), an online manual written by Per Cederqvist that extends the manpage written by Roland Peschand and the FAQ maintained by David G. Grubbs. While the Cederqvist is still useful, and has even been published as a book by Network Theory (*http://www.network-theory.co.uk*), there are now a number of other good books about CVS. The best ones are *Essential CVS,* by Jennifer Vesperman (O'Reilly); *Open Source Development with CVS,* by Moshe Bar and Karl Fogel (Paraglyph), which is also available online at *http://cvsbook.red-bean.com*; and *Pragmatic Version Control Using CVS,* by Dave Thomas and Andy Hunt (Pragmatic Bookshelf). There are also numerous how-to documents and tutorials all over the Internet, with particularly good ones at *http://en.wikipedia.org/wiki/Concurrent_Versions_System* and *http://www.devguy.com/fp/cfgmgmt/cvs*.

The biggest strength of CVS is that many developers are already familiar with it. It does scale well with reasonably large projects (hundreds of users, thousands of files, millions of lines of code) and large file sizes (tens of megabytes), though the time to tag files increases linearly with the number of files and their sizes. CVS is simple to set up and maintain; most CVS servers have the longest uptimes of any machine in a company. It's secure against casual attacks, though it has been cracked in the past (see "Security," earlier in this chapter).

Since CVS is both open source and mature, there are also dozens of separate tools to add extra functionality to CVS. A few of the most useful are:

ACLs

These allow you to control who can commit files, according to the user, the branch, and the directory name. The *cvs_acls* script from the *contrib* directory of the CVS source and the patches from *http://cvsacl.sourceforge.net* are examples of such add-ons.

Browsing CVS files

For web-based viewing of repositories, the Python-based ViewCVS interface (*http://viewcvs.sourceforge.net*) is excellent; it also supports browsing of Subversion repositories.

Graphical CVS clients

There are a number of graphical CVS clients in common use, and they all hide some of the details of the CVS command line. The oldest one is WinCVS (*http://www.wincvs.org*). TortoiseCVS (*http://www.tortoisecvs.org*) is well integrated with the Windows filesystem browser. My current favorite graphical CVS client is SmartCVS (*http://www.smartcvs.com*) because it runs on any platform with a JVM and provides all the add-ons of the other clients by default.

Commit email

The *activitymail* Perl script, available from *https://activitymail.cvshome.org*, has a large number of choices for sending email about commits. One particularly useful addition to email is to include links to a web-based view of the files' changes.

Change logs

The *cvs2cl* Perl script from *http://www.red-bean.com/cvs2cl* can generate change logs in HTML or XML. These change logs comply with the GNU standard for change logs, which is part of the coding standards at *http://www.gnu.org/prep/standards/standards.html#Change-Logs*. They can also act as a collection of "poor man's changesets" for CVS, and you can generate scripts to revert complete changesets or merge them to other branches.

Changesets

CVSps (*http://www.cobite.com/cvsps*) generates changesets from individual commits to a CVS repository.

Local changes

cvsdelta (*http://directory.fsf.org/cvsdelta.html*) creates summaries of what has changed locally in your sandbox.

Clients for CVS have been written in Java, Tcl, and C++. Most modern IDEs and many bug tracking systems have some level of integration with CVS. CVS is still the default SCM tool for many preconstructed environments, including SourceForge, which is probably the largest CVS user in the world. (The GNU project may have the largest single CVS repository.) Other products that tie all this extra information into one convenient web site for your project are the excellent FishEye (*http://www.cenqua.com*) and the open source CVS Monitor project (*http://ali.as/devel/cvsmonitor*).

The weaknesses of CVS in many ways reflect the fact that it evolved, rather than being designed as a whole. Interactions with a CVS server are atomic on only a per-directory basis, not per transaction. So if you update your local sandbox at the same time that another developer is checking in his changes, you may get only some of his changes. Alternatively, if something nasty happens to the CVS server during a commit, your commit may fail, with some files changed but with others unchanged. Try hitting Ctrl-C sometime during a CVS commit and then see which files were committed and which ones weren't. (Don't worry—another commit will catch the files that were missed by the first one.) When you create a tag, CVS doesn't let you record a message with a description of why the tag was created. Renaming a file causes a break in the recorded history of that file. Changing the name of a directory requires intervention in the repository by the CVS administrator and may not always be possible, so choose your directory names and hierarchy very carefully.

Living with branches and merging in CVS is somewhat of a headache, as described earlier in this chapter in "Branches and Tags" and "When to Branch? When to Tag?"; you should always tag CVS branches before merging from them. Using CVS to keep track of source code from a third party by *importing* it into your repository is a task to do with a clear head and a written set of notes in front of you, and be careful not to use the files that you just imported from again—check out a fresh copy instead. Authentication, authorization, and accounting support in CVS is rather rudimentary, and there is no support for an internationalized version of the tool. CVS works best with text files but can handle binary files, albeit inefficiently (and don't forget to use cvs add -kb to disable keyword substitution, in order to avoid corrupting such nontext files). Once an RCS file in a CVS repository exceeds about 10 versions and 100MB on a server with 1GB RAM, you can expect to see slower checkouts of that file, especially if it is on a branch.

Making your life with CVS easier

This section contains a number of ideas that can make administering more complex installations of CVS easier:

Use modules

The name of what you ask CVS to check out for you is referred to as a *module*. The top-level directories in your repository are the default modules. The interesting thing about modules is how they can be used to collect different directories from the repository together into a single target for checking out. For instance, if there is a project in the directory *projects/projectA* and projectA also wants to use files from a directory named *common/xml*, then entries in the *CVSROOT/modules* administrative file such as:

```
# The module named common refers to the top-level directory "common"
common          common
# The module named common_xml refers to the "xml" subdirectory
# in "common" but it will be named src/xml when checked out
common_xml      -d src/xml    common/xml
# The module named projectA is a combination of the
# projects/projectA directory and the common/xml directory
projectA        projects/projectA &common_xml
```

will cause the command cvs co projectA to create a local subdirectory *projectA* with sub-directories *src/xml* and the directories from projectA. This kind of indirection is important because it can create different directory structures simply by defining new modules. Be warned, though, that you can't tell CVS to use one particular version of the *modules* file, so be careful not to change the module definitions that are needed for older releases of projects. Modules are an aspect of CVS that are often overlooked, perhaps because they seem complicated to configure, but understanding what you can do with them will make your life with CVS much easier.

Avoid symbolic links

The temptation is so strong. You want to move a directory within the source tree and yet somehow preserve the change history of all its files. You know that just moving the directory in the repository will break your ability to go back in time, since CVS doesn't version directories, only files. But what if you moved the directory anyway and then created a symbolic link (a file that points to another file, also known as a *soft link*) from the old location to the new one? Yes, it works: developers will see the directory in both the old and new locations, and can commit files in either directory, though locking the directory may not work properly if you configure CVS to use LockDir to keep your locks elsewhere. But what about when the next directory move comes along three months from now? Then you'll have soft links to soft links, and so on. CVS does not keep track of different versions of soft links, so using soft links within a CVS repository always leads to extra work later on.

Sometimes the idea to use soft links arises from wanting to share a directory between two top-level directories without one group having to check out multiple modules. A better approach is to use alias and ampersand modules, as discussed in the previous item in this list.

Synchronize clocks

It's good practice, both for CVS and for build tools such as *make*, to synchronize the clocks on every machine that will use the tools. *ntp* is the most common synchronization client and server for Unix, and your local time server may well even be named something like *ntp.example.com*. Windows XP has its own synchronization client, and the Tardis tool works for all earlier versions of Windows.

Know which commands make immediate changes

After using CVS for a while, you may be lulled into believing that nothing you do in your sandbox can affect the rest of your team until you commit the changes. Wrong! CVS commands that modify the repository, apart from the tagging and branching ones (both the local and remote versions), include cvs add *directory*, which adds a directory immediately, and cvs import, which changes the head of the tree straightaway. (There is a -X argument with more recent versions of the import command to avoid this problem.) To make your life easier, pause to consider before using the tag, add *directory*, and import commands.

Save the output

When you are creating tags or branches with cvs tag, or merging versions with cvs update -j, or using cvs import, it's a good idea to save the lengthy output from these commands. Important information—such as existing tags not being moved or the names of files with merge conflicts in them—appears in the output and is not saved anywhere else. If you do lose the output from a command, you may be able to see which files have conflicts by running cvs -n update.

Be careful with top-level directories

Since renaming directories and moving them around is hard to do well with CVS, some CVS administrators find it helpful to keep all project directories under a single top-level directory. When the time comes to change the directory structure of the project, they can create a new top-level directory and copy the subdirectories into that. One problem with this approach is that it's now more complicated to merge changes into both the old and new top-level directory structures. The neater approach to this problem is to define a module per project and then have the module refer to the directories that make up the project.

Some CVS administrators also find it convenient to make the top-level directory in their repository unwritable by people who aren't also CVS administrators, so that accidental imports don't leave their mistakes there. This does mean that new top-level directories have to be created by a CVS administrator.

Avoid keywords and strings that complicate merges

CVS has some convenient keywords such as $Date$ and Id that are automatically expanded during commits to the current date or other information about the file. Unfortunately, when merging files from one branch to another, CVS does not treat the expanded versions of these variables as special, and merges can end up with hundreds of conflicts to be resolved by hand, where most of them are just changes in the date a file was modified. Many people avoid using these keywords and rely on cvs log for the same information. Still, the Id keyword can be useful if you suspect that releases might escape without their source code being tagged.

Another tip to make merges easier is to avoid using the strings <<<<< and >>>>> in your files. These strings are inserted by CVS to mark conflicts in merged files.

Beware of unexpected shell expansions

If the cvs commit command is used with the -m "*some comment here*" argument to make a comment about a commit, then shell characters in the comment are expanded. So a comment such as cvs commit -m "Changed the default $PATH value" will have $PATH replaced by its value in the current shell, and the commit message will end up looking something like "Changed the default /usr/local/bin:/usr/bin:/bin value" in your logs. This doesn't happen if you use an editor to add the comment or if you use single quotes instead of double quotes.

Change your shell prompt

When you have lots of different branches checked out in different sandboxes, it's easy to forget which one you're working on. Obviously, naming your local directory something suggestive helps, but you can also add the branch name to your shell prompt and even change the color of the cursor. The following incantation does this for the *bash* shell: just replace _branch with some text that appears in your branch names. Other shells have similar abilities.

```
PS1="[\u@\h\$(\
if [ -d CVS ]; then \
  if [ -e CVS/Tag ]; then \
    cat CVS/Tag | sed -e 's/^T/ /' | sed -e 's/^N/ /' \
    | sed -e 's/^D/ Date /' | sed -e 's/_branch/\[\033]12;blue\007\]/'; \
  else \
    echo ' \[\033]12;black\007\]MAIN' ; \
  fi; \
else \
  echo '\[\033]12;black\007\]' ; \
fi) \W]\\$ "
```

Avoid empty directories

You can create empty directories in your CVS repository, and when you check out a tree, the directories will appear as you would expect. There is a handy -P argument to cvs update to remove, or prune, empty directories. However, if you check out a tagged version of your tree, the empty directories are automatically pruned, and you have to run cvs update -d to get them back. The easiest thing to do is avoid empty directories in your source tree and instead create them as needed with your build tool. Adding empty dummy files is an ugly workaround.

Tag CVSROOT too

When you tag some files for a release, don't forget to tag the files in *CVSROOT* too. These files describe how CVS is configured and can change over time. If you want to know which directories a particular module represented at the time of a release, this will help.

CVS is the default choice for SCM for many open source and commercial projects. It is also the base standard by which other SCM tools, both commercial and open source, are measured. Subversion (described in the next section) is designed to be a replacement for CVS, but it will be a long time, if ever, before CVS goes away.

Subversion

Subversion (*http://subversion.tigris.org*) is an open source SCM tool designed as a "compelling replacement for CVS." Subversion development has been partially funded by CollabNet (*http://www.collabnet.com*), a commercial PDE discussed in "CollabNet" in Chapter 3. Subversion is released under the Apache Software Foundation license, with CollabNet given as the copyright holder.

THE HISTORY OF SUBVERSION

The first release of Subversion was in October 2000, and steady monthly releases finally led to Version 1.0 being released in February 2004. Key project members include Karl Fogel (who cowrote one of the CVS books referred to in "CVS," earlier in this chapter), Jim Blandy, C. Michael Pilato, Brian Fitzpatrick, Greg Stein, Kevin Hancock, and Ben Collins-Sussman.

Subversion (also known as SVN) really is like CVS 2.0. Even typing the main command svn feels somehow similar to typing cvs. Even apart from the fact that Subversion has an order of magnitude more code, there are substantial differences between Subversion and CVS under the hood, including a default Berkeley DB database backend rather than the flat-file RCS format used by CVS. (A filesystem backend called FSFS is also available.) However, the basic client/server model used by CVS is unchanged, and you still check files out, edit them, update, and commit them.

While using a Subversion client is as easy as using a CVS client, configuring a Subversion server can be a little harder. The default network protocol used to connect a Subversion server and its clients is based on an extension to HTTP that is called WebDAV. If you already have an Apache web server running on your Subversion server machine, you can configure it to use WebDAV and then install and configure the Berkeley DB database. Alternatively, you can use the svnserve executable, which is much more like CVS's cvs server process in concept.

The major changes in Subversion compared with CVS are:

Renaming directories and files
 Directories are now versioned, just like files. You can rename directories and files and still follow their commit history.

Atomic operations
 All Subversion operations either succeed fully, or fail with no changes made to the repository.

Versioned metadata

Every file and directory can have arbitrary information (*metadata*) associated with it as key/value pairs, and this information is versioned. Recording files' owners, ACLs, and any other information needed for specific sites can be implemented using this mechanism.

Full support for binary files

Subversion is designed to fully support both binary and text files much more efficiently than CVS does.

Cheaper branching and tagging

The cost of branching and tagging need not increase with the project size.

WHERE SUBVERSION AND CVS DIFFER MOST

The major difference about Subversion for most CVS users is what version numbers now mean. In CVS and many other SCM tools, version numbers are assigned per file. In Subversion, version numbers are per change to a repository. So "Version 23" of a file now means that the repository has had 23 commits to it, not that a particular file has had 23 commits to it. This also means that the version number of a file changes on every commit anywhere in the repository, even if the file hasn't changed at all.

Another difference is that tags and branches appear in the URL of the repository and look exactly like directories. For example, the URL for a subdirectory *subdir* in the main development of a project *myproject* could be *http://svn.example.com/myproject/trunk/subdir*, and a branch for release 1.0 could look like *http://svn.example.com/myproject/branches/rel_1_0_branch/subdir*.

Subversion can run on most Unix versions, Windows 2000 (and later for the server), and Mac OS X. Windows support is native and has always been part of the project. The limitation on the server for Windows is due to the use of Berkeley DB, which apparently doesn't run on Windows 95, 98, or ME. Using the FSFS filesystem backend should remove this limitation.

A number of tools to convert data from many other SCM tools to Subversion have been developed as part of the product. The script *cvs2svn* is one such useful tool; it converts existing CVS repositories to Subversion repositories. Some Apache projects have converted some of their repositories to Subversion, and GCC is in the process of doing so.

One of the most remarkable things about Subversion has been just how many other projects have sprung up around it, integrating it into existing IDEs and extending existing tools to support it. Even the effort to provide internationalized versions has been impressive. For web-based viewing of repositories, the Python-based ViewCVS (*http://viewcvs.sourceforge.net*) also supports browsing of Subversion repositories. TortoiseSVN (*http://www.tortoisesvn.org*) is one graphical client for Subversion that is well integrated with the Windows filesystem browser. Another graphical client for Subversion that can be used on Windows, Linux, and Macintosh machines is SmartSVN (*http://www.smartsvn.com*).

Development of all these supporting tools for Subversion has been made easier by clear documentation from the beginning of the project. One of the main sources of information is the book *Version Control with Subversion,* by Ben Collins-Sussman, Brian W. Fitzpatrick, and C. Michael Pilato (O'Reilly), which is also available online at *http://svnbook.red-bean.com.* Other books about Subversion include *Practical Subversion,* by Garrett Rooney (Apress), which is aimed more at SCM administrators; *Pragmatic Version Control Using Subversion,* by Mike Mason (Pragmatic Bookshelf); and *Subversion in Action,* by Jeffrey Machols (Manning). Another useful source of information and discussion about Subversion is the Subversionary web site at *http://www.subversionary.org.*

However, Subversion has limited support for ACLs and the *cvs2svn* script may have some difficulties handling complex branching schemes. The known bugs in Subversion are publicly available at the Subversion home page. Subversion still has plenty of room left to grow, with a number of ideas already scheduled for later releases. One such idea is the ability to track who is editing which files. Another is the ability to lock files so only one person can edit them at a time.

In summary, Subversion set out to build a replacement for CVS while keeping its familiar parts, and for the most part it has succeeded. Expect to see Subversion become the other choice for public SCM tools in PDEs like SourceForge and the Apache Project. CollabNet already uses Subversion as the underlying SCM tool in its PDE product, and more companies are likely to follow.

Arch

Arch (*http://www.gnu.org/software/gnu-arch*) is a distributed open source SCM tool, as opposed to the centralized servers of CVS and Subversion. It's designed to scale to tens of thousands of users, in the same way that peer-to-peer (P2P) tools such as BitTorrent have scaled well for distributing large files. Arch is licensed under the GNU General Public License. Note that Arch is still changing, and the version discussed here is tla-1.3, released in December 2004.

At its simplest, using Arch is like having a repository on your own machine, one that you can make commits to, branch, and generally rearrange as you wish, even on your laptop on an airplane. Then you synchronize from other repositories when you want, and they can accept your changes at their discretion.

Arch is carefully designed to minimize server-side work, so that it can scale well. It assumes that disk space is cheap and that network communication is the most costly operation. Just like Subversion, Arch provides atomic commits across entire source trees. Practically any shared resource such as a directory, FTP server, or web server can be used as an Arch server. Different versions of the metadata such as tags are stored, in addition to the

THE HISTORY OF ARCH

Arch began life as a collection of shell scripts by Tom Lord in 2002. Its growth since then has been rapid, driven by both the attractions of distributed SCM and some good publicity, and Arch has been rewritten in C. The personalities involved in developing Arch are definitely prickly at times, and Arch versus Subversion mudslinging has become something of a cliché in discussions about open source SCM tools.

versions of the files. Arch keeps track of file and directory rename operations by using unique identifiers for everything; these don't change, even when the name of a directory changes.

Changesets are a key part of Arch and use the familiar *diff* format, at least for text files. The unique identifiers for each file make it possible to automatically *patch* files, even when their names have changed. Arch also remembers which changesets have already been applied, so the potential multiple-merge problems of CVS can be avoided. The default format used for storing files and changesets is simple in the extreme—compressed tarballs and a file formatted exactly like an email message. These tarballs have checksums and can also be cryptographically signed to help ensure their integrity. The simple format means that only a few commonly available tools are required for Arch to work properly after installation.

Arch is known to work on GNU/Linux, FreeBSD, NetBSD, AIX, and Solaris. Portability to Windows is planned for the near future, but the main focus for Arch still seems to be Unix-based platforms. Other versions of Arch have been written in languages other than C, but *tla* by Tom Lord seems to be the most commonly used version of Arch.

Currently, the best sources of documentation on Arch are the "Arch Meets Hello World" tutorial at *http://www.gnu.org/software/gnu-arch/tutorial/arch.html* and the ever-changing Wiki at *http://wiki.gnuarch.org*. Documentation of the rather large number of Arch commands (over a hundred) is terse, which contributes to the generally steep learning curve for Arch.

Like any newer product, Arch has its rough edges. When it was evaluated in April 2005 for use with the Linux kernel, it was felt to be too slow for such a large project. Some people feel that the filenames used to refer to particular versions are too long to type comfortably, and that the choice of special characters in the names clashes awkwardly with the same characters used by common shells such as *bash* and also tools such as *vi* and *vim*. Arch has not yet been internationalized, though a fork of it named ArX has been. Other problem areas, which may or may not have been fixed by the time you read this, include the lack of symbolic links, the lack of file permissions (for controlling access), spaces not being allowed in filenames, and some Unix/Windows end-of-line formatting problems. One issue that is unlikely to have changed is that Arch developers can seem arrogant in their zeal for their project.

Arch is the best open source example of a trend in SCM tools toward tools that are distributed, rather than centralized on a single server. The emphasis on changes to a project's source code being seen as a collection of separate changesets is also a distinct trend in all modern SCM tools. In terms of development, Arch is roughly where CVS was 10 years ago: definitely usable for noncritical projects, but rough around the edges, particularly with regard to ease of use and documentation. Still, it has the backing that comes with being an official GNU project, and if development continues as it has, Arch could be a strong contender among open source SCM tools.

Perforce

Perforce (*http://www.perforce.com*) is a commercial SCM tool, currently licensed for around $750 per user, which includes a year of support. There are a range of licensing options, including free use for open source projects.

THE HISTORY OF PERFORCE

Perforce Software was founded by Christoper Seiwald in 1995. Seiwald also created the Jam build tool described in "Jam" in Chapter 5. Perforce sales have grown to include thousands of companies, including Microsoft (see "Visual SourceSafe," later in this chapter) and Google.

Perforce, also known as P4, is a modern, centralized, fully networked SCM tool. It provides atomic commits across entire *depots* (repositories) and supports branching and merging well, including automatically tracking when files were merged. Concurrent access to multiple files is the normal way of using Perforce, but unlike CVS, Perforce also keeps track of who is editing each file. Depots store binary files as compressed files and use an RCS-like format for text files. Metadata about the files and *changelists* (changesets), such as branch information and associated bugs, are stored in a separate, proprietary, journaled database. Backups of Perforce server depots can be made without stopping the server from being used, and no separate licensing server is used, which also reduces administrative work.

Perforce is supported on a wide variety of platforms, including almost all recent Unixes; Windows NT, 2000, and later; Macintosh Classic and Mac OS X; and VMS. Windows 95 and 98 are not supported for Perforce servers. Dozens of other platforms are supported for

Perforce clients. APIs to use Perforce as part of an application exist for C, C++, Java, Perl, and Python, among other languages.

Documentation for Perforce is extensive and of good quality. All the documentation is freely downloadable in convenient file formats from the company's web site. Judging by comments in newsgroups and weblogs and from what I've heard through other sources, the product support team at Perforce is excellent. Training and other consulting services are readily available.

Perforce has been carefully designed to scale well as projects grow. For instance, tagging and branching operations are fast, taking much less than the linear time seen with CVS. The Perforce web page *http://www.perforce.com/perforce/reviews.html* provides some useful comparisons of various SCM tools and tells how each one scales as a project grows.

Like any SCM tool that uses a database, Perforce requires attention to maintenance. Disk space allocation and tuning procedures are well documented in the *Perforce System Administrator's Guide*. Integrity-checking tools are provided to guard against database corruption. Renaming directories and files is a two-step process, but the history of each step is retained. Files on the client machine are read-only until the user tells Perforce that she wants to edit them. This can be awkward if you are working offline, or if an external application wants to write temporary changes to files that are stored in Perforce.

In summary, Perforce is similar in architecture to CVS but has stronger functionality and is much faster. The product is mature and well supported, and there are numerous tools that extend or integrate Perforce in various customized ways. Perforce is a good choice for larger groups of developers, especially within a company with the resources to administer it properly.

BitKeeper

BitKeeper (*http://www.bitkeeper.com*) is a commercial SCM product from BitMover. Bit-Keeper is licensed per person who modifies files, and licenses can either be purchased for around $1,750 or leased for around a third of the purchase cost. There is also a different license for using BitKeeper at no cost. The version described here is 3.2.3, released in August 2004.

BitKeeper, also known as BK, is a modern, distributed SCM tool, complete with atomic operations, changesets, file metadata, strong support for branching and merging, and a web-based graphical interface. Since BitKeeper is fully distributed, it has no central point of failure and it scales extremely well. It also helps that the bandwidth requirements for most common BitKeeper actions are relatively small. Every developer effectively has a copy of the repository on his machine, which makes working with the proverbial laptop on an airplane easy. You can make your local changes available (a *push*) using a wide variety of protocols from SSH to HTTP, or even using email.

BitKeeper handles all the complexity of pushing the changes in a local repository out to other developers' repositories. Renaming of files is handled well, including the tricky

THE HISTORY OF BITKEEPER

BitMover, Inc., the company that produces BitKeeper, was founded by Larry McVoy and others in 1998. McVoy was also the designer of TeamWare, the SCM tool used and sold by Sun. A huge success for BitKeeper was its choice by Linus Torvalds as the SCM tool to replace CVS for developing the GNU/Linux kernel. Some open source developers found the terms of the free license unpalatable, and there was some spirited discontent back in 2002, when a few Subversion developers clashed with Larry McVoy over the changing terms of the free license. The publicity doesn't seem to have hindered BitKeeper's sales. In early 2005, reverse engineering of BitKeeper's protocol led to the free version of BitKeeper no longer being offered by BitMover. Torvalds then began developing an SCM tool named *git*, which was designed as a possible replacement for BitKeeper in the Linux kernel project.

---

problem of two developers renaming the same file at the same time. You can add different comments to different files in a changeset, which is sometimes useful. The data format used by BitKeeper is based on SCCS, the original Unix SCM tool created by Marc Rochkind in 1972. SCCS files include checksums to help avoid corrupted data.

BitKeeper runs on most modern Unixes, Mac OS X, and Windows 98 and later releases. There is an long-standing offer from BitMover to support any platform for a sale of over 50 licenses, providing it is POSIX-compliant and not prohibitively expensive.

Documentation for BitKeeper is good, though the printable versions are available only with the product. Online documentation is extensive, and support is reportedly very responsive. There is a good demonstration of BitKeeper available at *http://www.bitkeeper.com/Test.html*. There is an open source BitKeeper client available from BitMover (*http://www.bitmover.com/bk-client.shar*), though this tool only extracts files from repositories. There is also an open source tool called SourcePuller (*http://sourceforge.net/projects/sourcepuller*) that can interact more generally with BitKeeper. Development of this tool was what led to the free version of BitKeeper ceasing in 2005.

BitKeeper is an attractive commercial SCM tool. The pricing scheme seems to indicate that BitKeeper is competing against ClearCase and is intended for use by large businesses, while still working closely with the open source community for the good publicity. Being chosen for GNU/Linux kernel development is a strong endorsement for any SCM tool.

ClearCase

ClearCase (*http://www.ibm.com/software/rational*) is the SCM part of a large change management environment known as the Rational Unified Process. ClearCase is licensed commercially at around $5,000 per developer, though this is negotiated on a per-site basis, and there is a "lite" version available for around $1,250.

THE HISTORY OF CLEARCASE

ClearCase grew out of the DSEE SCM tool by Apollo (which was later bought by HP) but was first developed and released by Atria in 1992. Atria merged with PureSoft, and the merged company was later bought by Rational, which in turn was bought by IBM. ClearCase is used by HP, 3Com, eBay, Cisco, and many other large computer-related companies.

ClearCase is unique among the major SCM tools in that it uses a separate, versioned, distributed filesystem on each developer's machine. Once in this filesystem, you automatically see the chosen versions of the files managed by ClearCase. So you never have to manually update your local copy of a file—the filesystem just makes it appear for you. Alternatively, you can freeze different parts of what you see at particular versions. Developers choose which versions of which sets of files they wish to see by modifying their "configuration specification" file, also known as the "config spec." These files can build on top of each other, allowing for complicated descriptions of which files you end up actually using.

WARNING
If the ClearCase server is unavailable, not only will developers be unable to use the SCM tool, they won't see the directories containing the ClearCase controlled files. To ensure that the networked filesystem remains available all the time, ClearCase supports redundant servers as well as the ability to distribute source trees across multiple servers.

Directories as well as files are versioned, and the ClearCase filesystem supports soft links. The branching and merging environment provided by ClearCase has good graphical support, and the merge tools seem particularly well liked. The ClearCase *make* tool, ClearMake, provides extensive information about all generated objects—you can even view the precise command used to generate an object file at any time. ClearCase can also use this information to *wink in* object files that have already been built, rather like *ccache* does (see "Slow Builds" in Chapter 5). However, ClearMake is noticeably slower than other versions of *make*, though the accuracy of dependency checking is much improved. ClearMake can also automatically produce a "bill of materials" (BOM) for a release, listing the specific version of each file used to construct the build. Of course, a BOM is only one part of what is needed to reproduce a release: the tools used and their versions are others.

ClearCase servers and clients are supported on AIX, HP-UX, IRIX, GNU/Linux, Solaris, and Windows NT, 2000, and later versions.

ClearCase comes with extensive documentation and support from IBM. Two useful books are *The Art of ClearCase Deployment: The Secrets to Successful Implementation*, by Darren W. Pulsipher and Christian D. Buckley (Addison-Wesley), and *Software Configuration Management Strategies and Rational ClearCase: A Practical Introduction*, by Brian A. White (Addison-Wesley).

The biggest drawback of ClearCase for many organizations is its cost, both the initial per-seat cost and the cost of the substantial administrative team required to keep ClearCase working. The large amount of administrative work needed to keep ClearCase running properly explains why it is rarely found in smaller companies. ClearCase can use large amounts of disk space on developers' machines, depending on how it is configured, and places substantial demands on networks. When either of these resources is limited, the performance of ClearCase can become very slow. For small to medium projects, ClearCase is usually seen as overkill.

Visual SourceSafe

Visual SourceSafe (*http://msdn.microsoft.com/vstudio/productinfo*) is a commercial centralized SCM tool from Microsoft. As of 2005, licenses are available for approximately $500 per seat.

THE HISTORY OF VISUAL SOURCESAFE

SourceSafe, originally written by Brian Harry and Kenny Felder, was purchased by Microsoft in 1994. Development continued, with the current release being Visual SourceSafe 6.0.

Interestingly, Microsoft itself used an internally developed version of RCS named SLM until 1999, when it began using a version of Perforce named SourceDepot.

Visual SourceSafe is a centralized SCM tool, usually used in a locking (*pinning*) manner, where only one developer can change a file at a time. It's designed to be used almost exclusively on Windows-based platforms by small groups of developers. One of its strengths is its tight integration with Visual Studio and other Microsoft tools. However, it is not unique in that respect, since Perforce, BitKeeper, and ClearCase also integrate well with Visual Studio. Commits are *not* atomic across a source tree.

There is one non-Microsoft book about Visual SourceSafe—*Essential SourceSafe*, by Ted Roche and Larry C. Whipple (Hentzenwerke Publishing)—but it doesn't cover the subjects that many developers find hard to use, such as branching. In the end, the tool's own online help and the MSDN library have the largest amount of information about Visual SourceSafe.

Visual SourceSafe is an older product, and frankly, it's showing its age. You can find some (mostly negative) opinions about it at *http://www.highprogrammer.com/alan/windev/sourcesafe.html* and *http://www.developsense.com/testing/VSSDefects.html*, and a more balanced discussion at *http://c2.com/cgi/wiki?SourceSafe*. You could also pay $99 for a formal report by Forrester (*http://www.forrester.com*). Some people claim that they have had their stored files corrupted using the tool, while others dismiss these claims. Using branches with Visual Studio projects seems to be more complicated than usual to get right, and performance is never fast enough. Supporting multiple time zones for developers requires other add-on products.

Some of these issues may be addressed in future releases, but I don't recommend using Visual SourceSafe for any new project. If you are looking for a product that feels like Visual Source-Safe, there is Vault, a commercial SCM tool from SourceGear (*http://www.sourcegear.com*) that uses the same terminology as Visual SourceSafe but does everything more robustly and over larger networks. There is also a new SCM product from Microsoft, provisionally named Visual Studio 2005 Team System, that's intended for larger groups of developers than is Visual SourceSafe; it is due for release sometime in late 2005.

Comparison of SCM Tools

Table 4-1 briefly summarizes my opinion of how each of the seven SCM tools described in this chapter matches up to the suggestions at the start of "SCM Tools," earlier in this chapter, about what to look for in such a tool. Several such comparisons exist on the Internet—for example, *http://better-scm.berlios.de/comparison* (which has no comparison of merging and is undated) and *http://wiki.gnuarch.org/moin.cgi/SubVersionAndCvsComparison* (which is a mutable Wiki). However, when comparing SCM tools using these tables, be careful to choose one that will work for your project; don't just go by the number of features the tool has. In Table 4-1, a plus sign (+) indicates a strength and a minus sign (-) indicates a relative weakness.

TABLE 4-1. Comparison of SCM tools

Requirement	CVS	Subversion	Arch	Perforce	BitKeeper	ClearCase	Visual SourceSafe
Data integrity	+	+	+	+	+	–	–
Fast tagging	–	+	+	+	+	+	–
Easy branching/merging	–	+	+	+	+	+	–
Integration	+	+	–	+	+	–	+
Web interface	+	+	–	+	+	+	–
Good support	+	+	–	+	+	+	+

Wider Uses of SCM

Most of this chapter has been about using SCM tools to control the source code for a product. To have confidence that you can repeat previous releases, you need to control much more than just the source code. Parts of the development environment to consider include all the tools used in the build process, the operating system as configured on the build machine, the test environment and the target operating systems, documentation, and finally how the SCM tool itself was configured at the time of the build. If all that sounds like too much load for your SCM tool, then at least create backups of the various tools and machines and store them somewhere safe off site.

One great use for SCM in your development environment is for people's personal machines, where the data is perhaps not backed up in any other way. On Unix machines, keeping a copy of each person's /etc directory and all the dotfiles from the home directory provides easy recovery when a disk fails. On Windows, a copy of each person's *My Documents* directory will let you recover key files at some point.

Checklist

This section contains a short list of questions that you should feel comfortable answering about how you use an existing SCM tool:

- What is saved in your SCM system? What is not in your SCM system? Why?
- What have you overlooked? Often the only time this question is carefully answered is when a hard disk dies and you try to recreate your environment. List all the files, tools, and other pieces of your environment that you use to build a release.
- Can you still recreate older releases if a file is renamed?
- Can you still recreate older releases if a directory is renamed?
- How do you know the date on which a file was branched?
- How do you know the intended purpose of each branch?
- Who can change permissions for write and read access to the SCM tool?
- What happens with your SCM tool if two files in the same directory have the same name, but one is uppercase and one is lowercase? What happens if a filename has spaces in it?
- How does the backup size of your SCM tool's files change over time? When will you next fill up a key disk, CD, DVD, or tape?
- Can you develop on a laptop on an airplane? How much of your SCM tool still works, and how do you resynchronize when you reconnect later on?
- How would you add a process to your SCM tool—for example, requiring each change to be reviewed by other people?
- Do you have good integration between your SCM tool and your bug tracking system?
- How do you decide when to upgrade your SCM tool, whether it's to fix bugs in the tool or for extra functionality?
- What is the most common mistake that people using your SCM tool make? How could you help them to avoid doing that?

## CHAPTER FIVE

Building Software

THIS CHAPTER DISCUSSES HOW SOFTWARE PRODUCTS ARE BUILT FROM THEIR SOURCE FILES. The first half of the chapter describes what a build tool is and what you might want a build tool to do. The second half compares six of the most commonly used build tools: shell scripts and batch files, *make*, GNU Autotools, Ant, Jam, and SCons.

One solid study, not written by a consultant working for a company that sells a build tool, suggests that between 10% and 30% of the time spent working on many complex software projects is spent wrestling with the build tool, waiting for slow builds, or investigating phantom bugs due to inconsistent builds.* That's a substantial amount of time! Whether you believe the figures or not, frustrating experiences with a build tool can certainly make any project far less productive. Conversely, a good build tool can fade into the background and let you get on with writing code.

The purpose of this chapter is to help you choose and use an appropriate build tool for your project. If that choice has already been made, then the examples and references for each build tool should help you use the build tool better. If you are using a build tool that isn't described here, then the general observations about builds should still be useful.

---

* G. Kumfert and T. Epperly, "Software in the DOE: The Hidden Overhead of 'The Build,'" Lawrence Livermore National Laboratory technical report, available at *http://www.osti.gov/energycitations/ product.biblio.jsp?osti_id=15005938* (2002).

How Software Gets Built

This section is a brief overview of how source code is turned into an *executable*, a program that can actually run on a computer. This is the process is known as "building software." A summary of the different stages of a build is shown in the next section, "The Different Stages of a Build." This summary is also used later on when considering how different build tools work in practice.

Source code (or "the program") is what developers (or "programmers") write. Source code can be written in high-level programming languages (such as C or Java), scripting or dynamic languages (such as Perl or Python), or low-level languages (such as assembly code). Source code can also be binary files such as images or precompiled libraries. Loosely speaking, anything needed by your product that cannot be generated from another place within your project is part of the source for your project. A *build* is the process in which a build tool uses other tools to convert the source code into a working product that can be used by other people.

How a product is used by other people varies for different customers and different machines. Some languages (such as Perl) are interpreted, which means that the source code is used directly by software that's already on the machine. This existing software is called an *interpreter*. Other languages (such as C and Java) are compiled, which means that another tool called a *compiler* converts the source code to the appropriate binary file format for the CPU to execute on each particular machine.

Writing source code is relatively straightforward until the amount of source code begins to grow. To help you keep track of what's going on in your program, you really want to divide up the source code. "Put the GUI code in these files, put the disk access code over here in this file, and then put all the database interface code into all these other files," and so on. Each of these parts depend on some of the other parts, but they probably don't depend on *all* of the other parts, and so dividing up the code in this way makes the product easier to imagine. Products depend upon these other parts being present, either when the product is compiled (at *compile time*) or when the program is run (at *runtime*).

To reduce the number of dependencies between different parts of the program, all kinds of simple and complex mechanisms have been invented over the years. Some of the commonly used ones are header files, data encapsulation, and interfaces. "Build Dependencies," later in this chapter, goes into more details. What all these approaches have in common is an attempt to make it very clear to different parts of the program how to use the other parts. These ideas do indeed help reduce the number of interfaces between different parts of a program, but at the cost of having to update them as the program grows.

The problem of building programs starts to get harder when different parts of the program have to be built in a certain order. For instance, with C programs you commonly build *.o* or *.obj* object files and then combine them into library files, before linking the generated files together to create an executable. With Java, you have to build *.class* files before you can create a *.jar* file. Before running your Java program, you'll also have to make sure that any other required *.class* or *.jar* files are present on your machine.

Whatever the particular requirements are for building the different parts of a program in a certain order, you might think that making sure that all those different steps are performed in the right order shouldn't be too hard. After all, it's just like a recipe for a meal with a large number of ingredients and lots of complicated steps to follow in order. Build tools are designed to perform the specified steps, using a defined build process—the *recipe*—which is usually described in *build files*. Once the recipe has been defined, then it just needs to be followed by the build tool.

If a program is not being changed, then even the simplest build tools should be able to follow a well-defined build process. However, change is inevitable in any program that is being developed or maintained. Changing just one source file means that the changed file has to be rebuilt. After that, other files that depend on the changed file have to be rebuilt. (The structure of which files depend on which is known as the *dependency tree*.) Shifting up to the next conceptual gear, the list of files that depend on the changed file also changes over time. That is, the parts of a program that need to be rebuilt for a particular change is *not* constant. Once the build tool has worked out which parts of the programs need rebuilding, it has to execute the appropriate commands to build just those parts. These commands may also have their own required order (e.g., compile before linking). Table 5-1 describes some of the ways that source code can change and what the build tools have to do to deal with the changes.

TABLE 5-1. When builds change

Type of change	What the build tool should do
New files were added.	[The developer needs to update the build files and check them for correctness.]
The contents of a file changed.	Rebuild the file; detect whether the compile failed or succeeded.
A file depends on some other file whose contents changed in some way.	Rebuild all the affected files.
A file now depends on a file that already exists.	Rebuild the dependency tree. Can the file be located properly?
A file now depends on a new file.	Rebuild the dependency tree. Does the new file already exist, or will it be created as part of the build?
A file no longer depends on another file.	Rebuild the dependency tree. Does the existence of the old file cause a problem? Should it be deleted?
A file now depends on a generated file.	Make sure that the dependency tree causes the file to be generated before it is needed.
A file now depends on a generated file whose own source has changed.	Regenerate all the necessary generated files.

NOTE

The hardest things to get right with build processes have to do with what happens when dependencies change, not when source code changes—it's like having a recipe change every time you try to use it.

Some concrete examples of the different types of changes shown in Table 5-1 are as follows ("*foo.c* → *foo.o*" means that *foo.o* depends on *foo.c*):

foo.c → *foo.o*
> The contents of the file *foo.c* were changed, so the file *foo.o* needs to be rebuilt.

foo.h → *foo.c* → *foo.o*
> The contents of the file *foo.h* were changed, and *foo.c* depends on *foo.h*, so *foo.o* needs to be rebuilt.

{*foo.h bar.h*} → *foo.c* → *foo.o*
> *foo.c* now depends on both *foo.h* and *bar.h*, so *foo.o* needs to be rebuilt.

bar.h → *foo.c* → *foo.o*
> *foo.c* now depends only on *bar.h*, so *foo.o* needs to be rebuilt. All information linking *foo.c* and *foo.h* should be forgotten.

foo.y → *foo.c* → *foo.o*
> *foo.c* is now a generated file, derived from *foo.y*, so *foo.c* (and consequently *foo.o*) needs to be rebuilt whenever *foo.y* is changed or if the tools that generate *foo.c* change.

The Different Stages of a Build

Builds are made up of a number of different stages, just as compilers can have preprocessing, compiling, and linking stages. Each stage is usually performed by the same build tool, though not always. For example, configuration and the calculation of dependencies may use separate tools, sometimes even using the compiler itself. In practice, some of these build stages are small or nonexistent with some build tools, but the order of the stages is usually the same for all build tools. The sequence of the different stages for a typical build tool is:

Define the targets
> What would you like to build? Everything? Just one file? A subset of files? The answer to this defines the *targets* of the build. By default, some build tools build as much as possible, while others just build the targets that are defined for the files in the current directory. The desired targets can usually be specified on the command line or as defaults in build files.

Read the build files
> The names of the executables and the source files for each executable are defined explicitly somewhere, often in build files. The contents of a generic build file are shown in the next section, "A Typical Build File." The build tool reads the build files so that it knows what it's trying to do. It also reports syntax errors in the build files.

Configuration
> The build tool discovers which platform and tools are to be used. The results of the build may be intended for a different platform than the one on which the build is executed (i.e., a cross-compilation), and this platform's details may be specified at the command line, along with the build targets. Some build tools assume that particular platforms have certain tools. Other build tools perform small experiments to discover precisely what works and how.

Calculate the dependencies

The build tool scans the build files and source files to work out which parts of the program depend on which other parts. Many dependencies are not specified in the build files, because there are too many of them and updating them by hand would be both error-prone and tedious. Instead, they are discovered by the build tool in this stage. This stage also reports any errors such as *circular dependencies*, where the chain of dependencies has a loop in it.

Determine what to build

Using the dependencies, the build tool works out which files need to be updated or generated. It reports errors such as nonexistent source files or files that couldn't be generated.

Construct the build commands

The build tool assembles the appropriate commands to update the out-of-date parts of the program. These commands are different for each platform and developer; even a tool such as *gcc* may be used with very different arguments on different platforms.

Execute the build commands

The build tool runs the commands to update the files that need updating and reports any errors returned by the commands. If there are errors, you can often choose whether to stop the whole build or to keep going.

Some of the stages may be repeated during a build. For instance, if source files are generated by executing some build commands, their dependencies will also need to be calculated. Likewise, the actual build commands that are executed may be constructed piece by piece.

A Typical Build File

Example 5-1 shows a generic build file, showing how some dependencies are specified; others will be discovered by the build tool. For example, the build tool does not specify what other files are required by *fileA*.

EXAMPLE 5-1. A build file

```
# The executable myproduct is made up of fileA and fileB and uses
# libraryX as well
executable("myproduct", "fileA, fileB", "libraryX")

# The library named libraryX is made up of file1 and file2
library("libraryX", "file1, file2")

# This list of tests comprises two files named test_alice and test_bob
# which are defined in some other build file
files("tests", "test_alice, test_bob")

# Installation targets which specify the files that are built for each
# different kind of user
install("testers", "myproduct, tests")
install("customer", "myproduct")
```

Build States: Virgin, Up-to-date, Changed, Interrupted, Clean

The *build state* is the state of the source files used by the build tool when it starts a build. However, except for references to "clean builds," the names for the different states that a build can be in don't seem to be standardized, certainly not in any well-known way. So I have invented names for each state: *virgin*, *up-to-date*, *changed*, *interrupted*, and *clean*. Each state is explained in more detail in this section.

> **WARNING**
>
> Build states refer to the state of the source code being used *at the start of the build*. This assumes that the build process has been correctly defined, with no syntax errors, circular dependencies, or similar mistakes in the build files. This means that whether a build succeeds or fails depends only on the state of the source code, not on the build process.

Understanding different build states is useful when talking about builds. Imagine the next time you want to describe to someone exactly how your product's build is broken. "Virgin builds are broken" is much more precise than just "the build's broken." The latter often receives a response of "well, it works for me," when what the person actually means is "changed builds work for me." Debugging a build problem often depends on the build state, and names for the specific kinds of build states help improve communication between developers.

Virgin

A completely fresh set of source code files, never before used in any build. Changes may have been made to source files, but no build has ever used them. Other names for this state could be *sterile* or *unbuilt*, but *virgin* reminds me of a virgin forest.

Up-to-date

No changes have been made in the source code files (or in any generated files) since the last build. If the build tool is performing correctly, this state is where builds end up, and every intended target is up-to-date.

Changed

Changes have been made in the set of source code files or generated files since the last time the build process was started. Typically, this happens by editing some of the source files, but sometimes there is information such as the time of the build or the build label that is different for every build. (Another name for this state could be *dirty*, in the sense of being the opposite of clean.)

Interrupted

The last time that the build tool was run it was interrupted, so some files may be incomplete or have unexpected contents. To use database terminology, running a build tool is not an atomic transaction, since no rollback capability is defined for the files that it changes.

Clean

All the files that were generated by a previous build have been deleted from the source files. Ideally, this state is identical to that of a virgin build, including the state of any modified source files. In practice, some generated files may get missed, or some files may have had their timestamps updated by the build or changed in some other way.

Figure 5-1 shows each of the different build states and how a set of source files moves from one state to another.

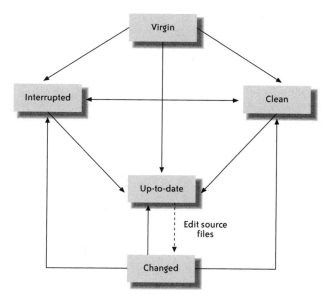

FIGURE 5-1. Five different build states

If a build process is working properly, then there are some assumptions that you can make to reduce the number of build states from five to three, which should make describing a build a little easier. If your build process has bugs in it, then you should use all five build states to make debugging it easier.

First, let's assume that our build files are carefully written so that the clean build state is the same as a virgin build state, and we can eliminate the virgin state.

Second, we can assume that interrupting a build is similar to modifying the source code, albeit in an unknown manner. This sounds rather scary, but it's a valid assumption—when you stop a build, you don't actually know what state the build tool has left various files in. This is especially true if you have written custom shell scripts and run them as part of your build. Figure 5-2 shows the different build states after making these two simplifications. Figure 5-2 is like Figure 5-1, but with the virgin state merged into the clean state and the interrupted state merged into the changed state.

Good Builds, Bad Builds

A successful or *good* build is one where the build tool was able to do what you asked it to do, such as building the product. A *broken*, *failed*, or *bad* build is one where the build tool was unable to do what you asked it to do. Builds can break for many reasons. Some of

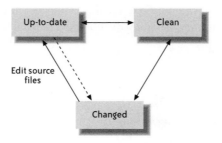

FIGURE 5-2. Three simplified build states

these are: incorrect source code, incorrect build dependencies (which are discussed in "When Build Dependencies Go Wrong," later in this chapter), changes in the tools or their options used in a build (especially for cross-compiles), lack of disk space, or network interruptions.

Build states refer to the state of the source code being used at the start of the build, but they don't say anything about whether the code will compile or even if it makes any sense. So whether a build was successful or failed has nothing to do with the build state. That is, a virgin build is still a virgin build, whether its first build turned out to be a good or bad one.

Build States and Different Targets

State diagrams such as Figure 5-1 and Figure 5-2 apply for every target that a build tool knows about. If you ask the build tool to build the whole project, then the source files needed to build the whole project are referred to in each state. If you ask the build tool just to build one small executable target, then the source files for the state diagrams are only the ones that matter for that particular target.

The size of the set of files related to each state depends on what you asked the build tool to do, but the different build states apply to each different target's set of files.

Build States in Practice

Let's assume that you have a local machine with a copy of the source code for your product. Perhaps you used an SCM tool to access an internal site in your company. Perhaps the source tree came as part of an open source distribution that you downloaded. Either way, now you have the source code, and you're ready to build it for the first time. This kind of build is a *virgin* build.

After you've tried to build the product, the set of files that the build tool knows about will have changed. You've probably generated some intermediate files. If you wanted to build the product and succeeded, then you have probably generated some file you could actually use. Some new source code files may have been generated as part of the build. The build state is now *changed*, because the set of files that is used by the build tool has changed. This is true whether the build succeeded or failed.

Since you have the source code, you decide to make some changes to it. Maybe your manager thinks that's what you're paid to do, or maybe you do it even though you don't get paid for it; it doesn't matter. After you've made your changes, you rerun the build tool to create a new version of the product. The changes you made may only have been small ones, perhaps a few lines in just a couple of files, but this kind of a build is still a changed build, just as it was after you first ran the build tool.

Now that particular build has finished, and ideally it just rebuilt the parts of the program that depend on the files you changed. However, you can't remember if you saved one particular change before you reran the build. "Never mind," you think, "I'll just rebuild it again to be safe." If in fact you had already saved all your changes, then you'll get an *up-to-date* build. This kind of build is one where the generated files are already up-to-date from the previous build. In a perfect world, no one would ever perform an up-to-date build—why would you rebuild something if there have been no changes and the generated files are already up-to-date? In practice, people perform up-to-date builds to convince themselves that they are not getting a changed build—that is, to make sure that nothing has changed unexpectedly. Since these builds do occur, they should be as short in duration as possible, because all they are doing is rechecking the build dependencies and they shouldn't actually have to execute any commands.

From past experience, you know that before you commit your changes, you want to make sure that they will work in a *clean* build. A clean build attempts to restore the source code to what it looked like when you first obtained it, except for any changes that you've made to the source files. A clean build does this by removing all the generated files, both generated source code and generated executable files. The reason that there are both clean and virgin build states is that not all clean builds really do restore the build to a virgin state. One easy way this difference can appear is when dependencies change, and the last versions of generated files (which no longer need to be built) still continue to exist. Another way is that some build tools leave *droppings*, small files scattered all over the source tree to maintain information about the state of the build; these droppings don't exist in virgin builds.

This time, you didn't interrupt your build tool in any way, so you never entered the other kind of build state, the *interrupted* build. This state, which is often quietly assumed to be the same as the changed build state, occurs when the build tool was in the middle of execution but was stopped somehow. Some tools can leave half-written or inconsistent sets of files in this case. As noted earlier, shell scripts that are executed as part of a build are particularly susceptible to creating this build state in their generated files. Programs that generate source code files are also vulnerable. Even compilers can leave incomplete object files if they are interrupted at just the wrong moment. Interrupted builds can produce very odd errors with build tools. Luckily, a virgin build will usually make things work again, but that does take time. The better approach is to make sure that generators and scripts clean up before and after themselves; also, such scripts should never assume that they ran to completion the last time they were run.

Build Dependencies

Untangling the complex and implicit dependencies between source files is one reason that a build tool is necessary for anything but small projects. This section describes what is meant by *build dependencies*, using C and Java source code as examples. It also looks at when build tools can automatically detect dependencies and when they cannot.

A source file has *explicit* dependencies, which are the files, classes, methods, and functions that can be seen directly in the source file itself. A source file also has *implicit* dependencies, which are all the dependencies of the file's explicit dependencies, extending in multiple steps right out to files that have no other dependencies (the *leaves* on the dependency tree).

In C source code, functions are usually defined in *.c* source files, also known as *implementation files*. A function f1 can use functions f2 and f3 only if the compiler already knows enough information about the functions f2 and f3 to work out how to generate the code to invoke them at runtime. If the functions f2 and f3 are defined in a different source file from function f1, then you have to tell the compiler about them somehow. This is usually done with a *header* or *.h* file, which contains *declarations* about the functions f2 and f3. For example, here is the contents of a header file named *wombat.h*:

```
extern void f2(int age);

extern int f3(char *name);
```

Each file that wants to use the functions named in *wombat.h* uses the preprocessor directive #include "wombat.h", usually somewhere near the start of the file. This causes the contents of the file *wombat.h* to be literally inserted in place of the #include line at compile time. Now the compiler will have enough information about the implementations of functions f2 and f3 to be able to compile the file. Locating the exact *wombat.h* file can be hard to make portable, so there are *include* or -I arguments that can be passed to the compiler to suggest where to look for header files and to specify the order in which to search directories for header files.

So if the file *wombat.h* is in a directory named */projects/phascolomys* (*phascolomys* happens to be the genus for wombats), but the file that's including *wombat.h* is in some other directory, then the compiler has to be called with an argument -I "/projects/phascolomys" so that it can locate *wombat.h*.

Dependency checking for C programs involves scanning *.c* and *.h* files for statements such as #include "wombat.h" and using the current -I arguments to locate the *wombat.h* file. The file *wombat.h* is marked as a file that the given *.c* file is dependent on, and then *wombat.h* can be scanned in turn for more #include lines. Figure 5-3 shows this idea more clearly with three header files and one file (*main.c*) that uses them.

The whole business of dependency checking by scanning files for #include directives is complicated by the use of #ifdef directives: the presence of an #ifdef means that, depending on how the preprocessor is invoked, particular #include directives may be used or ignored. So the dependency tree really needs to be generated uniquely for each set of flags passed to the tools used by a build tool.

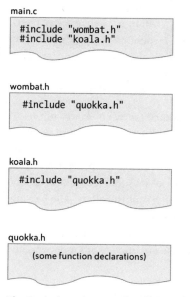

The simple dependency tree found by searching the source code for lines starting with #include looks like:

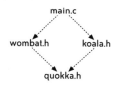

FIGURE 5-3. File dependency example for C source code

Figure 5-4 shows a dependency tree where the only things that can depend on source files are generated files. That is, source files don't depend on source files. This represents what you really want a build tool to do. For instance, if you have two instances of *main.o*, each one may have been built using a different set of #define flags. This issue is also discussed in "How Build Dependencies Change," later in this chapter.

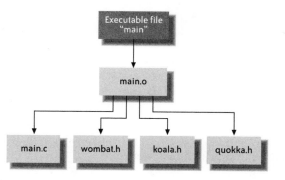

FIGURE 5-4. Dependency example for generated files

Java source code contains import lines, but these are just so that you can refer to things in a shortened format. Java also has the added complication for dependency checking that a single *.java* file can generate multiple *.class* files. Dependency checking for Java means analyzing the contents of the generated *.class* files. Java also has the concept of *reflection*, where you can use a class that is named only at runtime. Classes invoked by reflection are a good example of dependencies that build tools cannot be expected to identify automatically.

There is another kind of dependency analysis named *functional dependency analysis*, which is working out which functions call which other functions. This is part of what compilers do when they want to optimize code. This kind of dependency analysis is *not* what build tools do, because build tools are mostly independent of the details of the programming language that is being used in the source code. So when a build tool says that it supports dependency checking for a particular language, don't expect too much sophistication—the parsing of the source code files for dependencies is usually a simple search with a few regular expressions. Some build tools (including Jam and SCons) let you examine and extend the regular expressions that are used to decide which lines in a source file are important for dependency analysis.

When Build Dependencies Go Wrong

What happens if your build tool gets the build dependencies wrong? "Nothing good" is the short answer. If you're lucky, your builds will just take a little longer while some files are unnecessarily rebuilt. If you're unlucky, files that should have been rebuilt don't get rebuilt, and then not only do your changes not appear in the new version of the program, but you may also get very odd crashes and hard-to-debug output.

However, the really damaging effect of incorrect dependencies is that developers start to always do clean builds by default, just to be sure that their changes are correctly incorporated into the next build. Since the shortest clean build always takes longer than any changed build (unless dependency checking takes too long), the developers have just lost valuable coding time waiting for the longer clean build to complete.

Another approach that is sometimes used to try and survive in a project with incorrect build dependencies is to run the build tool multiple times. This may help with circular dependencies (where the dependency tree has a loop in it), but in general it just wastes more development time. How do you know how many times to rerun the build? The solution is to fix the explicit dependencies that are in your build files or to fix the build tool's analysis of implicit dependencies—not to cross your fingers and invoke *make* thrice.

There are some specific instances where calculating the correct build dependencies is harder. Reflection in Java classes is one example, as mentioned earlier. Working with generated source code is another example. With generated source files, the new files ought to be used when calculating the file dependencies, but this is often overlooked or is too hard to do well with many build tools. If generated source files are not added to the build dependencies, then the only way to regenerate a generated file may be to delete it before the build starts, which is awkward and prone to error.

Yet another example of difficult dependency analysis is when some of the build files themselves are generated as part of a build. This requires a build tool that can recalculate all its dependencies again after certain types of files are generated. I'm not aware of any current build tool that supports this concept well, so be careful when using this idea.

On a more positive note, what do you gain if you use a build tool that does get the build dependencies right? One capability is better support for *parallel builds*. Parallel builds are those in which a build is broken up into commands that can be executed in different threads or processes, or even on different machines, so that the overall build can be made much faster. Breaking up a build in this way is not always possible, or it may not be simple to do it elegantly. For instance, a useful parallel build generally requires accurate knowledge of dependencies or a build tool that can detect when files were built in the wrong order and redo that part of the build. (Electric Make takes the latter approach; see "make," later in this chapter.)

How Build Dependencies Change

The hardest part of building software with a build tool is calculating accurate dependencies and doing so quickly. Since part of what makes calculating accurate dependencies hard is that the dependencies change over time, this section considers some of the reasons why dependencies do change.

One good reason for dependencies changing is that projects grow. More software is written in new files, or other people's work is integrated with your product, and so you have new dependencies. These sorts of large-scale dependency changes tend to be relatively infrequent and are often explicitly added to the build files. Examples are adding a new file to the build or creating a whole new build file for a new library. One thing to be careful about with this type of explicit change is circular dependencies. Some build tools will detect these and warn you, but other build tools, including some versions of *make*, don't warn you about circular dependencies.

Another reason for dependency changes is modifications that were made to existing source files in order to use other parts of the product. This can be seen by the addition of include or import lines. If your changes are not being rebuilt by your build tool, check that the changed dependency has been detected; perhaps you've used a different way of referring to another file than the way that the build tool expected? This is one example of where the ability to display the dependency tree of a build is very helpful for debugging builds.

Changing the build variant (for example, by changing the precise arguments that are passed to the compiler) can create a different set of implicit dependencies that build processes need to be aware of. Compiler flags that commonly change include arguments to add debug symbols or for optimized versions of the product. The worst example of this is C source code that has a large number of #ifdef preprocessor directives scattered throughout the code. Depending on which arguments are passed to the compiler, the dependency tree can change radically. You really only want to use #include lines that are used with the current set of #ifdef directives when scanning for dependencies. Most build tools get around this by treating all potential dependencies as actual dependencies when scanning files, at the cost of increasing the time spent creating the dependency tree.

Similarly, the versions of the tools that are invoked by a build are part of the dependency tree. If a new version of a compiler or source file generator is used, then the build tool should be able to detect this and rebuild the appropriate files. The most common practical approach to this problem is to depend upon developers' doing a clean build after changing any tool that is used in the build.

The common themes for all these different kinds of dependency changes are that you should write your build files to expect such changes and that you should have to specify only the larger-scale ones manually.

Common Build Problems

Some commonly encountered problems with build processes include:

Command-line length
  The length of the commands executed by build tools can cause problems on different platforms. Shell commands are usually typed in by people, so they remain relatively short. It is not uncommon for commands that are thousands of characters long to be generated by build tools. Some reasons for this are absolute pathnames being used for all files, or long file lists being used to maximize the number of files processed each time that a slow-to-start compiler is invoked. Build tools can sometimes avoid this problem by using a temporary file containing the list of files to be used by another tool.

Filename formats
  The names for the same file on different filesystems are quite different. For instance, Windows filesystems have drive letters, plus backslashes separating directories, as opposed to Unix forward slashes. Older Windows filenames could have only up to eight characters, with a three-character extension. Older Unix filesystems did not support spaces in filenames. If you want to build your project on multiple platforms, then a build tool with good support for avoiding filesystem-specific names is helpful. The easiest build tools to use are ones that allow you to specify a filename in one format and then automatically convert the filename to the appropriate format for the intended platform.

Unit tests for build tools
  If you treat build tools like any other application, you might well expect to have a set of system tests to check that the tool is working as expected. Build tools are slightly unusual applications in that their input is so varied, but it is still useful to have a simple test project for testing your build tool. Detecting an error such as a file being rebuilt multiple times is hard to do purely by inspection of the build tool's output log. A collection of small test projects also provides an excellent place to develop new techniques for using your build tool.

Identifying builds
  Unique identifiers for all builds that are to be used by other people helps clear communication within a project. The idea of a *build label* is introduced in "Labeling Builds" in Chapter 3. A label such as QA#1_3_0#129#2005_07_09 can identify a build as build 129, for internal testing (QA), Version 1.3.0, which was built on July 9, 2005. This kind of build label has many uses for SCM tools, bug tracking systems, and file and directory names.

Slow Builds

When discussing builds with project members, the most common request is always how to make them faster. There are a number of approaches that can help speed up your builds:

Profile the build

The first thing to do with a slow build is find out where most of the time is being spent. You can do something as simple as logging the current time at various interesting points in your build files. Some build tools such as SCons can provide more complete profiling information by treating the build tools as an application to be profiled just like any other application.

Build only once

Incorrect dependencies in build files may mean that files are built more than once or that other files that aren't needed are being built. To make sure this isn't happening to you, extract filenames from the build log and make sure each one is expected and occurs only once. Profiling can sometimes help here too.

Use a build server

If developers' desktop machines seem underpowered for the size of the project, you can try using shared build machines with more disk space and RAM. If there are a lot of disk accesses during a build, then a RAM disk cache (a *ramdisk*) may help. Of course, using a single build server makes your development environment more vulnerable to a single point of failure.

Create staged builds

If the build for your product is taking more than an hour or two, it may be time to consider splitting it up into multiple builds, where each one builds a subsection of the product. The results of the builds can then be *staged*—that is, made available for other people in the project to use as starting points for their own builds.

Use ccache

When you compile a C file, the C preprocessor first creates an expanded source file, which is what is actually compiled into an object file. *ccache* (*http://ccache.samba.org*) is an application that keeps a copy of the generated object file, and if the expanded source file hasn't changed the next time that it needs to be compiled, then *ccache* just returns the saved copy instead of wasting time recompiling the file. If the file has changed, then *ccache* compiles it as usual. To do all this accurately, *ccache* has to also record which compiler flags were used when the saved object file was created. This idea is great for builds where you rebuild lots of files the same way every time (for instance, virgin builds), or if a build tool is rebuilding files by mistake.

Use parallel builds

Many build tools have arguments to run different parts of a build in parallel. Depending on how good the build tool is at separating the build into different parts, this may improve your build times, or it may not do much. The only way to find out is to try it, which is usually a straightforward matter of passing another command-line argument to your build tool. Another approach is to use a distributed compiler such as *distcc* instead of expecting the build tool to handle distributing the work for the build.

Use distributed compilation

Using a cluster of machines to build a product is sometimes helpful. One tool that does this is *distcc* (*http://distcc.samba.org*), an open source frontend to the GNU *gcc* compiler that distributes preprocessed files to remote machines for compilation. After being compiled remotely, the object files are then returned to the main build machine. *distcc* assumes that the build dependencies calculated by your build tool are correct and can be cleanly partitioned for a distributed compilation. Electric Make (mentioned in "make," later in this chapter) is another high-end distributed build tool.

Build Tools

The six different build tools examined in the second half of this chapter are: shell scripts and batch files, *make*, GNU Autotools, Ant, Jam, and SCons. These are all no-cost, open source build tools. This is not to say that there are no useful build tools from commercial vendors—there are a dozen or so listed at *http://www.softwareengineering.info/build/build_by_product.html*. They're just not used as commonly as the build tools that are listed below.

"The Different Stages of a Build," earlier in this chapter, described the different stages of a build. It is worth remembering each stage as you consider different build tools: configuration, target definition, reading build files, dependency calculation, deciding what to build, command construction, and execution of commands. Some of these stages in some build tools are very small or even nonexistent.

What should you look for in a build tool? In order of most important to least, my recommendations are:

1. It should have accurate dependency checking.

2. Startup and dependency checking should be fast. The build tool should use tools such as compilers intelligently.

3. Builds should be independent from the local user environment in which the build tool was started. This makes it easier to reproduce builds on different machines.

4. Variant builds for debugging or with extra optimization should be easy to specify, preferably with a single argument to the build tool on the command line.

5. It should include support for many platforms and languages, particularly if the product is open source. The ability to build using the same source tree on multiple platforms at the same time is helpful.

6. It should be easy to write and read the build files, and the build tool should already be understood by many of the project members.

7. It should be scalable, with support for parallel builds.

8. It should have support for debugging builds and build file problems. Graphical display of the dependencies and changes in dependencies is a bonus. Clear output from a build tool about what command-line arguments were used and which user started the build is helpful. Minimizing the number of complete commands that are displayed can also make build logs easier to read, though the complete commands and their output should also be logged somewhere for each build.

Good support from a tool vendor or the user community is also extremely helpful. And don't forget that almost all tools have won an award at some time or other!

Shell Scripts and Batch Files

The simplest possible build tool is a piece of paper with a list of the compilation commands to type in order. A shell script or Windows batch file is really just that same list of commands, with tests for success or failure added occasionally.

This approach has some advantages. It's quick to develop, since many of the commands can be cut and pasted straight from the command line after you work out what they should be. There is little or no confusion about why a certain command was executed. For simple projects, with a few dozen small files and with straightforward build dependencies, shell scripts or batch files can be an adequate build tool.

Unfortunately, there are many disadvantages to using scripts and batch files as build tools. Some of these are:

Rebuilding every file

The biggest issue is that simple build scripts rebuild every file, every time. You might not think that the difference between a 5-second build and a 25-second build is very much, but if you spend a day working on the project and recompile it 10 times per hour for 10 hours, then over half an hour (which is more than 5% of the working day) is wasted just waiting for the project to rebuild.

Failure detection

Another big disadvantage of scripts is having to make explicit tests to see whether a command failed before continuing with the next command. If these tests are not made, you may not notice that a command halfway through the build failed, making the whole build suspect.

Debugging

Debugging shell scripts is done mainly by printing out text messages and the values of interesting variables at strategic points in the script.* Some shells let you set a flag to display all the commands as they are executed in a script, which is really just a more verbose way of displaying interesting variables. It is also possible to run scripts in a "dry run" mode, where no commands are executed; instead, they're just displayed. This is helpful for scripts that would take a long time to execute, but if the behavior of the script depends on the contents of a file that is supposed to be generated by some other part of the script, then this approach doesn't work, unless you add echo statements to certain lines.

Portability

Making scripts and shell files portable, so that they can be executed on a variety of platforms, is tedious and prone to error. The names and arguments of even the familiar commands to copy a file or to find a named file vary from platform to platform. A good build tool can shield the developer from many of these details.

---

* There is an interesting project at *http://bashdb.sourceforge.net* to extend the *bash* shell to support debugging.

In conclusion, shell scripts and batch files are adequate build tools only for the smallest and simplest projects. If you ever expect your project to grow, then take the time to use a real build tool.

make

make is the original build tool and is probably still the most common one. *make* is generally most popular with developers of C and C++ applications, while those using other languages, particularly Java, more commonly use Ant (see "Ant," later in this chapter).

THE HISTORY OF MAKE

make was created by Stuart Feldman in 1977. The original paper about *make* is "Make—A Program for Maintaining Computer Programs" (Bell Labs Technical Report 57, April 1977), which can be found at *http://citeseer.ist.psu.edu/feldman79make.html*. Though most tools win awards at some time or other, Stuart Feldman and *make* won the prestigious ACM Software System Award in 2003, in recognition of the historical significance of *make*.

While much has been written about the advantages and shortcomings of *make*, nothing has been complained about as much as the trivial, but indeed irritating, requirement that some makefile lines must start with a tab character. Here's what *make*'s creator has to say on the matter:

> Why the tab in column 1? Yacc was new, Lex was brand new. I hadn't tried either, so I figured this would be a good excuse to learn. After getting myself snarled up with my first stab at Lex, I just did something simple with the pattern newline-tab. It worked, it stayed. And then a few weeks later I had a user population of about a dozen, most of them friends, and I didn't want to screw up my embedded base. The rest, sadly, is history. (Stuart Feldman, quoted in Eric S. Raymond, *The Art of Unix Programming*, Addison-Wesley, 2003)

Build dependencies are specified explicitly in build files, which are conventionally named *Makefile* or *makefile* and are written in *make*'s own programming language. The format of these *makefiles* is shown in Example 5-2. *make* maintains static definitions of dependencies in the makefiles and does not detect dependencies between files. Files are noted as changed only when their modification timestamps change or when they are absent.

EXAMPLE 5-2. A simple makefile

```
myproduct : file1.c file2.c
    gcc -o myproduct file1.c file2.c
    echo "Finished building"
```

In the Unix project shown in Example 5-2, the target myproduct depends on *file1.c* and *file2.c*. To create this target, *make* will execute the lines after the dependency line with the : on it (that is, the lines that begin with gcc and echo).

Note that both of the lines below the target myproduct start with a tab character, not four spaces. Let's say that *file1.c* is a C source file and that it contains the line: #include "file1.h"; that is, *file1.c* depends on *file1.h*. However, modifying or even deleting *file1.h* after myproduct has been built will never cause *make* to rebuild myproduct, because the dependency on *file1.h* is unknown. You could manually fix this problem by adding file1.h to the dependency line, changing the first line of the makefile to:

```
myproduct : file1.c file1.h file2.c
```

This lack of automatic dependency checking explains why most large projects that use *make* alone as their build tool have trouble rebuilding only those files that are affected by a change.

The are numerous implementations of *make* for almost every platform created in the last 25 years. The original *make* first became widely used with System V Release 2 Unix in 1984 but had been available since 1977. Compatible versions of *make* since then include a distributed *make* called *dmake* (1990), *gmake* (1991), BSD NET2 *make* (1991), and SunOS *make* (1989). *nmake*, the Microsoft version of *make*, is probably the most divergent *make*; it is one of the underlying build tools that are used when Visual Studio projects are built, whether from within the GUI or by using the *msdev* or *devenv* command-line tools.* *gmake* (*http://www.gnu.org/software/make*) is the GNU version of *make*; it was written by Richard Stallman and Roland McGrath. *gmake* is singled out from all the other versions of *make* since it has been ported to so many platforms and supports a wide set of all the different features from the other versions of *make*. *gmake* has been maintained and updated by Paul Smith since Version 3.76 in 1997.

Makealike (or should it be *makeoid*?) programs are build tools that are based on the concepts introduced by *make*. Some of these are *cake*, *cook* (which is used with the CMS tool Aegis), Lucent's *nmake* (no relation to Microsoft's *nmake*), Plan 9's *mk*, and *mms* for VMS. *makepp* (*http://makepp.sourceforge.net*) is a more recent replacement for *gmake*, designed to address many of the problems with *make* that are listed later in this section, with improvements including automatic dependency checking and using file signatures instead of timestamps. *bmake* (*http://www.crufty.net/help/sjg/bmake.html*) is derived from NetBSD's *make* and has some useful extensions in how variables and conditional targets are treated. All these tools have been used in projects, but none have achieved wide usage.

Documentation varies widely among the different versions of *make*. *gmake* is reasonably well documented (*http://www.gnu.org/software/make/manual*), but, as with many build tools, developers tend to write makefiles for large projects by copying fragments from

---

* Visual Studio 2005 has a tool named MSBuild that uses XML to represent projects and dependencies, in a similar way to that used by *nant*, which is Ant for .NET (see "Ant," later in this chapter).

existing makefiles. This is especially true if the project has a complicated or hierarchical directory structure. Beyond the *gmake* manual, there are two books for more information about *make*. The first is *Managing Projects with make*, by Robert Mecklenburg. The third edition covers much more than the previous two editions. The second book is more *gmake*-specific: *Programming with GNU Software*, by Mike Loukides and Andy Oram. Both books are published by O'Reilly.

Of the two books mentioned, only *Managing Projects with make* discusses how to create makefiles that scale well as a project grows. The classic article about this issue is "Recursive Make Considered Harmful," by Peter Miller (*http://www.canb.auug.org.au/~millerp/ rmch/recu-make-cons-harm.html*). Peter Miller is also the author of the CMS tool Aegis. His key observation is that if you have makefiles in many directories and subdirectories, then *make* can spend a lot of time and effort processing each makefile, reevaluating some of the same dependencies over and over, and still end up with a fragmented view of what the whole project needs. The better alternative is to use *make*'s include directive to gather all the makefiles into a single, logical makefile and then process just that one makefile. This approach is called *included* or *nonrecursive make*.

There is a good discussion of how the OpenRADIUS project implemented included makefiles at *http://www.xs4all.nl/~evbergen/nonrecursive-make.html*. If you are interested in practical comparisons of the two approaches, see Appendix A for some tests and their results, and some similar results by Boris Kolpackov at *http://kolpackov.net/projects/build/benchmark.xhtml*.

The greatest strength of *make* is that it's everywhere, and so it's already familiar to many developers. Unfortunately, the problems with *make* are numerous:

Incomplete dependency analysis

The common recursive use of *make*, with makefiles calling other makefiles, can lead to incomplete dependency graphs or even circular dependencies. The traditional workarounds for this are to change the order in which the subdirectories are visited; to repeat the execution of *make* multiple times; or to always run make clean first. This last choice is uncomfortably like just using a script for your build tool (as discussed earlier in this chapter, in "Shell Scripts and Batch Files").

Separate tools to help create and maintain dependencies for *make* do exist—*mkdepend* is one such tool, and the -M argument for the *gcc* preprocessor is another—but these are other tools that have to be configured in addition to *make*.

Portability

Not only do the versions of *make* commonly installed on different platforms differ significantly from each other, but the way that tools such as compilers are invoked varies widely from platform to platform. This means that either makefiles have to be written specifically for each platform, or a project-wide mechanism to set variables correctly on different platforms has to be created for each project.

As an aside, the largest project that I know of with custom makefiles for every platform is *libpng* (*http://www.libpng.org*), with 41 platform-specific makefiles for about 30,000 lines of C. That's a lot of makefiles to modify when you add a new source file.

Speed

Builds of large projects using *make* still take hours, if not days, despite the tremendous advances in CPU and disk speeds in recent years.

Debugging

Working out why *make* did or didn't choose to compile a file can be difficult. The -n argument to *make* can be used to perform a dry run, which doesn't actually execute any commands but instead just prints them out. Print statements such as echo can also help sometimes. *gmake* has better debugging output than most versions of *make* and supports a -d argument for choosing the desired type of debugging output, but the output is still overly verbose and hard to use.

Clock skew

The use of file-modification timestamps to determine when a file has been updated is imprecise and prone to error, especially across distributed filesystems such as NFS. Restoring a file from a backup copy, even on the same machine, can change the timestamp and cause *make* to rebuild source files unnecessarily or, even worse, not to rebuild source files when it should.

Makefile syntax

The *make* language does not have the conveniences of a carefully designed programming language. For example, *make* has the strange requirement of tabs rather than spaces at the beginning of certain makefile lines. A number of versions of *make* also behave strangely with lines longer than 80 characters in makefiles.

Once the problems with maintaining a large number of makefiles for multiple platforms became apparent, Prof. David Wheeler's observation that "all problems in computer science can be solved by another level of indirection" came into play, and numerous *makefile generators* were created.* The idea is to take a template file that lists both the files that you want from your build tool and also your source files, and then run the makefile generator with some platform-specific arguments to generate the appropriate makefiles. Some of the better-known ones are *imake* and Automake. Automake is by far the most common one nowadays in open source projects and is covered further in "Automake," later in this chapter. *imake* is primarily used for building the X11 Window System and is described further in the book *Software Portability with imake*, by Paul DuBois (O'Reilly).

Some products that attempt to solve the problems with using *make* for parallel or distributed builds include Electric Make (*http://www.electric-cloud.com*) and *distcc* (see "Slow Builds," earlier in this chapter). Electric Make is a commercial replacement for *make* (original *make*, GNU *gmake*, and Microsoft's *nmake* are all supported). For a starting price of $50,000, it monitors all the compilations and other build-related commands on multiple

---

* Wheeler was chief programmer for the EDSAC project in the early 1950s and is one of the inventors of the subroutine. He is also coinventor of the compression algorithm used by the popular Unix *bzip2* tool.

PAUL'S RULES OF MAKEFILES

These rules are taken verbatim from *http://make.paulandlesley.org/rules.html*, the personal web site of Paul Smith, the maintainer of GNU *gmake*; square brackets indicate my comments. The rules deserve wider exposure, even though some of the things that they refer to are not explained in this book. The same web site also has an informative article titled "How Not to Use VPATH" (*http://make.paulandlesley.org/vpath.html*).

1. Use GNU make

Don't hassle with writing portable makefiles, use a portable *make* instead! [There is some bias here perhaps, but *gmake is* an extensive, full-featured, and widely ported version of *make*.]

2. Every non-.PHONY *rule must update a file with the* exact *name of its target.*

Make sure every command script touches the file "$@"—not "../$@", or "$(notdir $@)", but *exactly* $@. That way you and GNU *make* always agree.

3. Life is simplest if the targets are built in the current working directory.

Use VPATH to locate the sources from the objects directory, not to locate the objects from the sources directory.

4. Follow the Principle of Least Repetition.

Try to never write a filename more than once. Do this through a combination of *make* variables, pattern rules, automatic variables, and *gmake* functions.

5. Every non-continued line that starts with a TAB is part of a command script, and vice versa.

If a non-continued line does not begin with a TAB character, it is never part of a command script: it is always interpreted as makefile syntax. If a non-continued line does begin with a TAB character, it is *always* part of a command script: it is never interpreted as makefile syntax.

Continued lines are always of the same type as their predecessor, regardless of what characters they start with.

Copyright © 1997,2002 Paul D. Smith. Verbatim copying and distribution is permitted in any medium, provided this notice is preserved.

---

machines, and when it detects an incorrect dependency it reschedules the erroneous compilation for later on. Even the logfiles are rewritten to show the correct build ordering.

To summarize, if your project is unlikely to grow too large, is intended for only a small number of platforms, and is written in C or C++, then *make* is still an appropriate build tool. If not, there are better alternatives; these are discussed in the rest of this chapter.

GNU Autotools

The GNU Autotools suite, also referred to simply as the Autotool suite, or sometimes as the GNU Build System, is probably the build suite most commonly used by open source C and C++ projects. The familiar incantation of ./configure; make; make install seems to build and install about 90% of the tarballs that you can download.

THE HISTORY OF GNU AUTOTOOLS

GNU Autotools were developed in the early 1990s for the GNU Project. Among the early contributors were David MacKenzie, Gary Vaughan, Ben Elliston, Tom Tromey, and Ian Lance Taylor. Judging by the rate of recent releases, it would seem safe to say that the tools are mature, but actually real functionality is still being added. The licensing scheme for GNU Autotools is, not surprisingly, the GPL.

The GNU Autotools suite actually consists of three separate tools—Autoconf, Automake, and Libtool—all of which use some common configuration files. Autoconf (*http://www.gnu.org/software/autoconf*) creates shell scripts named *configure*. These scripts can be executed to find out which features required by an application are present on a particular platform. Automake (*http://www.gnu.org/software/automake*) uses *Makefile.am* files to create *Makefile.in* template files, which Autoconf can then use to create GNU *gmake* makefiles. Libtool (*http://www.gnu.org/software/libtool*) helps create static and shared libraries in a portable and versioned manner for programs that are written in C. The most commonly used of these three tools seems to be Autoconf, judging by the number of *configure* files out there. Even if a project doesn't use Autoconf, the *configure* file is often the place where installation begins.

NOTE

Any filename that ends in *.ac* is probably an Autoconf-related file. Any filename that ends in *.am* is probably an Automake-related file. Any filename that ends in *.in* is probably an input file for one of the three GNU Autotools.

Autoconf

The concept of Autoconf is that all you should have to do to install a package is run the generated *configure* script to discover the precise details of how various features, such as compilation and linking, are actually working on your platform. This information is then passed to the build tool and also into the program by header files and preprocessor #define definitions. This concept alone may explain the popularity of the GNU Autotools suite; other build tools tend to make assumptions about what is provided on each version of each platform, but the GNU Autotools suite confirms this information when the application is actually installed. Other factors that explain the suite's popularity are that only the basic Bourne shell, the necessary C or C++ compilers, and *make* are usually needed for the *configure* script to work. Also, the default make dist command creates a convenient tarball of all the files that you need to package a release.

The *configure* script has a number of different arguments that you can use to enable and disable various parts of the program that you are building. The default of using no arguments Should Just Work, and if *configure* fails to run due to a missing dependency for the project, then the error message is usually clear enough. However, if running *configure* fails in any other way, then debugging the problem can be hard. "Debugging GNU Autotools installs," later in this chapter, describes some helpful approaches for debugging installations from the perspective of a user.

From the perspective of a developer working with Autoconf, you create a file *configure.ac* to be the input for Autoconf. *configure.ac* (which used to be named *configure.in*) is written in a mixture of GNU *m4* (a macro processing language) and Unix shell commands. However, you need to ship only the generated *configure* file, not its precursors.

Automake

Automake produces makefiles that will work with GNU *make*, and they should also work with many of the other variants of *make*. Automake uses the file *Makefile.am* to describe the desired executables, libraries, and other files for the project. The language used for *Makefile.am* is specific to Automake, but Automake also reads the same *configure.ac* configuration file that is used by Autoconf. Using the *Makefile.am* file, Automake produces *Makefile.in* files that Autoconf can use to produce makefiles.

The *make* targets in the makefiles that are created by Automake and then Autoconf include well-known targets such as all, install, and clean. Other useful targets are uninstall, which simplistically undoes whatever install did, and check, which executes any tests defined by the package developer. The target dist creates a distribution archive file, and distcheck creates a distribution, then untars the archive into a new directory, builds the package there, installs it, and finally runs make check.

> **NOTE**
>
> Since Autoconf and Automake are separate tools, one can imagine creating build files other than makefiles. For instance, the AutoJam prototype (*http://developer.berlios.de/projects/autojam*) creates the equivalent of *Jamfile.in* files for Autoconf to use to create the build files named *Jamfile* used by the build tool Jam (see "Jam," later in this chapter). SCons (see "SCons," later in this chapter) already has its own Autoconf-like functionality that does at least some of what Autoconf does, so a separate AutoSCons tool is less likely to be developed.

Libtool

Libtool is designed to hide the implementation details of creating libraries, especially shared libraries, on different platforms. It's fully integrated with Autoconf and Automake but can be used even without them. The contents of the desired libraries are defined in *Makefile.am*, just as executables were for Automake. Libtool also includes support for versioning of libraries and for tracking which versions are expected for a particular package.

When it comes to finding out which libraries have already been installed and using them in other packages, *pkg-config* (*http://pkgconfig.sourceforge.net*) is a separate tool that integrates well with the GNU Autotools suite and is useful for discovering the particular arguments that are necessary to use an installed library on your platform.

An Autotools "Hello World" program

None of the half dozen or so tutorials that I found while researching this section worked exactly as written. So I've provided the precise steps that I used to create my own "Hello World" program with GNU Autotools. These instructions are for Autoconf 2.53 and Automake v1.6.3. Libtool was not used here.

1. Create a new directory with two simple C source files named *hello.c* and *hello.h*. *hello.c* should contain at least the standard `main` function and can also contain lines such as:

   ```
   #ifdef HAVE_STDLIB_H
   .
   .
   (any code that depends on stdlib.h goes here)
   .
   .
   #endif
   ```

   At the top of *hello.c*, add the line:

   ```
   #include "hello.h"
   ```

   The other C file, *hello.h*, should contain:

   ```
   #ifdef HAVE_CONFIG_H
   #  include <config.h>
   #endif
   #ifdef HAVE_STDLIB_H
   #  include <stdlib.h>
   #endif
   ```

   Eventually, `HAVE_STDLIB_H` will be defined or not defined in *config.h*, depending on whether *configure* finds the header file *stdlib.h* on your platform.

2. In the same directory as *hello.c*, create a file named *Makefile.am* containing the two lines:

   ```
   bin_PROGRAMS = hello
   hello_SOURCES = hello.c
   ```

3. In the same directory, run the `autoscan` command to create the file *configure.scan*. This command emitted a warning about an uninitialized value for me, but succeeded. Since autoscan does not overwrite *configure.ac*, you can run it periodically to detect potential portability problems in your project.

4. Rename the file *configure.scan* to *configure.ac* and edit that file as follows:

   a. Change `AC_INIT(FULL-PACKAGE-NAME, VERSION, BUG-REPORT-ADDRESS)` to `AC_INIT(hello, 0.1, yourname@example.org)`.

   b. Add a line containing only `AM_INIT_AUTOMAKE` below the top `AC_INIT` line.

   c. Change `AC_CONFIG_HEADER([config.h])` to `AM_CONFIG_HEADER([config.h])`.

   d. Change `AC_CONFIG_FILES([ ])` to `AC_CONFIG_FILES([Makefile])`.

5. Now create four empty placeholder files with the command touch NEWS README AUTHORS ChangeLog. This step can be avoided if the --foreign argument is used when automake is run later on.

6. Run aclocal to produce the file *aclocal.m4*, which contains *m4* macro definitions such as AM_INIT_AUTOMAKE.

7. Run autoconf to produce the *configure* file and a cache directory.

8. Run autoheader to produce *config.h.in*, which contains #define directives that will be set up when configure is run.

9. Run automake --add-missing to produce *Makefile.in* and some other necessary scripts. Note that the last four commands (starting at aclocal, in step 6) should be run as a group if any subsequent changes are made.

10. This is the step that a customer downloading the source for this project starts at. Run configure to produce the file *Makefile*. The line in the generated file *Makefile* that starts with DEFS shows what was found by running configure, as does the generated file *config.h*.

11. Run make to produce the "Hello World" executable named *hello*, the result of compiling *hello.c* in a portable way.

Debugging GNU Autotools installs

The advice in this section refers to what you can do when ./configure; make; make install doesn't do what it should, but you have faith that compiling the package on your machine should be possible. Problems of what to do when Autoconf, Automake, and Libtool don't work when you are developing the *configure* file itself are a different issue. For those kinds of problems, the manuals and the mailing lists at *http://lists.gnu.org/archive/html/autoconf*, *http://lists.gnu.org/archive/html/automake*, and *http://lists.gnu.org/archive/html/libtool* are good places to start. Also, since the actual Autotools programs are themselves written in shell script and Perl, familiarity with using a Perl debugger may help.

Some problems that you may see during installation and build include:

Could not find...
    If configure fails with a message saying that it could not find some dependency, your first action should be to check whether the required files are installed and, for dependencies involving libraries, that the installed versions are adequate. There may also be arguments to configure to let you tell it where to find particular packages. configure --help will show the available options.

Wrong Autotools version
    If configure fails with an error about needing a different version of one of the Autotools, you should be able to download and install it safely, since the Autotools are written with the intent that multiple versions will coexist on one machine. This usually happens only

if you are trying to modify a package, in which case it's not unreasonable to require that you use the same versions of the Autotools as the package's developers.

configure *succeeded,* make *failed*

Let's assume that you can see the text of the command that failed. First cut and paste the offending command to a shell script file and execute this file to confirm that the command fails using your own environment, as well as the environment being used by the Autotools.

If the command succeeds, then change the environment, preferably in *configure.ac*. If the command fails, do what is necessary by hand to the command line or source code to make it succeed. If success can be defined as "ignore this failure," then many versions of *make* support a -i argument to simply ignore errors and keep on going.

If you had to change the source to get the command to run successfully, then it is possible that the source wasn't written portably. Email the maintainers with the diffs and platform details. If changes in -D defines or other command-line arguments were necessary, apply the minimal set of changes to the files *config.h* or *Makefile*, understanding that these are generated files and thus may be overwritten.

Finally, make the effort to send the package maintainers the details of the problem: your package and Autotools versions, your platform, the broken command line and the working command line, and, ideally, the changes that fixed the problem.

I just want to add one file!

The proper way to do this is to modify *Makefile.am* and then to rerun the Autotools. A temporary hack is to modify the generated *Makefile*, adding the new source file to the _SOURCES variables. Of course, you run the risk of the modified *Makefile* being overwritten if the Autotools are rerun at any time.

make install *failed*

If the prefix directory is owned by root, you may need to run make install with root privileges, or rerun configure and specify a different prefix directory for which you do have write permission.

More Autotools

Documentation for the individual GNU Autotools is good enough, but the current sources of information about how to use them all together are barely adequate. There are the standard GNU manuals for each tool at *http://www.gnu.org/software/autoconf/manual*, *http://www.gnu.org/software/automake/manual*, and *http://www.gnu.org/software/libtool/manual.html*. There is also one book that aims to bind all three tools together, *GNU Autoconf, Automake, and Libtool*, by Gary Vaughan, Ben Elliston, Tom Tromey, and Ian Lance Taylor (New Riders). It's also known as the "Goat book" because of its cover picture. Even though it's rather dated now, it is still strongly recommended for anyone trying to do more than cut and paste from other projects. The contents of the Goat book are also available online at *http://sources.redhat.com/autobook*. Another useful (though dated) article, which includes a well-written example, is "The GNU Configure and Build System," by Ian Lance Taylor (*http://www.airs.com/ian/configure*).

The GNU Autotools were originally developed for Unix systems and only later modified to work for Windows machines. The recommended way to use them in Windows is to install the Cygwin environment and the necessary Perl and Microsoft tools. The project at *http://gnuwin32.sourceforge.net* has more information on how to do this. Mac OS X is supported by GNU Autotools. Languages that are supported by the default installations of the GNU Autotools include C, C++, Fortran, Perl, Lex, Yacc, TEX, Emacs Lisp, and, to a lesser degree, Java and Python.

The Autotools are a well-established way of making sure that software is portable to a very large number of platforms. Since developers can write their own *m4* macros for *configure.ac* files, the Autotools are extensible. Indeed, there is a public archive of useful *m4* macros at *http://autoconf-archive.cryp.to*, and the GNULIB project (*http://savannah.gnu.org/cgi-bin/viewcvs/gnulib/gnulib/m4*) has more examples. The Autotools have good support for localization of text strings in products, using the GNU *gettext* utilities (*http://www.gnu.org/software/gettext*).

Still, opinion is divided about GNU Autotools. On one hand, thousands of people use the results of Autoconf and run *configure* quite happily every day. On the other hand, when an install does fail, they have little hope of understanding or fixing the problem without substantial effort. Most of the problems with GNU Autotools seem to be voiced by developers who are trying to write the makefiles. These issues generally fall into the following categories:

Layers upon layers
It can be confusing when different files are used as input to tools that generate files, which are then used as input to yet more tools. Debugging the results of such a complicated scheme can be hard and time-consuming. If you want to add a source file to a downloaded package, you (understandably) have to have the GNU Autotools installed in order to regenerate the makefiles; otherwise, you have to temporarily modify complex makefiles.

Large and complex generated files
The generated files can become quite large, starting at around 3,000 lines and often growing to more than 30,000 lines of shell script. *configure* scripts are written using only the simplest shell constructs in order to ensure portability, but this ends up creating convoluted scripts not really intended for reading by humans. Also, even using cached results, running *configure* can take a fair amount of time. Supporting all the standard targets and options for *make* also adds to the size of the hierarchical makefiles.

Mixed and arcane languages
The macro processing language *m4* is not a particularly common language (the only other applications that are using it seem to be Sendmail and *fvwm*), so it's a barrier for developers wanting to use GNU Autotools. The total number of languages used by all the Autotools is quite large: GNU *m4*, Perl, shell languages, *make*, Autoconf macros, and the Automake language.

NAMES OF BUILD FILES

The first build tool was *make*. Make uses files named *makefile*, in various combinations of upper- and lowercase. These files have come to be known as "makefiles." By generalization, build tools use "build files" for their configuration, but of course the actual names of the build files are different for each tool. Many build tools have one special top-level build file and then many other build files. The filenames that are used by convention for the tools discussed in the following sections are:

Tool	Top-level build file	Other build files
Ant	*build.xml*	*build.xml*
Jam	*Jamrules*	*Jamfile*
SCons	*SConstruct*	*SConscript*

Ant

Ant (*http://ant.apache.org*) is an open source build tool, part of the Apache community of open source software projects. Ant is licensed under the Apache License.

Originally designed as an extensible replacement for *make* but "without *make*'s wrinkles," Ant quickly found favor as the build tool for projects written in Java. Ant comes with a large number of ready-to-use *tasks*. Each task allows users to define a small part of a build process in their build files. The ease with which Ant can have other tasks added to it has resulted in a build tool with a diverse set of abilities. You could go so far as to say that if you want your Java tool to be used nowadays, it has to have an Ant task to run it. All IDEs, whether open or closed, that are intended for developing Java projects now have built-in support for using Ant.

The build files for Ant are written in XML. The core of Ant itself is written in Java, as are the Ant tasks that are used in the build files. The build files have <project> XML elements, which contain <target> elements, which are the names of targets that can be passed to Ant on the command line. target elements can specify that they depend on other target elements. Each target contains one or more <task> elements, which are the elements that control what Ant actually executes during the build.

Ant build files are conventionally named *build.xml*. For the Java project shown in Figure 5-5, a *build.xml* that uses the jar, javac, and the delete Ant tasks would look like that shown in Example 5-3.

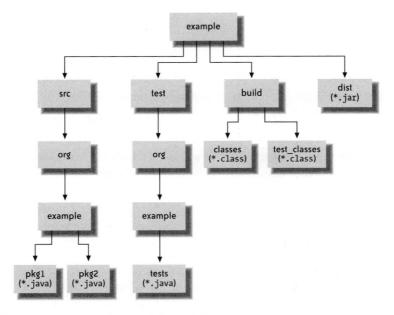

FIGURE 5-5. Directory tree of an example Java project

The default task is named dist and it calls the run_tests target, which in turn calls the compile and compile_tests targets to compile the product and compile the tests, using the javac task. Where there is just an echo task in this example build file, you would add tasks to actually run the tests. Finally, the first target, dist, uses the jar task to create a distributable JAR archive of the product.

EXAMPLE 5-3. An Ant build.xml file

```xml
<?xml version="1.0" encoding="ISO-8859-1"?>
<project name="My Project" basedir="." default="dist">

  <target name="dist"
          description="Jar up the project ready for distribution"
          depends="run_tests">
    <jar destfile="dist/project.jar" basedir="build/classes"/>
  </target>

  <target name="run_tests" depends="compile, compile_tests"
          description="Test the project class files">
    <echo>Call an Ant task to test the project</echo>
  </target>

  <target name="compile"
          description="Compile the source files">
    <javac srcdir="src" destdir="build/classes"/>
  </target>

  <target name="compile_tests"
          description="Compile the test source files">
    <javac srcdir="test" destdir="build/test_classes"/>
  </target>

  <target name="clean"
          description="Remove all generated files">
    <delete dir="build/classes/org"/>
    <delete dir="build/test_classes/org"/>
    <delete dir="dist/*"/>
  </target>

</project>
```

The output from executing ant with no arguments (so that the default dist target is used) shows the target names and the tasks that they call. Note that while this minimal build took 15 seconds from start to finish on a rather underpowered laptop, it only took 3 seconds on a more modern desktop machine:

```
[theo@theo-laptop example]$ ant

Buildfile: build.xml

compile:
    [javac] Compiling 2 source files to /home/theo/example/build/classes

compile_tests:
    [javac] Compiling 1 source file to /home/theo/example/build/test_classes

run_tests:
     [echo] Call an Ant task to test the project here.

dist:
     [jar] Building jar: /home/theo/example/dist/project.jar

BUILD SUCCESSFUL
Total time: 15 seconds
```

Since Ant is written in Java, it runs unchanged on all platforms that support Java. The common ones are Solaris, GNU/Linux, and Windows, using the downloads from Sun (*http://java.sun.com*). Dozens of other platforms have had other Java Virtual Machines (JVMs) written for them; there is an extensive list available at *http://www.geocities.com/ marcoschmidt.geo/jvm.html*. All official Ant tasks are written to operate correctly regardless of the underlying platform; that this mostly works as designed is due to plenty of testing. Troublesome areas include the Cygwin environment and older versions of Windows. If you write a task yourself, be careful about portability when using native commands, especially ones like ps, the Unix command for listing processes, which seems to have different arguments wherever it is found.

The documentation for Ant is generally good and certainly extensive, with standardized descriptions of what each Ant task does.* The Ant documentation includes FAQs, reference manuals, API manuals, Wikis, presentations, and half a dozen books at last count. The books include O'Reilly's *Ant: The Definitive Guide*, now in a second edition, by Steve Holzner, and *Java Development with Ant* (Manning Publications), by Erik Hatcher and Steve Loughran, who are two members of the Ant project. There is also a different O'Reilly Ant book only in German: *Ant—kurz und gut*, by Stefan Edlich. Be warned, though: the first editions of the O'Reilly books cover only up to Ant 1.4.

Ant has many strengths. It runs on all the platforms for which you can find a JVM, and that's every major platform I've used in the past 10 years. Ant uses XML to describe the build dependencies for a project, so you don't have to be able to write Java to use Ant. Using XML also means that the information can be easily transformed—for instance, into a graphical representation of the dependencies, as is done by Vizant (*http://vizant.sourceforge.net*) and AntGraph (at the time of this writing, the download site is no longer valid, but AntGraph's author can be contacted via *http://www.ericburke.com*).

Another major strength of Ant is the large number of Ant tasks that already exist. Over 80 core tasks are shipped with Ant, and they provide support for Java compilation, filesystem commands, archiving, mail, and CVS commands. The 60 optional tasks that are also part of the Ant project provide access to other SCM tools, unit testing, and much more. There are hundreds of other public Ant tasks freely available to do everything a project could require, including source code and document generation, web page maintenance, and even automated blogging.

Creating your own Ant task is not hard if you can write basic Java, since the documentation is clear and there are a plethora of available examples. You can also use the exec task to specify the precise commands to be executed as part of the build, though this tends to create platform-specific build files and makes it harder to determine whether a task succeeded or failed.

---

* This may be partly due to Javadoc (see "Internal Project Documentation" in Chapter 8), the standard tool that makes it easy to create API reference documents for Java programs; it is installed with Java by default. Perhaps Java programmers have come to expect more from their documentation?

WRITING AN ANT TASK FOR JDIFF

Everything I had read said that writing your own Ant task was easy, but I wanted to confirm it for myself. There had been a few requests for an Ant task for JDiff (*http://www.jdiff.org*), an open source tool I wrote that compares two different versions of a set of Java files. JDiff produces a Javadoc-like report of all the parameters whose types have been changed, the methods and classes that have been added and removed, and so on. JDiff is implemented as a Javadoc *doclet* (an application that uses Javadoc to parse Java source files) and had already graduated from build scripts to Ant a few years before. I had been testing JDiff using Ant's ready-made Javadoc task, but there were a lot of knobs to twiddle to use JDiff with that task. What was wanted was a simple Ant task to make it easier to generate a no-frills comparison of two Java projects.

I started with Ant's tutorial "Writing Your Own Task" (*http://ant.apache.org/manual/develop.html*), and after less than 30 minutes of carefully following along, I had my first working custom Ant task. Adding support for attributes and nested elements in the XML for the task took another hour or so to get working, with the help of the *Java Development with Ant* book. Then I decided to create my own JDiff task by extending the Javadoc task class, rather than the ordinary Task class. Documentation for this was mainly the Javadoc task API pages, which told me enough to generate my first call to Javadoc. The trouble was that my task wanted to make three calls to Javadoc, not just one, and I couldn't see any easy way to reset the parent Javadoc task object to a clean state so that I could execute it again and again.

It was time to get away from that Javadoc task class. Instead of the JDiff task class inheriting from the Javadoc task class, I changed the JDiff task class to use three different instances of the Javadoc class. That worked nicely, after I eventually discovered that you have to call the method setProject yourself on such separate Task objects. The documentation is skimpy for this particular approach to custom Ant tasks, so if you are considering writing your own Ant task, extending an existing class for a task still seems to be the easiest way to proceed. The quality of the Javadoc documentation for your chosen parent task will make a big difference in how easy the process is. Of course, if you really want to be sure of how that parent task works, the source code is where the answers are. Ant 1.7 should have some improvements in how tasks can be reused.

Overall, writing my own Ant task for JDiff was not too hard. It took about a day to complete, mainly because of trying the two different approaches. The errors and warnings generated by Ant when there were errors in the build file were clear enough. The verbose and debug arguments for Ant helped me to see what my task was really executing. If I had needed more details, I could have run Ant inside a Java debugger or added the time-honored println or log statements, which both appear nicely interleaved with the output from Ant.

Some of Ant's weaknesses are:

XML limitations

One of Ant's weaknesses is that large projects have large build files. XML was not designed to be particularly concise; thus a good XML editor such as XMLSpy or even Emacs becomes vital for larger projects. Keeping track of all the different parts of large build files can be complex, though each target XML element can have a textual description conveniently associated with it.

XML is fine as a format for build files until you try to use Ant as a scripting language or want to add conditional (if-then-else) constructs to your build files (though there now is a condition task). One specific example of the issues of using XML is that if you want to execute a shell command that uses a < input redirection operator, you have to write < in the XML. Quoting of arguments is another messy area. The use of XML can be frustrating when a particular task doesn't do quite what you want it to do. You can either tweak the Java source for the task and then recompile it or try writing XSLT scripts to transform your XML files into the kind of XML that Ant build files need.

Complex dependency chains

Another nonobvious feature of Ant is that if target 3 depends on targets 1 and 2, and target 2 also depends on target 1 (i.e., a triangle), and if you invoke Ant as ant target2 target3, then target 1 will be executed *twice*: once for target 2 and once for target 3. The way to avoid this is to always invoke target 3 from the command line, which will do the right thing.

This can sometimes create challenges when defining the target dependencies as projects grow. One way to avoid this is to eschew the depends attribute altogether and define the required dependencies in another target, using the antcall task to invoke each target in turn. The ant task can be useful when creating a hierarchy of recursive build files, though this approach can result in slower builds, just as with recursive *make*. The import task, new in Ant 1.6, promises to make large, modular builds somewhat easier.

Limited properties

Ant build files use properties to store values, but these are not as powerful as variables in a regular programming language. For instance, once a property has been set, it cannot be changed later on in the build file. Also, you cannot use one property to hold the name of another property; one level of redirection is all you get. Many XML editors don't know how to expand Ant properties.

Parallel builds and dry runs

Parallel builds are not as straightforward with Ant as with other build tools (and they're not particularly easy in some of those tools either). Dry runs (seeing what Ant would do if it were run but not actually executing any commands) are not supported by Ant, though individual tasks may support them.

Slow startup

Since most JVMs seem to take some time to start up, subjectively Ant is not a particularly fast build tool. However, most Java developers find it to be much faster than *make*. This is primarily because Ant uses a single JVM for multiple tasks, but it may also be because Ant can reduce the number of times that a Java compiler has to be invoked—for example, by compiling more files at a time with each compilation command. The dependency checking of the default Java compilation task is not particularly robust, so other build dependency tools have emerged. There is Ant's own optional depend task. I've had good results using Misha Dmitriev's Javamake (*http://www.experimentalstuff.com/ Technologies/JavaMake/index.html*). You can also use faster Java compilers, such as the open source Jikes compiler, originally from IBM (*http://jikes.sourceforge.net*). For small to medium-sized Java projects, many experts take the approach that a clean build using a fast compiler beats complex, and sometimes error-prone, dependency analysis.

Platform-dependent issues

Platform-dependent issues such as the use of forward or backward slashes in filenames can be minimized through careful use of Ant tasks such as PathConvert to generate the platform-specific version of a filename. For more information on this and other issues about using Ant in real development, see Steve Loughran's article "Ant in Anger" at *http://ant.apache.org/ant_in_anger.html*.

Ant does not support internationalization directly, nor is any of the Ant logging output localized, but given the good support in Java for both, this should be easier to do than with most build tools.

Numerous Ant-related projects have been developed; some add to the list of tasks for Ant, some providing alternate ways such as GUIs to create build files for Ant, and some reimplement Ant for other environments. Examples of each of these include:

More tasks

AntContrib (*http://ant-contrib.sourceforge.net*) provides support for compiling C and C++ source files with Ant on a variety of platforms.

Build file generators

Antelope (*http://antelope.tigris.org*) is a UI for creating Ant build files that can also help with profiling and debugging Ant build files.

Other variants on Ant

nant (*http://nant.sourceforge.net*) is a build tool for the Microsoft .NET Framework that is written in C#. *nant* uses XML build files very much like Ant's and includes a convenient slingshot task to create an Ant build file from an existing Visual Studio .NET project. Visual Studio 2005 has a tool named MSBuild that uses XML similarly to the way *nant* does.

As many other IDEs already do, Microsoft's Visual Studio and Borland's JBuilder both save their lists of the source files that are associated with a project in XML files, and these files are used by the IDE's internal build tool to build the project. XSLT scripts can transform these tool-specific XML project files into Ant or *nant* build files. This often makes it easier or cheaper to build projects entirely without the IDE, since you may be able to avoid installing the full and sometimes costly IDE on multiple build machines.

Another popular use of Ant is as the basis for an automation environment. Automation environments are discussed in detail in "Automation Environments" in Chapter 3; basically, they are applications to help you automate the *checkout-build-test-deploy* parts of your build process (this is known as "continuous integration" in the XP literature). Typical tasks for automated environments are downloading the source for a project using an SCM tool and then running a build and unit tests, and doing all this continually, or every hour or night. Reports of the current state of the project are created and made available, often through a web site or by email.

Some automation environments that use Ant are Anthill (*http://www.urbancode.com/projects/anthill*), which is a commercial tool that also has a no-cost version, and CruiseControl (*http://cruisecontrol.sourceforge.net*), an open source automation environment. Both these and other automation environments are discussed further in "Automation Environments" in Chapter 3.

Another outgrowth of Ant is Maven (*http://maven.apache.org*), a project management tool from the Apache Project. While you can use Ant to manage other parts of your project such as releases and tracking multiple *.jar* file dependencies, large *build.xml* files can become hard to understand. Maven lets you describe your project's structure using a version of XML with programming constructs named Jelly. You can still call Ant tasks from Maven, but Maven can also download the required files for a project as necessary; Ant 1.7 will also be able to do this. Many of the Apache projects use Maven to describe their structure. The idea of having an overall structured description of a project is a good one and seems likely to become common in all automated environments.

In summary, Ant has become the default build tool for Java projects: if a project is written in Java, it's most likely being built with Ant. The exceptions are those projects tied to an IDE with its own build tool, and even these IDEs now support building products by using Ant. In addition, if you want a definition of a build that can be transformed into formats suitable for use by other tools, then using XML for your build file language is very convenient.

Jam

Jam (*http://www.perforce.com/jam/jam.html*) is an open source build tool from Perforce Software, written by Christoper Seiwald and aimed squarely at projects written in C and C++. Jam costs nothing, and is licensed in a very free manner:

> License is hereby granted to use this software and distribute it freely, as long as this copyright notice is retained and modifications are clearly marked. ALL WARRANTIES ARE HEREBY DISCLAIMED.

That's the entirety of the license for Jam. As you might guess from it, Jam is not supported by Perforce; Perforce's business is more focused on its own SCM tool, which is discussed in "Perforce" in Chapter 4.

In Jam, build dependencies are specified in build files called Jamfiles, and these Jamfiles can include each other in a hierarchical fashion (the top-level build file is named *Jamrules*). Example 5-4 shows a typical Jamfile. First, note the quirky but required spaces before the

THE HISTORY OF JAM

Jam (which may have once stood for "just another *make*") was originally created in the early 1990s by Christoper Seiwald for internal use at Sybase. Release 1.0 was in November 1993. Seiwald went on to found the SCM tool company Perforce Software in 1995 and is still the CEO there.

Jam is still used to build the various SCM-related products that are sold by Perforce, but new releases of Jam have appeared on average only once every two years. The current version of Jam is 2.5rc3. Since Jam is free, work has continued on it outside Perforce. The most active fork of Jam is BoostJam (*http://www.boost.org*) by Dave Abrahams, Rene Rivera, Vladimir Prus, and others. It was originally developed to build the Boost libraries, which are a suite of free, peer-reviewed, portable C++ source libraries. BoostJam was actually derived from FT Jam (*http://www.freetype.org/jam*), an extension of Jam by David Turner for the FreeType software font engine project. Jam has also been used internally by Cisco and other related networking companies to build large pieces of networking software.

---

semicolons at the end of the lines. The top line of the Jamfile specifies the location of the Jamfile in the directory hierarchy; this one is in a directory named *src*. The next two lines show how there are two other Jamfiles included by this Jamfile. The line beginning with Main shows an executable named *hello* being defined as containing the four *.c* source files and needing to be linked with the libraries listed after LinkLibraries. This Jamfile will create an executable *hello* on any one of the many platforms supported by Jam. The appropriate file suffixes and prefix are supplied by Jam for each platform.

EXAMPLE 5-4. A Jamfile

```
SubDir TOP src ;

SubInclude TOP src subdir1 ;
SubInclude TOP src subdir2 ;

Main hello : hello.c foo.c bar.c baz.c ;
LinkLibraries hello : libother libcommon ;
```

There are three internal stages of execution when Jam is run. In the first stage, all the Jamfiles are opened and (re)read, and for all the Jam targets that could be named on the command line, such as *hello*, a dependency tree is created. Source files are automatically scanned for other dependencies using extensible rules. Just as with *make*, file modification timestamps are used to decide whether files have changed, as opposed to the digest scheme used by SCons.

In the second stage, Jam calculates which files need to be updated as part of building (or rebuilding) the specified targets.

In the third stage, the specific Jam rules such as Main that were used in the Jamfiles are used to create the Jam variables that are later used to create the commands that are actually executed. Jam rules are written in the Jam language, and each Jam rule has an action associated with it, which is written as a snippet of shell script.

Unix platforms that are supported by Jam include GNU/Linux, AIX, the BSD Unixes, HP-UX, IRIX, QNX, Solaris, and a number of other less well-known Unixes. Other platforms include Windows and Mac OS X, and also VMS, OS/2, and BeOS. Compilers that are supported by default include *gcc*, Microsoft Visual C++, MinGW, the Borland compiler *bcc*, HP-UX aCC, AIX Visual Age, Solaris CC, and IRIX MIPSpro. Other recognized tools and file formats include Lex and Yacc.

Documentation for Jam is accurate, but woefully thin. What is most obviously missing is a cookbook of recipes for various kinds of projects. The next place to search for help is the Jamming mailing list (*http://maillist.perforce.com/pipermail/jamming*). Another surprising lack is that of a central list of bugs related to Jam (BoostJam does have such a service).

Jam's strengths are many compared with *make*. First, the idea of a global understanding of dependencies works well; just what is needed for the target that you specify is what gets built. Jam is also fast. One commercial project is able to build all the targets that are found in a million lines of C source code in over 4,000 files in under 10 minutes on an unremarkable desktop machine. Jam is also relatively small; its source code is under 15,000 lines of C source, which makes porting it to different platforms somewhat easier than with larger build tools. Indeed, Jam has already been ported to many different platforms, probably second in number only to *make*. Extending Jam is relatively easy, since new or overriding rules and actions can be defined in the Jamfiles that are parsed at startup, as shown in Example 5-5. This example also shows that Jam rules and actions are easy to customize, but are often hard to understand.

EXAMPLE 5-5. Extending Jam

```
#
# Generate C source using a CORBA interface defined in an
# IDL file.
#
# Argument $(1) is the name of the output file
# Argument $(2) is the name of the IDL source file
# Argument $(3) is an optional string argument passed to
# the IDL compiler.
#
rule Idl
{
    # A Jam idiom to extract the directory from the # first
    # argument. outdir is a local variable also available to the
    # action defined below.
    local outdir = $(<[1]:D) ;
    # Set a global Jam variable named IDLFLAGS
    IDLFLAGS on $(<) = $(3) ;
    # Specify that the C source depends upon the IDL file and
    # also on the output directory
    Depends $(<) : $(outdir) $(>) ;
```

EXAMPLE 5-5. Extending Jam (continued)

```
    # Make sure that the output directory exists
    MkDir $(outdir) ;
}


#
# Actually generate the source files using the IDL compiler
# and the IDL source file.
#
# An action is made up of shell script commands, so doesn't
# have to have the space-semicolon line endings, but semicolons
# are still used to separate the shell commands.
#
actions Idl
{
    cd $(outdir);
    idlcompiler $(IDLFLAGS) $(>);
}


#
# An example of using the new rule in a Jamfile
# to generate the file def.c from def.idl with some verbose
# output
#
Idl build/project1/idl/def.c : def.idl : -Dverbose=true ;
```

Jam's weaknesses are mainly in debuggability and documentation. Jam's debugging output is extremely verbose and hard to follow or restrict in any useful way. This leads to one of the common complaints about Jam, along the lines of "Jam didn't build my new library." This complaint is often due to the differences between *make* and Jam: if nothing depended on your new library, then Jam knew it didn't have to build it, so it didn't. In *make*, you probably defined every target explicitly, so some target or other probably ended up building it for you.

Other weaknesses of Jam include:

The Jam language

The Jam language itself can sometimes prove irritating. Rather oddly, many lines must end with a space and a semicolon. Omitting the space will lead to all kinds of cryptic messages and hard-to-debug build problems, especially if the line in question is the last one in a Jamfile. Using an editor such as Emacs with a mode to color Jamfiles syntactically helps a little with this. The language is also entirely string based, so it has no increment operator—which is fine until you really want one. Jam currently has no support for internationalization.

Grist

Another awkward part of using Jam is the concept of *grist*. Grist is a string associated with every file in a build used by Jam; it tells Jam where to find or write that file. Some of the built-in rules for Jam expect the grist to be implicit, while others expect it to be explicitly provided. When a file's grist is wrong, it can be hard to work out why Jam can't locate the file. Naming a very specific target on the command line, such as a single *.o* object file, is harder than necessary because of the format of grist, which contains characters such as < and ! that have to be escaped to avoid confusing most shells.

Separate phases

Jam operates strictly in phases: it first evaluates dependencies and all the files that need rebuilding and then executes the commands to rebuild them. This means that the dependency calculations and any included Jam rules in the first stage cannot use files that are generated as part of the second stage. One way around this problem is to call Jam from a shell script or batch file and then use this script to create any generated *Jamrules* files, for example.

Local header files

There is a current bug that proves surprising to newcomers to Jam. Header files included without a directory name (e.g., include "myproject.h") will be found just fine by the compiler (since the current directory is usually part of the default include path), but Jam may not recognize the dependencies on the included files. This means that changes to header files such as *myproject.h* will not result in the proper rebuilding of the files in which they were included. Including the file with a directory name (e.g., include "subdir/myproject.h") is a rather long-winded workaround for this bug.

BoostJam is a frontend to Jam and includes explicit support for building object files somewhere other than in the source directory. It also supports building variants (debug, optimize) and multiple targets with multiple compilers better than Jam does. BoostJam also has a better way of quoting arguments passed on the command line, much improved debugging output, and a number of other helpful additions. As of 2005, the BoostJam team is actively developing Version 2 of BoostJam.

In summary, Jam is an accurate, free, and fast build tool, probably the fastest of all the build tools examined in this chapter. A wide range of different platforms and C and C++ compilers are supported by default, and adding more is possible. Weighing against these benefits is the difficulty of debugging Jamfiles, minimal documentation, and lack of any impetus from Perforce to develop Jam any further. The current developments in BoostJam, particularly Version 2, are the brightest hope for improvements to Jam.

SCons

SCons (*http://www.scons.org*) is an open source build tool written by Steven Knight and others. Among its early contributors were Chad Austin, Charles Crain, Steve Leblanc, and Anthony Roach. The current licensing scheme is the MIT license.

SCons is implemented in Python (*http://www.python.org*), a modern, interpreted, object-oriented language freely available under the Python license on many platforms. Python is often compared to Tcl, Perl, Scheme, and Java, and is reportedly one of the easiest languages to learn.* For its build files, SCons uses script files that are written in Python and named *SConscript*.

Unix platforms that are supported by SCons include GNU/Linux, AIX, the BSD Unixes, HP-UX, IRIX, and Solaris. Other platforms include Windows and Mac OS X, and also OS/2.

---

* The argument that Python is the easiest language to learn is in a persuasively presented paper available at *http://www.python10.org/p10-papers/14/index.htm*. It's a good paper, but it was presented at a conference about Python.

THE HISTORY OF SCONS

A build tool named Cons, for "construction," was created by Bob Sidebotham in 1996. It was eventually released under the GPL and is an FSF-connected project. Cons was originally inspired by Jam but used Perl as the language for its build files instead of the Jam language. A key idea of Cons was that you should be able to use the full power of an ordinary programming language within the build files. However, Cons was hard to extend for different file types and didn't handle parallel builds very well; also, some people felt that Perl was not the easiest language in which to write build files. Cons is currently in maintenance mode at *http://www.dsmit.com/cons*, but the last release was back in 2002.

SCons was conceived as a rewriting of Cons in Python for the Software Carpentry competition, which was sponsored in 2000 by Lawrence Livermore National Laboratory and O'Reilly, among others. More details of the competition can be found at *http://www.onlamp.com/pub/a/python/2001/09/13/pythonnews.html*. ScCons (for "Software Carpentry Cons") was renamed SCons (for "software construction") after it won the build tool part of the competition in August 2000. Opinions on pronouncing SCons differ, but "ess-cons" seems to be the most common way. The first release of SCons, modestly versioned at 0.01 alpha, was released in December 2001. The first beta release was 0.90 in June 2003, and the first nonbeta release is expected sometime soon.

Compilers that are supported include *gcc*, Java, Microsoft Visual C++ (including the use of precompiled headers), MinGW, the Intel compiler tools, .NET tools, the Borland compiler *bcc*, HP-UX aCC, AIX Visual Age, Solaris CC, and IRIX MIPSpro, among others. Other recognized tools and file formats include Lex, Yacc, *tar*, L^AT_EX, *m4*, Qt, SWIG, PostScript, PDF, and *zip*.

Some distinguishing aspects of SCons are:

Portable build files
The way that programs are specified in the *SConscript* build files is independent of the platform; this permits most platform-dependent decisions to be made in a single configuration file, rather than in each build file. Judicious use of the os.sep string rather than the /, \\, or : characters can help maintain portability. Actually, Python and SCons understand that foo/bar refers to the file *bar* in the directory *foo* on both Unix and Windows, so even this may be unnecessary.

Automatic dependency scanning
The dependency checking for SCons is reliable, and a number of languages are supported by default (C, C++, D, Java, and Fortran). You can also extend SCons to support dependencies on objects that are not files—for example, entries in a database.

Signature files
An MD5 signature of each preprocessed file and the arguments to the compiler is created for every generated file. This makes it easy to detect when a file really does or does not need to be recompiled, which saves a lot of build time. However, just "touching" a

key file no longer causes the expected rebuild, which at first can confuse people familiar with *make*. It also makes it possible to share generated files between different people with more confidence in the correctness of such files.

Parallel build support

The SCons model for performing distributed builds is a carefully considered one. There are multiple threads, with a single job executing per thread. Each thread synchronizes with a task master, which gives it more jobs to work on. In comparison, older versions of *make* can end up spawning a process for every recursive makefile, making the number of jobs executing at any moment dependent on the structure of the source directories.

Programming language for build files

The use of a full-fledged programming language for the build files means that all the usual features such as conditional branching, loops, text formatting for output, and a sane syntax are present in SCons. You also gain the advantages of having a debugger, profiler, and other such tools that are already part of most programming languages but have historically been missing from most build tools.

SCM tool integration

SCons contains native support for checking out files from various SCM tools, including SCCS, RCS, CVS, BitKeeper, and Perforce. Subversion is not yet supported.

Extensibility and modularity

Adding support for building from new file types is relatively easy. Using small parts of SCons in other applications such as installers is also possible since SCons was designed to be modular. The part of SCons that does the dependency checking and the execution of commands (the "build engine") is separate from the part of SCons that specifies which files to compile. In theory, you could even write the build files in a language other than Python (this idea is explored further in "Custom Build Tools," later in this chapter).

Example 5-6 shows an *SConscript* file. It is written in Python, which has no semicolons at the end of lines and uses the indentation of each line to identify a block of code, instead of curly braces as seen in C and Java. Comments are preceded by the # character. A single top-level file named *SConstruct* can be used to tell SCons about the *SConscript* files, potentially one in each subdirectory.

EXAMPLE 5-6. An SCons SConscript file

```
# Explicitly allow this file to use a common environment defined elsewhere.
Import('env')

# Define an executable named 'hello'
env.Program(target = 'hello',
            source = ['hello.c', 'foo.c', 'bar.c', 'baz.c'],
            LIBS = ['other', 'common'])
```

The line with the Program method call shows an executable named *hello* being defined as containing the four *.c* source files and needing to be linked with the libraries listed in the LIBS argument. This *SConscript* file will create an executable *hello* on all of the platforms supported by SCons. The appropriate file suffixes and prefix are supplied by SCons for each platform.

The output shown in Example 5-7 is a small section of the results of using the --debug=tree command-line argument with SCons. It shows how *libA.a* depends on the three object files, which in turn depend on the *.c* three source files. Note that if this were a build on a Windows platform, then the file extensions and directory separators would be changed appropriately. Another very useful debug option is --debug=explain, which tells you why a file was recompiled.

EXAMPLE 5-7. SCons debug output

```
+-dir1/libA.a
  +-dir1/a1.o
  | +-dir1/a1.c
  +-dir1/a2.o
  | +-dir1/a2.c
  +-dir1/a3.o
    +-dir1/a3.c
```

Documentation of SCons is of good quality. There is a 5,000-line manpage installed with the package, which is also available from the SCons home page. The Wiki on the home page is well laid-out and has a number of cookbook examples about how to use SCons. Basic examples for using SCons can also be found at the end of the manpage. The mailing lists for SCons are friendly and a good source of help. No book has yet been published about SCons, but it seems to be only a matter of time before one is.

Some other well-considered aspects of SCons include the fact that the environment in which the build is performed is defined independently of the user's own environment. This helps to avoid the awkward situation of leaving departed developers' machines untouched just to perform builds. Variables in the Python build files are properly scoped, which is not true of many other build tools, though of course this does mean that variables have to be explicitly imported between *SConscript* files. Scalability of SCons for long command lines (lengths of over 10,000 characters) has also been demonstrated, at least for Windows.

Other things that make SCons easier to debug than most build tools are options to display the time spent in different major parts of a build, access to full-scale profiling data for the Python profiler *pstats*, and an option to start the build from within *pdb*, the Python debugger.

SCons even has enough confidence in the correctness of its dependency checking to provide a command-line argument to explicitly build the product in a random order! This unique idea helps performance when building different versions of a product simultaneously from the same source code, since it avoids performance problems that occur when multiple processes try to access the same file at the same time. The SCons core developers have an extensive set of unit tests and system tests, and changes to SCons are controlled using the change management tool Aegis.

Weaknesses and irritations of SCons seem to be relatively few. One complaint is about how long an already up-to-date build can take (up to 10 seconds when nothing actually needs to be built). The time spent checking dependencies can be reduced by using the SCons arguments --max-drift=1 and --implicit-deps-unchanged. Still, the startup time for SCons can feel slow. If you make an error in an *SConscript* file, the Python backtrace at the command line can be quite long, and you have to get used to the most recent part of the trace being at the bottom of the screen, not the top. The *.sconsign* MD5 signature files exist for each generated file, but these droppings can be made to occur in the directory where the files are built, or even in a single file, as opposed to the source directory. Internationalization is not currently supported.

SCons does require Python, which may not be installed on your machine by default. However, it deliberately does not require cutting-edge versions of Python (though it is tested with them), and Python isn't hard to learn, with many good tutorials available online. *Python in a Nutshell*, by Alex Martelli (O'Reilly), is one good introduction to Python, as is *Dive into Python*, by Mark Pilgrim (Apress), which is also available at *http://diveintopython.org*. The *Python Cookbook*, by Alex Martelli and David Ascher (O'Reilly), is also handy when you want just an example of how to do something with Python.

In summary, SCons is a well-designed build tool for a range of languages and platforms, and one that has been developed carefully by a knowledgeable group of developers. The choice of Python as a build tool does introduce yet another language dependency to any project, but this overhead seems to be small in practice. If you are starting a project from scratch, or your current build tool is just too much to bear any longer, SCons is the build tool to use.

A VISION OF THE FUTURE?

As few years ago, I had a vision of a *language-independent* build tool. With this tool, you would write the build files in whatever language was most appropriate and familiar for the project—Java, C, Python, or even Visual Basic. The build files would be small programs and would make use of a well-defined API to a build engine. Each section of the build file would make calls such as CreateExecutable("hello", *SomeFiles*), where *SomeFiles* is the collection of files that are used to create the executable file *hello*. Dependency checking would be completely automatic, so you would need to recompile or reinterpret the build files only when a file was added to or removed from a target. Detecting this could be done using the digest or signature of the build file itself.

Sound a bit far-fetched? Interprocess communication (IPC) mechanisms such as CORBA have been enabling communication between applications written in different languages for years. Distributed build tools already use IPC mechanisms to communicate between the different processes. Build engines such as the one developed for SCons are already constructed to exist as separate pieces of functionality. All the pieces are coming together for such a build tool—watch the skies!

Custom Build Tools

As projects grow, there is often a need to generate some part of the source code automatically using generic code structures, in the same sense as C++ templates. Common areas for generated code are logging functions, class skeletons, and header files. The input specification can be a simple text file, an XML file, or a whole hierarchy of definitions in different files. A generator tool that uses these input files is invoked as part of the build process to generate the required files. Whatever mechanism is chosen, the generator is essentially a custom build tool, complete with all the potential advantages and frustrations that all the other build tools in this chapter possess. Before writing or using such a generator tool, consider all the things that you want in a regular build tool, such as accurate dependency calculation, easy debugging, and fast up-to-date builds.

Comparison of Build Tools

Table 5-2 briefly summarizes how each of the six build tools described in this chapter compare to the suggestions at the start of "Build Tools," earlier in this chapter, about what to look for in a build tool. This table summarizes the observations of the previous section, which discussed each tool in more detail. A plus sign (+) indicates a strength and a minus sign (–) indicates a relative weakness.

TABLE 5-2. Comparison of build tools

Requirement	Shell scripts	make	GNU Autotools	Ant	Jam	SCons
Dependency checking	–	–	+	+	+	+
Fast and smart	–	–	–	+	+	+
Independence from local environment	–	–	+	–	+	+
Variant builds	–	–	+	+	+	+
Multiple platforms	–	–	+	+	–	+
Easy to read and write build files	–	–	–	+	–	+
Scales well, parallel builds	–	–	+	–	–	+
Debugging/readable output	–	–	–	+	–	+
User community	–	+	–	+	-	+

Changing Your Build Tool

If you do decide to change your build tool, here are some tips for making the transition a little easier. "Steps When Changing Tools" in Chapter 3 also has some more general advice on choosing new tools.

Search for advice

Search carefully for examples of how other people have used the new build tool. Create a few local prototypes before going to the effort of creating all of the new build files. Subscribe to the appropriate mailing lists and browse the documentation and any books about the tool.

Start with a working build

Make sure that the existing build is working, at least for the major targets that are used by the project. This will remove a whole range of uncertainties from the conversion process.

Capture all the output from a working build

Generate a text logfile that shows the complete details of every command that the build currently executes, including any warnings from compilers and other tools. Now make your new build tool do what the old one did, as closely as possible. Then when your new build fails in some mysterious way, you will have a working example to compare against the output from the new build. Your existing build tool may well have an argument to increase verbosity and to show the actual command lines that were run.

Use the existing directories

If at all possible, create the new build files for the new build tool using the existing directory structure. This is one less variable changing at the same time. Later, after the build is working, you can start to rearrange directories and rename or split up the source code files.

Use temporary scripts

If there are parts of the original build files that the new build tool doesn't support until you customize it in some way, you can still make progress by hardcoding the old build commands into a script file and calling that with your new build tool.

Compare the results

If you run both the old and new build tool in parallel for a few days or weeks, then you can compare every generated file. It's also reassuring to see how many generated files are identical at a binary level and to understand the differences when they aren't—often this is due to timestamps. Ideally, when you do change over to using the new build tool, no one should see any difference in the files that are generated. You can also run tests to compare the performance of the old and new build tools, which helps encourage other people to use the new build tool.

Checklist

This section contains some questions that the person responsible for your builds should feel comfortable answering about your current build process:

- When you build the product, do the generated files end up mixed in with the source files, or are they in a separate location?

- You made a small change to a few files, but then rebuilding the product took *much* longer than you expected. Can you find out why it took so long? Exactly which files were rebuilt, and why was each one rebuilt?

- How long does an up-to-date build take with your build tool? (As explained in the earlier section "Build States: Virgin, Up-to-date, Changed, Interrupted, Clean," an *up-to-date* build is one where nothing has changed since the last build and so the generated files are already up-to-date.)

- How long do the other kinds of build (virgin, changed, interrupted, and clean) typically take for your product?

- How do you cause just a subset of your product to be rebuilt? Do you have to delete a magic file? Specify some target name to the build tool? Change to a special location in your source tree?

- How do you debug a build process? Can you debug where incorrect dependencies come from?

- Can you use different versions of your build tools on the same machine with confidence?

- Can you list all the other tools (and their versions) that your build tool depends on? Are they safely stored somewhere in such a way that you could recover them after a disaster? When was this backup last updated?

- Can you list all the operating systems (and their versions) that your build tool depends on? Are they safely stored somewhere in such a way you could recover them after a disaster? When was this backup last updated?

- How long did all the different kinds of builds take in the past? Can you predict when your build will become too slow?

- Do you think that a parallel build would improve your build times? How do you configure your build tool to run parallel builds?

- If you want to produce a different product using the same build tool and build files, in how many places do you have to add information about the new product?

- If you want to add a new type of build (e.g., with a different set of debugging arguments to a compiler or to generate PDF files instead of HTML), how many of the build files do you have to change? How many places do you have to make these changes in each build file?

- If you had to change the name of a product or a project, or the name of the company, how many build files would you have to change?

- Finally, the real motivation for this chapter: how much time per week do the project's developers spend wrestling with the build tool, waiting for slow builds, and investigating phantom bugs that are due to inconsistent builds?

## CHAPTER SIX

Testing Software

The single most important rule of testing is to *do it*.

— Brian Kernighan and Rob Pike
The Practice of Programming

THIS CHAPTER IS ABOUT HOW A GOOD TEST ENVIRONMENT can make testing your product much easier. A test environment is made up of the tools that you use to run your tests and report the results, together with the processes and policies for how to use the tools. Test environments are also referred to synonymously as "test infrastructures," "test harnesses," and "test scaffolds."

This chapter describes what to look for in a good test environment and summarizes a few different test environments. Automation of all the different kinds of tests is emphasized, along with integrating the tests with your SCM and build tools and communicating the test results to the rest of the project. Finally, some of the practical aspects of testing that always seem hard to get right are examined.

NOTE

This book takes a somewhat simplified view of testing because the focus is on the tools used to write and run tests, not on how to write good tests, or testing methodologies. For more information about testing in general, there are many books and web sites. Some that I have found particularly useful are listed in Appendix B.

This book also uses the term *tester* generally to mean anyone who runs a test, including developers, Quality Assurance (QA) engineers, and toolsmiths. This is because everyone in a project is involved in testing the product, in one way or another. Of course, testing is just one part of creating a quality product.

Different Kinds of Tests

There are many different ways to test software products. The tests that are described in this section are all tests that are separate from the product—that is, tests that don't have to be shipped to a customer. Other kinds of tests not discussed here are written directly into the product, checking for sane data values at the start of a function or testing for consistent states at other places in the source code.

All tests contain assumptions about what is correct and incorrect behavior for the product. Few products are ever mathematically specified to their most precise details, so most test results can only be as accurate as their assumptions are about how the product should work. Tests that check for both known correct and known incorrect behavior at least catch each end of the range of a product's behavior. The area between these two extremes is where carefully constructed tests can detect any poorly specified or inconsistent parts of a product, in addition to errors in the implementation of the product.

Unit Tests

Unit tests are designed to test smaller parts of a product, ideally just a single part per unit test. Exactly what a "single part" means in practice depends on how the product is designed: it could be a whole feature, a class, or just a single method or function. Unit tests are often written by the same developers who wrote the source code that is being tested. They may in fact be the best source of documentation of how to write applications that use their particular part of the product. Unit tests generally don't make assumptions that a network is accessible and working, or that a database or any other large product is available.

Unit tests are closely tied to the code that they test, and indeed the unit tests for the functions in a file *foo.c* will often be found in a file named *foo_test.c* in the same directory. The ability to identify source files for tests by their names is often useful, so don't just put unit test code anywhere. Unit tests are useful only if they stay in step with what they are testing, so it's good practice to build the unit tests whenever the product is built. The extra time for a build is a one-off cost, since a good build tool will rebuild unit tests only when something changes. Sometimes unit test files are placed in a top-level directory parallel to the product source code, but this doesn't encourage checking out, compiling, and running the tests, so I don't recommend doing this. Separate top-level directories can sometimes make running the preprocessor more complicated for C and C++ test files, but they may also make packaging Java class files a little easier.

Some programming methodologies such as XP stress that unit tests should be written before the code that they will test is written. This kind of test-driven development (TDD) approach does give a clearer understanding of what the code should do and what its APIs should look like. Of course, this also involves more work in the short term, and testing every get and set method may be unnecessary. As with all testing, the art of writing unit tests lies in deciding where to test for the maximum likely reward for your effort.

> **NOTE**
>
> *Regression tests* are defined as any tests that confirm that a program hasn't regressed and reintroduced bugs. Not regressing has also come to mean that a program still produces the same test results as it did before some changes were made to the program. Using regression tests can reduce the risk of making changes.

System Tests

System tests are designed to test the whole product. They may well be written by testers, often a separate group of people from the developers who wrote the source code for the product. Having two groups of people provides a useful confirmation when both groups have the same understanding about how the product is supposed to work. Testers who write system tests may or may not know how the product works at the source code level, so these kinds of tests are sometimes referred to as "black box testing." Testing that depends upon being able to see inside some imaginary box is known as "white box testing."

System tests generally assume that the product has been installed as the customer will install it and that everything that the product requires is present. This may include a working connection to the Internet or access to a database. Specifying exactly what a product requires to operate correctly is discussed in "System Requirements" in Chapter 9.

Customer Tests

Customer tests involve using the product just as a customer might. This might include installing the product in different ways or updating the product to a newer version. Customer testing may involve beta releases with real customers. Usability tests, which try to decide how easy a product is to use, are often conducted as part of customer tests. Both novice and experienced users of the product are needed for usability tests to be able to improve the design of a product.

Other Tests

Other kinds of tests include:

Comparison tests
Similar products are compared directly against each other, often in terms of features, robustness, and price.

Conformance tests
Testing that a product conforms to a particular specification.

Interoperability tests
Products are tested for how well they work together, usually by assuming that they all conform to a particular specification and then connecting the different products together in some way.

Many of these kinds of tests are performed by an external organization on behalf of a company, a standards body, or an industry magazine. Some of these organizations are more rigorous and objective than others, just like the industry analysts who write product reports for their magazines.

Such testing organizations may permit support staff from a company to be present but will not usually allow them to actually configure their own product except by proxy. It's also hard for testing organizations to be sure that the product they are testing is anything like the version that a customer reading the test results six months later will be able to purchase.

The design of these kinds of tests is often a matter of much discussion and careful market maneuvering. If you can influence the test configuration and parameters, then you can help ensure that your product will succeed, even before the test is performed. Indeed, products are sometimes specifically designed to perform well in benchmark tests, even if their performance in more common, real-life situations is less spectacular.

Why Automate Your Tests?

The motivation for automating tests is pretty simple: the easier it is to run the tests, the more the tests will be run, and the more tests you will be able to run. Tests that are not run regularly begin to rot and become useless. Automating unit tests and system tests also makes it easier to run them regularly as part of an automation environment (see "Automation Environments" in Chapter 3). As the number of tests and the different things that you want to test grows, automation becomes the only way to run the tests in a reasonable amount of time. Some tests, such as load testing with many hundreds of machines, are hard to imagine wanting to do by hand!

However, despite what the glossy brochures for test automation tools tell you, automated testing will not magically solve all your testing problems. For each test, you need to first decide how much effort it will take to automate it and what the likely payback is. For instance, imagine that a large, long-running system test costs X each time you run it manually, or costs Y for the first time you automate it and then nothing thereafter. If Y is 10 times X, then there is no benefit to automating the test unless you know that you are going to run the test more than 10 times in the life of the product.

Tests with more human interaction (such as conformance tests, customer tests, and "bake-offs") benefit less from automation, so this section doesn't discuss automating those kinds of tests.

As a general guideline, all the developers on a project should be able to build and run the unit tests, and there should be an agreed-on set of unit tests to be run whenever developers want assurance that their changes haven't broken anything—the CYA process.* Some

---

* CYA—cover your assets. This can involve anything from a "How Not to Break the Build" document, to a script that must be run before committing changes, to having all your diffs reviewed by other developers.

projects in fact require that unit tests are run before committing any changes to the project. There is a balance to be struck here for each project between the time spent running the unit tests and the increased perceived stability of the product. Running the unit tests automatically elsewhere and then mailing failures to developers who have changed the code since the unit tests last passed is another way to approach this issue.

System tests are often a larger collection of tests that are more complex than unit tests; thus system tests may take much longer to run. Whenever a release is created for testing purposes, the system tests should be run automatically, ideally before any time is spent manually installing and testing the new release. These system tests can be viewed as a contract between developers and testers about what has to work, at a minimum, before testers bother to look at the rest of the product.

Automation of both unit and system tests will also help greatly when the product has to be maintained later on, after the first release. The fewer steps it takes to build and run the tests, the fewer steps there are to forget or to run incorrectly.

Evaluating Test Environments

At a minimum, a test environment should allow you to:

- Run a number of tests.
- Decide whether the tests ran properly and whether any tests hung. A hung test should not prevent other tests from being run.
- Determine what the result of each test was—error (in the test), failure, or success—and also explain why.
- Summarize the results of the tests in a report.

It is my opinion that a good test environment keeps its tests separate from the mechanism used to run them. To see why, imagine that you want to use a different way of running your tests. You really don't want to have to actually change how any of your tests are written, since the tests are still testing the same parts of your product. A good analogy here is that if you change your build tool from *make* to SCons, you shouldn't have to change the source code for your product, just the build files.

Just like build tools and their build files, test environments benefit from having a good scripting language, one that has full support for familiar programming constructs. If you have to write your scripts and tests using a language that is supported by only one test environment, then changing test environments in the future will be more effort than it needs to be. And frankly, vendor-specific scripting languages are rarely as good as other, better-known scripting languages. Beware vendor lock-in!

Preparing to Test

Before you run a single test, make sure that you have a test plan that clearly describes the different parts of the product that will be tested—and how, on which platforms, and what the expected results are for each test. Make a list of the required machines and applications for each test, so that you can decide which groups of tests can be run in parallel. When the inevitable time crunch comes for your project, a clear and comprehensive test plan will help you in discussions about which parts of the product perhaps don't need as much testing as other parts.

Performance tests should be written with clear expectations of what their approximate results should be. Numbers by themselves are rarely meaningful, so the usefulness of performance tests is often more about how the results change as the values of different dimensions of the product are changed. You should at least be able to predict whether changing a parameter will make a particular result increase or decrease. You should also run performance tests for different durations until you can see the results tending toward a final value or range of values—for a short time, a man can outrun a horse, but I wouldn't call it a particularly useful test result.

It's also important to make sure that you've identified all the different dimensions that will be considered during testing. For example, for an application that runs on a single machine, you will need values for the operating system and version, disk size, and available memory. Once these dimensions are known, specific combinations of them can be chosen and used during testing. Getting the dimensions wrong is very frustrating for testers; it's annoying enough to have to repeat tests because the product changes, but it's infuriating to have to rerun tests because insufficient data was collected the first time that they were run.

Preparing to run the tests should now be a matter of deciding which tests to run, specifying the expected results, checking for the necessary resources, and, most importantly, deciding who will be told about any test failures and who will own any broken (failed) tests. If test results are never used, then the time spent testing is wasted. This sounds obvious, but if developers are not made aware of test results, then it's as though the tests had never been run.

A good test environment can help with the following before any tests are run:

Checking resources
   If an external resource (such as a database or a web site) is a prerequisite for running a group of tests, then it often makes sense to check that the resource is available just once, not before every one of the tests.

Defining expected results
   Defining the expected results is part of defining a test. Some tests may be expected to fail. This is true when a bug has been found and a test has been written to demonstrate this failure, but the bug has not yet been fixed. Other failing tests may be tests that are themselves waiting to be fixed.

Tracking primary owners
   Test environments can make it easy to change who owns each test, ideally by using a UI or a simple text search and replace. It should always be easy to identify who will be

asked to make a broken test work again. With bugs, even if it's not clear until the bug has been investigated more thoroughly who really owns the faulty code, at least there's a name to start from. If the same test keeps failing due to changes in an unrelated area, then the owner of the test can offer to let the owner of the other area own the test, without having to change who owns the source code.

Tracking secondary owners

Providing a secondary owner of a test in case the primary owner leaves the project is another useful idea. That way, email messages about failed tests should always reach someone, who may well feel motivated to reassign the tests to a new primary owner, if only to stop the email.

Generating test data

Some edge cases or *boundary conditions* can be tested for automatically. For instance, if a method accepts an integer as an argument, then values of 0, −1, and 1 are probably worth using in a unit test. Similarly, very short and very long strings, strings with spaces and punctuation, and non-ASCII strings are all good candidates for testing APIs that have string parameters. If your product uses text files, try passing an executable file to it as an input test.

Handling input data

If you are using fixed data, make sure it is stored in such a way that it is easy to change, such as in a file that's used for input by the test, rather than being compiled into the test executable. This also implies that test environments should be able to read from datafiles.

Generating random numbers

A test environment should have a good random number generator for generating data and for making choices in tests. Good ones are hard to find, and they're easy to use in ways that make the results decidedly nonrandom, so guidelines about using them properly are helpful.

Somewhat paradoxically, if you do need a random number generator, you should make sure that its output can be precisely repeated, so that you can debug your tests. This is usually done by passing in a "seed value" to the function that initializes the random number generator. Using the same seed value will produce the same sequence of random numbers—it's where you start in the sequence that isn't random.

Running the Tests

Some aspects of a test environment that help when running tests are:

Single tests

The ability to run just one test quickly dramatically improves the turnaround time for retesting small parts of a product.

Groups of tests

Being able to refer to tests in groups and to have the same test be part of multiple groups means that you can run test groups such as "the ones that failed last time" or "just the tests for Windows."

Independent, idempotent tests

Ideally, tests should have no side effects and should leave the environment in a known state. This means that you should be able to run the same test over and over again, or run the tests in any order. Test environments that help you get this right will save you hours of time trying to debug tests that failed only because the test that was run just before them failed. Running the tests in a different order also simulates more closely how customers may use the product.

Parallel processes

Tests that have to be run at the same time and be synchronized with each other are hard to run in most test environments. Most testers simply try to avoid these tests or design the product so that it can be put into states where it will wait for certain inputs for synchronization. The useful software clock resolution on many machines without real-time operating systems is only tens of milliseconds, so microsecond synchronization of software is most unlikely to be supported by test environments.

Background processes

Even if parallel processes don't have to be synchronized with each other, some tests will need processes to run in the background, and output logging and deadlock detection should work for these processes just as they do for other tests. A test environment should also provide a clean way to check for orphaned background processes before the next test starts.

Multiple machines

The use of multiple machines for a test means that the test environment has to provide a way of executing commands on remote machines, and also a way to collect the results of the commands for processing as part of creating a report. The test itself may have to be written so that it can be started and then wait for a signal to proceed.

Multiple platforms

Tests that run on many different platforms (for example, both Unix and Windows) benefit greatly from a test environment that hides the differences between the platforms from the person writing tests.

Capturing output

Good test environments can make capturing both the output and any errors from each test much easier. Keeping textual output and errors in the same place makes it easier to see when errors occurred relative to other output. If they have to remain separate, then timestamps are required, with as much resolution as the platform will provide. It's also helpful to be able to tee the output from each test to be able to monitor the progress of each test.

Scanning output

When the output of a test has been captured, usually into a file, the result of a test is often determined by searching for certain strings in the output. A good test environment can help by making the common cases simple to implement, while also supporting complex regular expressions or even state machines driven by the content of the output file. If there is some part of the output (such as the starting time or memory addresses) that changes every time a test is run, make sure that this output either is separate from other output or can be filtered by the comparison tools that are being used.

Note that the Unix tool *grep* does not support matches over multiple lines, so you can't use it to search for `Number of failures:\n1`, where `\n` is the newline character. However, both Perl and Python do support this.

After the Tests

Some features of a test environment that are helpful after tests have been executed include:

Distinguishing between failures and test errors
Tests can fail; this is expected when a product isn't behaving as expected. Tests can also have errors—that is, when the tests themselves fail to run correctly. Test environments that make a clear distinction in their test definitions and test reports between these two cases help reduce confusion. Test reports also have to make it clear when a test failure was expected. Of course, tests that fail intermittently without a clear explanation eventually tend to not get run.

Tracking which files were tested
Since tests may have names like *test019* that are unrelated to the source code that they are testing, all other clues about which files, classes, methods, and functions a particular test was exercising are helpful. For instance, you could look at the definition of a test to see which methods it called; or your test environment could provide you with that information and maybe add links to those methods to the detailed parts of test reports.

Flexible report formats
A wide variety of ways of communicating results is useful. Generating a set of HTML web pages is one common way to present reports, but text-based email, PDF, Word, or spreadsheet files are sometimes more appropriate. To make generating test reports in a variety of formats easier, it's often useful to store the results in a structured file format such as XML. Some test environments use databases to store their test results.

Storing test information
Once tests have become stable enough to be run automatically as part of a build, it's a good idea to use an SCM tool to store both the source code for the tests and the test results. The tests and their results should be tagged with the same build label that the build was tagged with (see "Labeling Builds" in Chapter 3). That way, you know which tests were run against a particular build, and also which versions of those tests were used.

Historical reports
Some test environments provide tools to create historical reports about test results. Graphs showing the total number and proportion of tests that pass or fail against time can provide a sense of a product's stability. Like any project statistic, these figures are useful only if you understand how the information was gathered and what kinds of errors exist in the data.

Creating bugs

Once a test has failed, it should be easy to create a bug about the failure. Creating a bug should always have a human involved to act as a filter for what is added to the bug tracking system. However, once the failure has been identified as a genuine bug, filling in the fields of the bug and attaching logfiles should be handled as automatically as possible.

> **NOTE**
>
> Did your test fail with a cryptic error message? After you've searched the open source code for clues about where the message might have come from, your best bet may be to try the Google Universal Debugger. Simply cut and paste the error into a Google search box, optionally add double quotes (") at the start and end of the phrase to keep it together, and then see whether other people have seen the same error. Don't forget to try searching the Google Groups too.

Good Test Reports

What should a good test report contain? The answer depends on whom the reports are intended for and how often the reports appear. A manager of a project may be interested only in the total number of tests, the percentage that failed, and perhaps the changes in these numbers since the last test report. Most importantly, a manager will want to know who's going to fix the broken tests.

Developers and testers tend to require more detail in test reports. Such information includes a unique name for the test or group of tests, an error state (maybe more than just "passed" or "failed"), links to the logfiles gathered when the tests were run, the duration of the tests, and possibly the expected duration. Output logs should be available in both raw and preprocessed form to highlight warnings, errors, and any other locally interesting text. Since test reports may well be printed on monochrome printers, highlighting of any text should use fonts and border thicknesses, not just color. Another helpful idea is to add links to reports to allow readers to browse each test definition and the areas of the source code that are being tested. Figure 6-1 shows an example of a crisp and clear test report.

The more information that appears in a test report about the environment in which the tests were run, the easier it is to recreate that environment later on, or in a different location. "Release Information" in Chapter 9 discusses the kind of information to gather for releases, and much of the same information is useful for test reports.

A useful guideline for the design of a good test report is to remove everything that doesn't directly provide information to the reader. Every line on every page is a potentially distracting piece of clutter for someone scanning the report in a hurry. A classic book on this subject that I can thoroughly recommend is Edward Tufte's *The Visual Display of Quantitative Information* (Graphics Press). Examples from all of his excellent books can be found at *http://www.edwardtufte.com*.

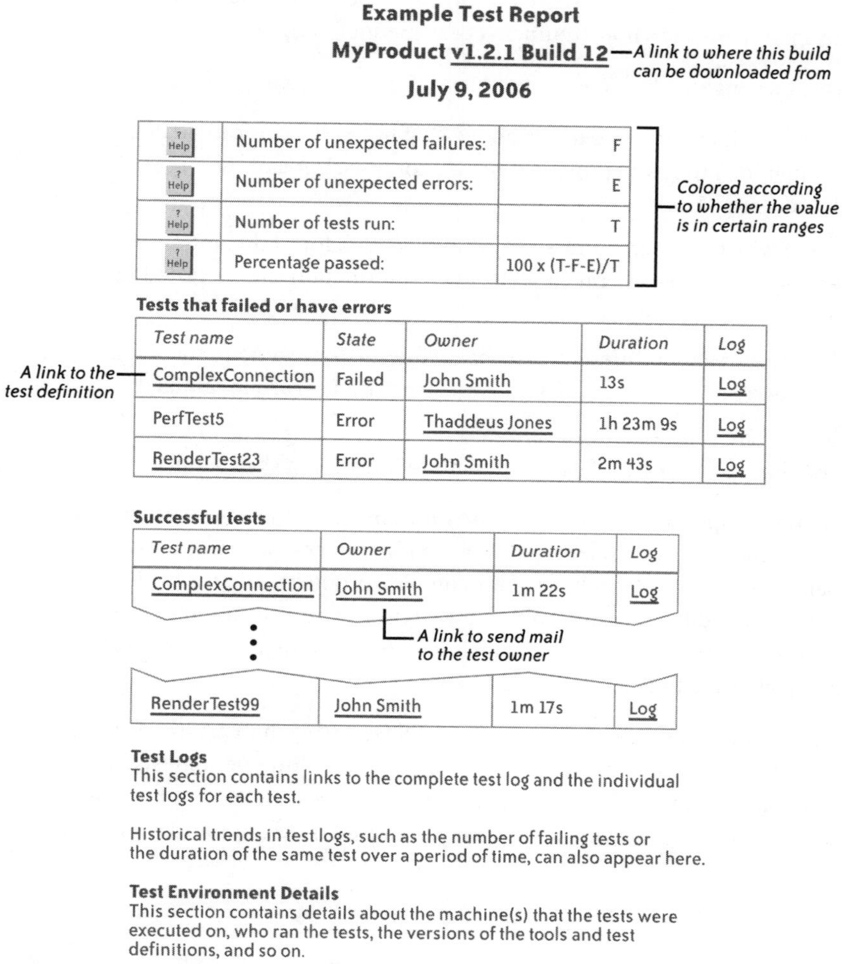

Example Test Report

MyProduct v1.2.1 Build 12 —*A link to where this build can be downloaded from*

July 9, 2006

? Help	Number of unexpected failures:	F
? Help	Number of unexpected errors:	E
? Help	Number of tests run:	T
? Help	Percentage passed:	100 x (T-F-E)/T

Colored according to whether the value is in certain ranges

Tests that failed or have errors

Test name	State	Owner	Duration	Log
ComplexConnection	Failed	John Smith	13s	Log
PerfTest5	Error	Thaddeus Jones	1h 23m 9s	Log
RenderTest23	Error	John Smith	2m 43s	Log

A link to the test definition

Successful tests

Test name	Owner	Duration	Log
ComplexConnection	John Smith	1m 22s	Log
⋮			
RenderTest99	John Smith	1m 17s	Log

A link to send mail to the test owner

Test Logs
This section contains links to the complete test log and the individual test logs for each test.

Historical trends in test logs, such as the number of failing tests or the duration of the same test over a period of time, can also appear here.

Test Environment Details
This section contains details about the machine(s) that the tests were executed on, who ran the tests, the versions of the tools and test definitions, and so on.

FIGURE 6-1. An example of a clear set of test results

Test Environments

This section examines some examples of different test environments that are currently available.

Shell Scripts and Batch Files

The simplest ad hoc test environments are just collections of a number of different test commands. Unix shell scripts and Windows batch files provide one way to collect these commands together. Scripting languages (such as Perl, Python, and Tcl) can also be used. Failure of a test written for these environments can often be detected by the value of each program's return code, with nonzero generally indicating a problem. Output is usually simple: the test name and pass or fail, with the error code. Single tests can be run by simply invoking them with the same arguments that the shell script uses.

Some aspects of testing that become more difficult if you use shell scripts and batch files are:

- Checking for deadlocks when a test is not ending properly. This can be done by using a separate watchdog process to provide timeouts for tests, but a program can do this more efficiently by using threads.

- Coordinating which regular expression patterns to look for in the output from each particular test. With a more general language, this information can be stored in the same place as each test definition.

- Gathering statistics about different parts of each test—for example, startup times and response times. A program can offer a better structure for running different parts of tests separately.

- Generating reports in HTML. This is just plain tedious using shell scripts.

For fewer than perhaps a hundred straightforward unit tests, this approach at least gets you started, and has very little overhead. However, the overall awkwardness of shell scripts explains why they are rarely used for complex products. The major drawback of this approach is that adding features to the test environment gets progressively harder as the shell script becomes more complex, which in turn discourages you from writing more tests or making changes to the test environment.

As a practical example of some of these issues, CVS (see "CVS" in Chapter 4) is released with a 34,000-line shell script named *sanity.sh* for running a number of tests on different platforms. The file *TESTING*, which is also part of the source code distribution for CVS, discusses various alternatives to *sanity.sh*, precisely because it is hard to understand such a monolithic shell script.

xUnit

The first of the series of xUnit test environments to become popular was JUnit (*http://junit.sourceforge.net* and *http://junit.org*), originally written by Erich Gamma and Kent Beck, which is a well-known open source test environment for Java classes. JUnit is now integrated into the Java build tool Ant and also into most IDEs for Java developers.

The xUnit test environments all use the same basic architecture as JUnit, but each one is intended for implementing tests for different languages. Each test inherits from a TestCase class and implements setUp and tearDown methods to prepare a class for testing and to clean up after testing, respectively. The author of the test class then defines methods whose names start with "test" to perform the tests, and uses a variety of assert methods to determine the result of each test. Generally, each test class should test a small part of the application (the "unit" part of xUnit). Multiple tests can be combined into TestSuite classes. You can also use a TestResult parameter within the tests for the collection of runtime statistics.

There is a long list of all the available xUnit test environments at *http://c2.com/cgi/ wiki?TestingFramework*, and there is an even longer list at *http://www.xprogramming.com/ software.htm*. The book *Unit Test Frameworks,* by Paul Hamill (O'Reilly), provides a good overview of the test frameworks for Java, C++, .NET, Python, and generated XML documents. The *Pragmatic Unit Testing* series, by Andy Hunt and Dave Thomas (Pragmatic Bookshelf), covers JUnit and NUnit in the authors' classic back-to-basics style.

One large advantage of the xUnit test environments is that since the architecture and classes are similar from one language to another, it becomes easier to write tests in different languages and easier to understand other people's tests. There are a number of command-line and GUI tools for running xUnit-based tests and collecting their results. However, the tests that you write are closely tied to the xUnit environment; it's harder to run such tests directly from the command line or by using a different test environment. Writing your tests in the same language that your project is using is a popular way to make developing tests easier.

DejaGnu

DejaGnu (*http://www.gnu.org/software/dejagnu*) is an open source test environment written in Expect that uses Tcl as the language for defining tests. Like the bug tracking system GNATS (see "GNATS" in Chapter 7), DejaGnu was originally developed at Cygnus. It's now maintained by Rob Savoye and Ben Elliston, and it is the test environment used by *gcc, gdb,* and some other GNU projects.

TCL AND EXPECT

Tcl (*http://tcl.sourceforge.net*) is a scripting language commonly used by testing teams, though you can also use it to build larger applications. The graphical interface for BitKeeper (see "BitKeeper" in Chapter 4) is one such application.

Expect (*http://expect.nist.gov*) is an open source tool written in Tcl that helps you automate interactive tasks such as FTP sessions, remote logins, and complex system tests.

DejaGnu's main focus is on running system tests, which are usually defined in Tcl, but you can also run existing tests in the same environment. There is strong support for running remote tests on many different platforms (though to run it on Windows, you must have the Cygwin environment) and there is good integration with the GNU Autotools suite (see "GNU Autotools" in Chapter 5). Running the tests automatically generates both a summary of the results and details of the tests' output. One benefit of using Expect is that DejaGnu can be used to test interactive applications such as *gdb*, the GNU debugger, which uses an interactive CLI by default. DejaGnu is also one of only a few available test environments that are POSIX-compliant.

The manual for DejaGnu is well written and contains an excellent step-by-step guide to getting started. Test debugging is mostly done by increasing the verbosity of various logfiles, but there is also more information on debugging remote tests available at *http://kegel.com/ crosstool/current/doc/dejagnu-remote-howto.html*.

If you need to test your product on many platforms (basically anything that *gcc* runs on) or if you want a lot of text-based user interaction as part of your testing, then you should consider DejaGnu for your testing environment.

SilkTest

SilkTest is a commercial test environment from Segue Software (*http://www.segue.com*). First released in 1993 as QA Partner, the latest release of SilkTest was Version 7.1 in 2004. Pricing starts above $6,500 per user for the test design tool; the runtime part costs less.

SilkTest is one of the industry-standard test environments (the other one being WinRunner) that is commonly used for testing everything from GUIs to browsers to databases to network management applications. The design tool runs only on Windows platforms and allows you to record and play back test actions, and to extend them with different data. SilkTest has its own test-scripting language named 4Test, which has support for multiple platforms and many existing applications. There is support for testing Java applications on Unix platforms, and the separate runtime part of SilkTest can be used on multiple platforms in parallel.

SilkTest is highly customizable; hence it has a fairly steep learning curve. The quality of support from Segue seems to have gone through cycles, but is sometimes excellent. Alternative sources of information include the QA forums at BetaSoft (*http://www.betasoft.com*).

Types of Test Tools

There are many different tools that can be used to test and debug very specific aspects of products. Some of these tools are more commonly used by developers than testers, but these tools can also be part of automated testing. For instance, knowing *when* a program started to leak memory during tests makes it easier to identify the particular changes that caused the memory leak. This section looks at a number of different kinds of tools that can be used as part of a test environment.

Memory Analyzers

One of the classic problems with programming languages such as C and C++ is that developers are responsible for keeping track of the memory that their programs use. If the memory leaks—that is, if it isn't freed properly for later reuse—then the program will eventually run out of memory and probably crash. In addition to permitting leaks, many languages don't check for programming errors such as reading or writing past the end of an array, which corrupts memory. The alternative to all of this is to use a language such as Java that support *garbage collection*, the process whereby unused memory is automatically managed while the program runs (at the cost of somewhat less control over when memory is reclaimed).

Memory analyzers are tools to keep track of how and when memory is allocated and freed by a program. They may also check for errors including ignoring an array's length; using a variable that is no longer valid in a later part of a program; reading from memory that hasn't been used yet; and a whole host of other common coding mistakes.

One of the oldest commercial memory analyzers is Purify (*http://www.ibm.com/software/awdtools/purify*), originally from Pure Software, then Rational, and now IBM. For many developers, Purify defined the expectations for what a memory analyzer should be able to do and how easy it should be to use. Purify runs on Windows, HP-UX, IRIX, GNU/Linux, and Solaris. It works by instrumenting the executable and the libraries that make up a program, adding code to every function to track when each part of it is called. No recompilation of source code is necessary, though more information can be collected if the source code is recompiled. There is a related product named PurifyPlus that provides code coverage (see the next section, "Coverage Tools") as well as memory checking, but PurifyPlus does require recompilation of the program. Other good commercial memory analyzers include TotalView (*http://www.etnus.com*), which is also a graphical debugger, and Insure++ (*http://www.parasoft.com*).

There are a number of open source memory analyzers (see *http://en.wikipedia.org/wiki/Memory_debugger* for a long list of them), but the best-known ones are Electric Fence (*http://perens.com/FreeSoftware/ElectricFence*), Valgrind (*http://valgrind.kde.org*), and *dmalloc* (*http://dmalloc.com*). If you're willing to recompile *gcc,* there are also patches available at *http://gcc.gnu.org/extensions.html* to add the -fbounds-checking command-line argument.

Electric Fence uses lots of memory but is particularly good at detecting out-of-bounds memory reads or writes. *dmalloc* is a replacement library for the standard memory allocation library, so it is likely to detect any bug that involves incorrect allocation or freeing of memory. *dmalloc* is also relatively portable and fast. Valgrind is actually an entire simulated x86 processor for GNU/Linux programs, and memory analysis is just one part of what it can do. Valgrind is probably the closest open source equivalent to Purify. A basic comparison of Electric Fence, *dmalloc,* and Valgrind can be found in "A Survey of Static and Dynamic Analyzer Tools," by Elise Hewett and Paul DiPalma (*http://www.cs.wm.edu/~coppit/csci780-fall2003/final-papers/hewett-dipalma.pdf*).

An alternative approach is to add some form of memory analysis to your product yourself. This can be particularly useful when you allocate one large block of memory at startup and then have your own memory allocation functions. It's not hard to make sure that every allocation is tracked and then to provide a way to display how much memory is being used by each part of the product. A useful idea is to provide not just the amount of memory used, but also the change since the last time the value was displayed. This lets you see more easily which parts of your product are leaking the most memory.

Of course, all this monitoring and analysis comes at a price. The executables are somewhat larger, but the main effect is that applications run more slowly when using memory analyzer tools. This is not usually a problem when the tool is being used to catch mistakes that are triggered by simply starting up a product, but using them to help debug errors that occur only after running a product for a long time can be very tedious indeed. The different speeds can also make timing-dependent bugs go away. This difficult class of bugs, where monitoring something changes the bug, are sometimes known as Heisenbugs.*

Even languages such as Java that do support garbage collection can benefit from the use of analysis tools such as JProbe (*http://www.quest.com/jprobe*), which can show where memory is not being garbage collected as expected and can also suggest why. Fine-tuning exactly when garbage collection occurs in order to improve interactive performance is another use for this kind of memory analyzer.

Coverage Tools

Coverage tools report how much of a product's source code is used when the product is tested. Of course, just because a line of source code has been executed doesn't mean that it has been fully tested and found to behave correctly in all cases. But if a line of code has never even been executed, you don't know anything at all about it.

> **WARNING**
>
> Some coverage tools are better than others at tracking exceptions. Exceptions are a way of making a function immediately return from any line of its source code if certain error situations occur; the lines after an exception is thrown will not be executed, so should they not be counted as covered.

Another kind of coverage testing is *branch coverage*. This measures the number of different places where a particular condition was never fully exercised. For example, were both the true and false branches in a particular if-then-else statement executed? Still another kind of coverage is *condition* coverage, where every Boolean in a conditional statement's condition is monitored to make sure that it has been tested as both true and false. For example, given the following:

```
if (var1 && var2 && var3) { ... }
```

the Booleans var1, var2, and var3 are expected to have been both true and false during the tests. Tests that set every group of Booleans used in such conditional statements to

---

* Like a fundamental particle bound by Heisenberg's uncertainty principle, the bug resists all attempts to pin down both its effect and its location at a particular instant. The act of observing a Heisenbug seemingly destroys information about it.

all possible combinations of values take an exponentially long time to run, depending on the number of Booleans, but using a coverage tool to tell you which conditions were never tested at all can still be useful.

Good coverage tools summarize their results so that you can see which files or classes have received lower than average testing with your current tests. Summary reports that allow you to drill down to the details of each function or method can also help you avoid rerunning the coverage tests.

As with any testing, the art of coverage testing is to focus on areas of concern and not to expect 100% coverage. Coverage is a worthwhile endeavor, but the lure of concrete numbers can encourage an unwarranted overreliance on coverage for judging how well testing is going.

Performance Tools

For developers, the idea of performance tools usually suggests *profilers*. Just like coverage tools, profilers record how often each line, function or method, and class were called, but they also record how much time was spent in each place in the source code. This information can help a developer understand where the product spends most of its time (the *bottlenecks*) and may suggest some areas to focus on for improving the product's performance. It's a good idea to profile only the released version of the product, since nonoptimized code, or code with debugging enabled, will often change the results of profiling.

Many compilers including *gcc* already support profiling abilities with separate tools such as *gprof*. Compiling the product with the correct arguments will cause profiling data to be saved when the product is run. This data can then be processed separately later on. Compiler-driven profiling tends to be text only, and it can be hard to follow the results for large programs. One of the best-known commercial profilers is Quantify, originally from Rational, now IBM (*http://www.ibm.com/software/awdtools/quantify*). It has good graphical summaries of the results, which can be expanded and followed through different parts of the source code. Valgrind (see "Memory Analyzers," earlier in this chapter) also has profiling abilities, and there is a graphical frontend to these named *KCachegrind* (*http://kcachegrind.sourceforge.net*).

For testers, performance is usually about loading the product with unusual amounts of data, large numbers of users, huge numbers of files, or any other parameter that can be modified. The idea is to discover what the limits of the product are, not necessarily to understand the causes of these limits. Once the limits are known, that information can be used to set customers' expectations and to guide them as they configure the product. Stress testing differs from load testing in that stress testing examines how the product behaves when the resources that it needs (memory, CPU cycles, disk space) are in short supply.

Static Code Analyzers

Another entire class of testing tools is *static code analyzers*. These tools take the source code of the product as input and analyze it. Some of the more common kinds of information provided by these tools are:

Language conformance

This is how closely the source code conforms to a standard for the language it is written in. Compilers for each language often deviate from the standard for the language, which can make code that compiles on one machine fail to compile when using a different compiler or when compiling on a different machine. When compiling C source code with *gcc,* there is a -std argument to specify which language standard is being used.

Security

Source code can be analyzed for statements that are vulnerable to cracking by potential stack smashing or other buffer overruns. Examples of tools that do this are StackGuard, Stack Shield, ProPolice, and Libsafe, all of which are conveniently compared in the paper "A Comparison of Publicly Available Tools for Dynamic Buffer Overflow Prevention," by John Wilander and Mariam Kamkar (*http://www.ida.liu.se/~johwi/research_publications*).

Correctness

Usually this involves proving, in the mathematical sense, that a program correctly implements what was intended. Far less formal, but still very useful, are tools such as the open source FindBugs (*http://findbugs.sourceforge.net*), which analyzes Java source code for different bug patterns, even looking for silly little bugs. FindBugs has a good track record of finding real bugs in many well-known applications that were already in production. Other similar tools are listed at *http://findbugs.sourceforge.net/links.html*, and there is a comparison of such tools for Java at *http://www.cs.umd.edu/~jfoster/papers/ issre04.pdf.*

Size

How large is your product? One simple way to check in a Unix shell is by typing:

```
find . -name "*.[ch]" -print0 | xargs --null wc
```

to count the number of lines in each of the *.c* and *.h* C source files in the current directory and its subdirectories. You could even count only lines that end with a semicolon by replacing wc with grep ';' | wc.

A more robust way of doing all this is to use SLOCCount (*http://www.dwheeler.com/ sloccount*), an easy-to-use open source line-counting application that works with most languages. If you want to track how the size of your product changes over time, StatCVS (*http://statcvs.sourceforge.net*) can do so for CVS repositories and can also generate lots of other CVS-related information; however, what's defined as a line of code is not as sophisticated as in SLOCCount.

Complexity

Counting the number of lines of source code is only the simplest (and some would say an almost meaningless) way of measuring a software product. There are a number of different ways to measure the complexity of source code, and tools for each different method exist for a variety of languages. An introduction to different software metrics and their history can be found at *http://irb.cs.tu-berlin.de/~zuse/metrics/3-hist.html*.

As well as measuring the size of your product, SLOCCount calculates the COCOMOII (*http://sunset.usc.edu/research/COCOMOII*) complexity of a product and uses the results to make an estimate of the cost of recreating the product. The resulting figures always seem high until you count the number of hours everyone has spent on the project.

Documentation

Tools such as Javadoc and *doxygen* generate documentation for developers from the comments embedded in the source code. These tools are described in more detail in "Internal Project Documentation" in Chapter 8.

A more unusual example of static analysis of a product's source code is measuring the stability of its API. A *stable* API is one that doesn't change greatly between two versions of a product. I wrote such a tool for Java applications (JDiff; see *http://jdiff.org*). The statistic that it uses doesn't seem to published anywhere else, so I have included it here. JDiff counts the number of *program elements* (Java packages, classes, constructors, methods, and fields) that have been added, removed, or changed between versions. The percentage change of the API between versions is then defined as:

$$\text{Percentage change} = \frac{100 \times (\text{added} + \text{removed} + 2 \times \text{changed})}{\text{sum of public elements in both APIs}}$$

For example, if there were 15 packages in the old API, and then 2 packages were removed and 4 packages were added, there are now 17 packages in the new API. If another 3 existing packages have changed between versions, then the simple percentage difference would be:

$$\text{Percentage change} = \frac{100 \times (4 + 2 + 2 \times 3)}{15 + 17} = 38\%$$

A change of 100% means that there is nothing in common between the two APIs; a change of 0% indicates that nothing changed between the two APIs. In practice, this formula is applied recursively for every package's classes and class members. That is, the value for the number of packages changed (3 in the example) is not an integer, but instead is the value obtained by applying the same formula to all the classes in the changed packages, and then to all the constructors, methods, and fields of the changed classes. This results in a more accurate percentage difference. Real-world figures are a 28% difference between Java J2SE™ 1.2 and J2SE 1.3, and a 46% difference between Versions 1.3.1 and 1.4. As might be expected, patch releases of J2SE have much lower percentage differences.

Finally, one location for a somewhat dated, but still useful list of static analysis tools is *http://testingfaqs.org/t-static.html*.

The Difficult Parts of Testing

There are two ways to write error-free programs; only the third one works.

—Alan Perlis
"Epigrams in Programming"
ACM SIGPLAN, September 1982

Personally, I find that testing a piece of software is full of activities that somehow turn out to be harder than I feel they ought to be. This section looks at some of these difficult parts of testing.

Faults of Omission

No matter how systematic and thorough you've been, there are always missing tests and the bugs that they never caught. These missing tests often seem so obvious after they are noticed. Of course, there are plenty of these faults of omission in the source code too, and some are found by the tests that you *did* remember to write and run.*

A general intent that is helpful when thinking of tests is to not only test for what the product should do, but also test that it hasn't done anything that it shouldn't do. For example, when you add a value to a complex data structure, consider not just whether that value is present, but also whether any extra values were added or other structures were changed.

It takes a particularly doubting outlook about software products to be able to consistently imagine conditions that the designers and developers of a product overlooked. Great testers can be psychologically exhausting for a team, since they can *always* find something wrong. Still, a good bug can be as surprising as seeing how someone cracked your product, and it can generate the same sneaky admiration in developers for the technical insight shown.

There is an interesting quote from Donald Knuth, who has written and tested plenty of complex software products, as well as having written the classic *Art of Programming* series of books. In a paper describing his experiences testing the typesetting program T$_E$X, he wrote:

> I get into the meanest, nastiest frame of mind I can manage, and I write the nastiest [testing] code I can think of. Then I turn around and embed that in even nastier constructions that are nearly obscene. (D. E. Knuth, "The Errors of TeX," *Software Practice & Experience* 19, no. 7 [1989]: 625–626)

Which at least has passion to recommend it. The next sentence is quoted less frequently, though it has some serious implications for anyone else maintaining his tests:

> The resulting test program is so crazy that I could not possibly explain to anybody else what it is supposed to do.

---

* According to Brian Marick at *http://www.testing.com/writings/omissions.html*, 20% to 50% of bugs in shipped products are faults of omission—source code that needed to be written, but never was.

Capturing Output

Many tests display text as messages while they are running, and the final result of the test may be part of this output, which then has to be searched for by some tool or other. (Other tests are more silent and simply indicate the test's status by their exit code.) One of the hardest parts of creating a good test environment is making sure that all the text output can be captured in a synchronized and complete way on many platforms.

Most operating systems support the idea of *input*, *output*, and *error streams* for programs, though in very different ways at their lowest levels. By default, there is an input stream for the program to receive data on, an output stream on which text appears, and an error stream for displaying error messages. Other streams can be defined for raw file-based input and output. Each of these streams can be redirected to and from files, or merged together. Some recurring problems when using this model are:

Merged output

If two threads in a program write to the same output stream at the same time, the text is mangled, with parts of both messages appearing together. The program has to provide a way to synchronize access to the stream. Windows locks its files so that only one source can write to them at a time.

Buffered output

If you are using buffered streams, then to improve performance no data is written until a certain number of bytes have accumulated in the buffer. However, if your program stops unexpectedly without flushing the output buffer, you may lose the critical messages that would tell you why the program stopped.

Child processes

If one process starts another process, then arranging for the output from the child process to be redirected along with the output of the parent process is prone to error.

Complex code

Neither Windows nor Unix primitive operations in the area of input and output are particularly easy to use correctly.

This is a good area in which to look for working examples in any test environment.

Using Multiple Machines

Running tests on multiple machines creates a whole level of difficulty beyond testing on a single machine. Just the time taken to run these tests manually can quickly become overwhelming. I recall trying to test an application that used multicast without a lab full of test machines or any way to reliably run commands remotely on the machines that we did have. We ended up using everyone's desktop machines on the weekend and ran from one machine to another to start and stop the tests!

The difficulties here can be broken down into three parts: sending commands to remote machines, starting and stopping the tests, and collecting the resulting data.

Sending commands

For less than about 16 machines, especially if they are all running the same operating system, a KVM (keyboard, video, monitor) switch, a shared monitor, and a programmable keyboard can take you a surprisingly long way. Many KVM switches allow you to change between machines by using a short sequence of cryptic keystrokes. First, create an executable script to run the test on one machine and name the script using a single letter; then program the keyboard to change machines using a single function key. To run the script on all the machines, simply peck away at the two keys until everything is running. VNC (*http://www.realvnc.com*) is a program that lets you see the desktops of different machines, and you can do a similar thing with VNC screens. All of this isn't very elegant at all, but sometimes it's all that's needed.

Rather more general ways of sending commands to remote machines are to use *rsh* and its more secure descendant *ssh*. Two open source tools that can run commands remotely are *fanout* (*http://www.stearns.org/fanout/README.html*) and BitCluster (from BitKeeper, the eponymous maker of the SCM tool described in "BitKeeper" in Chapter 4), which is available as an alpha release from *http://www.bitmover.com/bitcluster*.

Using CORBA ORBs is another way to communicate with remote machines. Applications can send command strings to multiple machines using different languages and on different platforms. You do still have to write the code that actually executes the commands on each platform, and most ORBs don't support multicast, so commands are sent to each machine in turn.

Starting the tests

Once you have a way to send commands to multiple machines, you'll need to administer the machines so that they all have the desired version of the operating systems and the correct copies of the test programs. Doing this can take a fair amount of time in itself. Now you need a master test-control tool to send the correct commands to each machine. You may want to be able to take snapshots of the test results during the tests in order to see what's happening on each machine. Without regular peeks at each machine and good logfiles with synchronized timestamps on each machine, it's often hard to work out why a test or product crashed on only a few machines out of many. Some of the tests may also require more input from the master machine after some time has passed. In this case, you'll need a way for each machine to indicate that it's waiting and is ready for more commands.

Collecting the data

Once the tests have finished on every machine, the amount of data to be processed becomes an issue. Copying all the results that are on the test machines back to a central location can overload that one machine's resources and slow down the network. If affecting the local network while the tests are running is not a concern, then you could copy results during the tests or use a single file server mounted remotely on each of the test machines.

One good idea is to preprocess the results while the data is still on the test machines and then copy just the summaries to the central location, where they can be assembled into the report for the whole test.

To ensure that your collected data is meaningful, you should make sure that the clocks on all the machines involved in the tests are synchronized (for example, by using *ntp* on Unix, or the Windows synchronization client or Tardis on Windows machines). You might also need to postprocess results that come from different time zones and watch out for daylight savings time occurring on different days in different countries.

One interesting project that shows what can be done with a distributed test environment is SmartFrog (*http://sourceforge.net/projects/smartfrog*), a framework developed by Hewlett-Packard and released as open source software.

Only a Developer Can Do That!

There always seem to be some bugs where the only person who can test the fix is the developer who made the fix. This is irritating, since it was usually a tester who noticed the problem and filed the bug. One example of this sort of bug is in stress testing, where to overload the product, a developer may need to change the values of array sizes, file sizes, or connection speeds, and these changes have to be made in the product's source code.

For instance, suppose that the product crashed during some long-running tests, and it was eventually determined that this was due to the rest of the internal network being over-loaded for more than 15 minutes. A bug is filed, and the assigned developer believes she has a fix. It's more than a little inconvenient to overload the internal network again, so she makes changes in the source code that affect the way the product accesses the net-work, in order to simulate the extended network overload. How is a tester supposed to confirm that the bug is fixed? Without simulating the entire network, the closest to confir-mation anyone can come to is to have the developer explain the changes and to provide test versions of the product with and without the changes.

The most common example of bugs that only developers can test occurs when part of the product has no API, and that part is where the bug is. If the bug needs to be tested by someone other than a developer, then the best solution is to add a test API to that part of the product. It's quite likely to be similar to the debugging code added by the developers anyway. Of course, you have to be careful that the test APIs are not enabled when the product is shipped, and that they are not relied on by developers and testers during the ordinary use of the product.

One way to get around this whole problem is to make sure that the testers on the project are comfortable inspecting source code, can build and execute the unit tests, and can add hooks into the product for easier testing. If the project's testers are not comfortable with these activities, then at least make sure that developers and testers are using the product in the same way, so you can avoid the equally irritating opposite of this section's title: "Only a tester can do that!"

Accessibility Testing

Testing a product to make sure that it can be used by people with different needs from the developers is always hard to do automatically. So much of what a customer can or cannot use is hard to embed in tests, particularly in automated tests. The classic example is making sure that information on web pages can be read by people with vision problems. Since accessibility is now required by law in various countries, this is an area that would really benefit from better automated testing tools.

My personal frustration is with the use of color alone to add information to a report or web page. Along with up to 10% of all men, I was born red/green color-blind, so some common color combinations look identical to me.* This doesn't mean that all colors appear the same, or that I can't tell what red looks like (to me). It does mean that certain colors that appear quite different to my wife look the same to me, just as some people can't tell two close musical notes apart. Some practical examples are that red chalk on a green blackboard is hard to see, and maps and diagrams that have regions with similar colors are pretty much useless to me.

Perhaps you've seen products that change tiny little images from green to red to tell you when something has gone wrong? These products just don't get purchased by color-blind people, because we can't see any of the changes. Products that have considered this issue will allow you to configure the colors used in different parts of the product and may even provide some different color schemes or *skins*. (Skins are not there just to make the product look cool.)

As this issue has become better understood by web designers, web sites have been created with suggestions of color combinations to avoid, or even to show you what your web site looks like to a color-blind person. One good site as a starting point for more information is *http://more.btexact.com/people/rigdence*. There is also a wonderful tool at *http://www.vischeck.com/vischeck/vischeckURL.php* that simulates how web pages appear to color-blind people.

Checklist

This section contains a short list of questions that you should feel comfortable answering about your existing test environment:

- Can you use your test environment to run just one test?
- How do you decide when to automate a test?
- Do you ever discard tests? If so, how do you decide when? If not, do all of your tests actually help you to test the product?
- When are automated tests run? Is someone automatically informed about failed tests?

---

* Color-blindness is also known as "color variance" or "Daltonism."

- Can your test environment detect when a test has become deadlocked? Can you kill it, and can the other tests still be executed?

- How do you know who to contact about a particular test when it stops working?

- How do you know which parts of your product are the least tested?

- When was each aspect of the product last tested, and where are the results?

- What resources do each of your tests require?

- How could you change your product to make it easier to test?

- How much work would it be to test your product on a new platform? Does your test environment help you with this?

- When a bug is fixed, do you know which precise test will confirm that it is fixed?

- Which versions of the tests and test environment tools were used with which release?

- If your product uses color anywhere in it at all, have you had a color-blind person test those parts?

- Most importantly, does your test environment make testing your product easier?

## CHAPTER SEVEN

Tracking Bugs

THIS CHAPTER IS ABOUT KEEPING TRACK OF BUGS IN SOFTWARE PRODUCTS. Doing this well turns out to be one of the harder things for a development environment. Few people ever seem to really like using their bug tracking system, perhaps because different groups of people want very different things from the same bug tracking system. Bug tracking systems are one example of *collaborative* tools, which help groups of people work together efficiently on many small tasks. Similar systems include the tools that help customer support teams track customers' issues and the tools that help a salesforce coordinate its efforts, but those tools are outside the scope of this book.

The first part of this chapter discusses what kinds of things you might want a bug tracking system to do for you. The second part describes six different bug tracking systems: spreadsheets, Bugzilla, GNATS, FogBugz, JIRA, and TestTrack. The last part of the chapter discusses some commonly encountered annoyances of bug tracking systems and has some suggestions for how to avoid the worst of these. Most of these suggestions are independent of any particular bug tracking system.

Tool Requirements

At a minimum, a tool for tracking bugs needs a way to uniquely identify each bug and somewhere to store the information that describes each bug. The word *bug* is used here to refer to both an actual bug in a product and the information about a bug that is stored in a bug tracking system. Bug tracking tools usually store this information in a database. Most tools add the ability to generate reports in various file formats. The contents of these reports are often the results of queries that have been run against the underlying database. Sometimes bugs have states assigned to them, and each bug's state is changed as work is done on the bug. Other information that is often recorded with a bug includes who found it, who is working on it now, which releases the bug exists in, and which releases it was fixed in.

There are a number of characteristics to look for in any bug tracking system:

Easy to enter new bugs

There should be a minimum number of fields that have to be filled in, just enough so that if any of them were empty, then the entire bug would be useless. These required fields should be the easiest ones to find on a screen or in a list (and simply making the field names red instead of black doesn't cut it for color-blind people). You should be able to leave the screen to copy and paste text from other screens, and return to find the screen just as you left it. Drop-down lists can help ensure that data is consistent, but they should not be allowed to grow too long. Fields that aren't available should be disabled, not just made invisible. If there are obvious choices for whom a bug should be assigned to, then these should be filled in automatically. You should also be able to attach other files to a bug.

Easy to change the state of a bug

The different states that a bug can be in varies widely with different products and projects, so a convenient state diagram that shows how bug states are expected (and permitted) to change is very useful. If bugs are allowed to change states only according to the state diagram, then it's helpful if the bug tracking tool suggests only the valid states for changes.

Easy to change many bugs

The ability to change a number of bugs with a single operation can save a lot of time, especially if the list of bugs is the result of running a report.

Easy to review a particular bug

Given a particular bug identifier, you should be able to view and edit that bug quickly and intuitively. All of a bug's information should be accessible from a single screen of the UI.

Easy to watch a bug

It should be easy to become aware that something in a bug has changed. Email is the usual way to notify people about this. It should be easy to change when and how different groups of people are notified. Notifications may be related to groups of bugs or to changes in the state of bugs.

Easy to search using brute force

When all other ways of finding a particular bug fail, you should be able to search all the text fields for a given string. It may not be efficient, but when you are stuck, you really need to be able to do this.

Easy to trace the history of a bug

You should be able to see how a particular bug has changed over time—what changed, who made the change, and when. Snapshots of the bug at each change and a list of the differences between the snapshots are both useful.

Easy to connect to source code changes

If a bug tracking system is integrated with an SCM tool, then you should be able to find all the changes to the source code that are related to a bug or multiple bugs. This could be reported as the affected filenames and their versions, the differences between versions, or the changesets.

Characteristics you should look for that relate to using the bug tracking system to manage a project are:

Easy to generate reports

How easy it is to generate different reports is often a major factor in people's perception of how easy it is to use a particular bug tracking system. It should be possible to generate simple reports by using a simple interface. It should also be possible to generate more complex reports with AND, OR, and XOR Boolean operations, selection of multiple values, and range comparisons. You should be able to save all reports, along with text explaining the purpose of the report. Formats for reports can include HTML, comma-delimited text, XML, Microsoft Word, and PDF.

Easy to produce historical reports

Not all bug tracking systems let you produce reports about how the bugs have changed over time. These kinds of historical reports are very useful for seeing how a project is progressing.

Easy to connect to a schedule

The list of which bugs should be fixed for a particular release should be straightforward to enter and to create reports about. If one bug depends on another, then that also should be made very obvious. Some projects like to be able to have project members vote for the bugs that they really want to be fixed, which can help when assigning bugs to planned releases.

Desirable features that are more closely related to administering a bug tracking system include:

Easy to modify the definition of a bug

The administrators of a bug tracking tool will probably need to change the different fields that make up a bug. This should be straightforward, with clear documentation about what kind of data is expected in each type of field that can be added. Adding new fields to UI screens should be as intuitive as possible. Removing a field should also be integrated with the report and screen design areas of the bug tracking system.

Easy to modify the workflow

It should be easy to change the states that a bug can be in—that is, to change the names of the possible states and also how the states are related to each other. Adding or removing states should also be possible.

Easy to manage the list of users

Many companies already have their users defined—for instance, in an LDAP server. Bug tracking systems that can work with existing lists of users make maintenance easier. There should at least be a way to import a list of users, so that the administrator doesn't have to enter each one manually.

Scalable

As the number of bugs, groups, and users in a bug tracking system grows, the interface design must also scale well. Drop-down lists with hundreds of users don't work very well. Searching text fields may become painfully slow. Backups may become more than an overnight job. Additional features to help with detecting duplicate bugs also become more necessary as the number of bugs increases.

Accessible through external clients; good API

You should be able to read and modify data in the bug tracking system from outside the GUI or browser. This is a generally useful ability (e.g., for adding the latest build label to the bug tracking system as part of an automated build process). A well-considered and well-tested API, beyond just writing SQL statements, is a good sign.

Easy to change the text displayed

It should be easy to change the text that is displayed onscreen for usernames, release numbers, and other field names. This is partly to help localization and customization, but also because product names can change, so embedding them directly in a database field name makes maintenance harder than is necessary.

Easy to back up different parts of the bug tracking system

You should be able to save copies of reports and UI screens before modifying them, in case of errors. This also allows you to design complex reports and screens on a development system and then import them into a production system, rather than having to re-enter them by hand. Backing up the actual data in the bug tracking system should be possible on a live system and easy to automate.

The features listed so far in this section are the positive requirements for bug tracking tools. The following is a list of some general issues with bug tracking systems that come up again and again in practice. More specific annoyances, and ideas to help work around them, are described in "Bug Tracking Annoyances," later in this chapter.

Huge attachments

Many tools claim that the size of file attachments that can be added to their bugs is limited only by the underlying filesystem or database. That may or may not be true, but you should check how the performance is affected. "Cleaning Up," later in this chapter, has some more ideas about cleaning up your data to help with this.

Spam magnets

If you create a public email address for customers to send bugs to, you risk filling your bug tracking system with spam when the address falls into the wrong hands. Good spam filtering will help stop most of this, but be sure you can delete information from all the fields in your bugs.

Mystery data formats

Migrating from one bug tracking system to another is often very tedious, even more so than with SCM build tools. If the data is in an open format, and if there are published schemas for each tool's database, then the process becomes somewhat easier. Before you add data to a bug tracking system, consider how you would extract it if the system failed to perform in some way.

Internationalization

Some bug tracking systems don't handle non-Latin text and other characters well in their input fields, or even in the names of users. Many are not localized for any language except English.

Default values

If no data was added to a field, what value does that field have when you want to search on it? If a field is added or removed, how does it appear in historical reports? Not surprisingly, the classic database issues of nulls and defaults also exist for bug tracking systems.

Databases need administrators

If a bug tracking tool uses a complex database such as Oracle, then there will probably be occasions when Oracle administration will be a necessary skill for the tool administrator. Make sure this is clearly understood from the start and arrange for consulting and training if the necessary skills aren't available within the project.

Multiple platforms

Different people will want to use the bug tracking system from different platforms. Since supporting client applications for multiple platforms is a lot of work, many bug tracking tools have chosen to use web servers and browsers instead. This is mostly portable, but not all browsers will work with complicated web pages, and many browsers don't do very well at displaying XML or HTML text when it's entered as data for a bug.

A related problem is that some users, and most system administrators who are integrating a bug tracking tool, will want to use CLI commands. The CLI ought to work uniformly across the different supported platforms, but in my experience it often doesn't.

Bug Tracking Tools

There are easily a hundred different tools available for tracking bugs. A good place to start if you want to see a list of choices is the Open Directory's Bug Tracking section at *http://dmoz.org/Computers/Software/Configuration_Management/Bug_Tracking*. Another good location for a list of tools is *http://testingfaqs.org/t-track.html*. Yet another list of open source bug tracking tools is *http://usefulinc.com/edd/notes/IssueTrackers*.

Spreadsheets

The simplest structured way to keep track of a small number of bugs is to use a spreadsheet program, such as Excel or OpenOffice Calc. You could use an ordinary text file or a Wiki, but then it's hard to sort the information. Each row in the spreadsheet is a single bug. Some typical column titles might be Bug Number, Summary, Description, State, Owner, and Priority. Sorting and summarizing by different columns can show the bug counts per person, the highest-priority bugs, and so on. Many spreadsheets will let you restrict the kind of data entered into each field—for instance, to make sure that the bug number is unique.

The main advantage of this approach is its simplicity. Spreadsheets are commonly available tools and are reasonably well documented. Basic reports are easy enough to produce. Adding a new field to the definition of a bug is as simple as naming another column.

However, the disadvantages of this approach are significant. Most of these are the same reasons why people use databases rather than spreadsheets. As a project grows, the first problem that is likely to be encountered is that only one person can modify the spreadsheet at a time. Another problem is that, unlike with a good database, if the machine running the spreadsheet crashes during modification of a bug, then the data can be inconsistent. Also, as the number of bugs in the spreadsheet grows into the thousands, the time taken for the different reports can grow significantly.

Using a spreadsheet to keep track of bugs should be viewed as a temporary measure, one that will not scale as a project grows. There are many simple, low-cost bug tracking tools available that will scale better than a spreadsheet. Still, a spreadsheet is better than an email folder of reports of possible bugs or a wall full of Post-it notes, but not by much.

Different Server Technologies

There are many bug tracking systems to choose from—perhaps more than all the available SCM tools and build tools combined. Most of these tools meet a fair number of the requirements and goals for a bug tracking system that were listed in "Tool Requirements," earlier in this chapter. So how to choose tools for evaluation? Some tools are easy to reject because they're no longer actively developed—when was their last real release? A useful reference for checking up on this is Danny Faught's Boneyard page (*http://www.testingfaqs.org/boneyard.html*), which is a list of many corporate changes and dead products in this area. Other tools are easy to reject because you can't justify their cost for the project at hand.

Between these two extremes there are still hundreds of tools, both commercial and free, all of which have a dozen or so customer sites and a few glowing testimonials. My suggestion is that if you have used one of these tools before—or even better, if you've administered it and it worked for a similar project—then use it again if at all possible (and if you still can bear it). That way you'll avoid spending time discovering bugs in a new product.

If you are interested in knowing what other people and projects are using, then the next five sections should be helpful to you. The tools in these sections (Bugzilla, GNATS, FogBugz, JIRA, and TestTrack) were chosen because each one is relatively well known and represents a different underlying technology. The different server-side technologies used by each tool are:

Bugzilla
> Perl scripts called from a web server

GNATS
> A standalone server using C and shell scripts

FogBugz
> PHP scripts called from a web server

JIRA
> A Java servlet running inside an application server

TestTrack
> A separate server closely coupled to a web server

Bugzilla

Bugzilla (*http://www.bugzilla.org*) was one of the first projects to be released by the Mozilla organization. Written entirely in Perl, Bugzilla is licensed under the open source Mozilla Public License. The version described here is 2.18rc3.

THE HISTORY OF BUGZILLA

Bugzilla grew out of the bug tracking systems developed for use inside Netscape in the late 1990s. Terry Weissman wrote the first version in Tcl and then ported it to Perl for Version 2. Since April 2000, the project has been led by Tara Hernandez and then Dave Miller. Several forks have occurred and merged, including the Bugzilla used by Red Hat, and IssueZilla, which was used in CollabNet's preconstructed development environment (see "CollabNet" in Chapter 3).

Bugzilla has all the basic features that you would expect from any bug tracking system, and a good number of more advanced ones. Interaction is via a web browser, and notification is by email. Configuration is done by modifying Perl source files, so the local source of Bugzilla can (and should) be versioned with an SCM tool. Other features include the following:

- Regular expressions can be used in text searches. The web page for queries can seem daunting when first encountered, but the defaults mostly just work. More complex queries using Boolean operators are also supported.

- Reports are a separate feature from queries and are really quite impressive. Three kinds of information can be chosen, then filtered according to interest, and then displayed as tables, various graphs, or pie charts. Data can be exported as comma-delimited values. The historical reports are also of generally good quality.

- LDAP is used to control access rights, so there is no need for a separate set of Bugzilla usernames.

- The history of each bug is available; it displays in a table which fields were changed by whom and when, and what the changes were.

- Each person can configure to a fine level which types of changes to a bug will trigger an email to them.

- Email addresses in bugs can optionally be obfuscated to stop address harvesting on public web sites.

- Bugzilla supports people *voting* for different bugs. Bugs with more votes are considered more irritating to more people.

- Links from within text to other bugs, URLs, and email addresses are created automatically.

- Adding dependencies between bugs is supported.

- Spellchecking is available.

- There is some limited support for measuring the time spent working on each bug.

- Bugzilla is well localized in at least nine different languages and can use multiple language templates at once.

- There are tools to check the configuration and to check that the data in the database makes sense to Bugzilla.

The list of projects and companies that use Bugzilla is impressive and includes some of the largest open source projects. The Apache web server, the Linux kernel, and *gcc* all have thousands of bugs recorded in their Bugzilla systems. There were discussions within Apache about using other bug trackers after Apache's insecurely configured Bugzilla led to the defacing of the main Apache web site, but better security seems to have meant that Bugzilla is still in use there, though some projects are now moving to JIRA.

Documentation for Bugzilla is sufficient but improving, and the mailing list and other resources are very active due to the large number of users and system administrators. Consulting is offered from numerous sites all over the world. Another useful page about Bugzilla administration is Byron Jones's *http://bugzilla.glob.com.au*, especially for Windows servers. References for how to integrate CVS with Bugzilla appear in "Integrating with SCM Tools," later in this chapter.

Bugzilla's biggest strength is that it is open source. If you are comfortable with Perl and the Perl ways of doing things, then customization is possible. However, because Bugzilla has grown organically, some of the interfaces are not defined clearly enough to make it easy to maintain your modifications as new versions are released. Also, modifying the workflow by adding new states is not easy at all. That said, the many features that already exist in the newer versions of Bugzilla may well be complete enough so that only minor customizations are necessary for your project. Another approach is to purchase a server already configured with Bugzilla—for example, from Bugopolis (*http://www.bugopolis.com*)—or to use a Bugzilla hosting service such as BugHost (*http://www.bughost.com*).

Bugzilla was developed for Unix-based web servers and has only recently begun to support Windows as a server platform. Likewise, it was written to use MySQL as the underlying database and has only recently begun to support other databases (PostgreSQL is one). Documentation of the database schema is sparse. In general, configuration of Bugzilla is still quite complex, even if you are comfortable with Perl and Unix.

Bugzilla is the most popular open source bug tracking tool available. It's used by a large number of projects and companies and does provide a wide range of features after careful installation and configuration, preferably by someone who is comfortable with Perl. One area still under careful scrutiny is security (*http://www.bugzilla.org/security*), so make sure you read all the documentation when using it on a public server.

GNATS

GNATS (*http://www.gnu.org/software/gnats*) is a bug tracking system from the Free Software Foundation and is licensed under the GPL.* It's written mainly in C and shell scripts, and has a long history of extensive customizations by each project that has used it. All interaction with GNATS was originally by Unix shell commands and email, but other interfaces also exist. There is a Web interface (Gnatsweb), an Emacs mode, and a GUI written in Tcl/Tk (TkGnats) that runs on Unix and some older versions of Windows. The source's *contrib* directory also contains a web interface for administering GNATS itself, which is particularly useful since GNATS comes with a fair number of different configuration files.

THE HISTORY OF GNATS

GNATS (recursively defined as "GNats: A Tracking System") has been in existence since the early 1990s. It was originally written by Heinz G. Seidl, and then for a number of years it was developed by Brendan Kehoe and Jason Merrill at Cygnus, and it's still sometimes referred to as the GNU Problem Report Management System (PRMS). Releases based on the 3.1 source continued even after the 3.2 release. Version 4.0 was a major rewrite by Bob Manson, Milan Zamazal, and Yngve Svendsen; it was released in August 2003. As of early 2005, Chad Walstrom is the maintainer of the project.

GNATS is really intended for use on Unix machines, though the Tcl/Tk, email, and web interfaces do allow it to be used from Windows machines. Releases prior to 4.0 used text files to store the data. Release 4.0 changed the data format to a binary one. By default, the states for bugs are:

Open
   Initial state for all bugs.

Analyzed
   Work has begun on the bug.

Feedback
   A fix is being tested.

Closed
   The bug has been fixed.

Suspended
   Work on the bug has been suspended.

---

* GNATS should not be confused with GNAT, which is the GNU Ada Toolchain project.

Large projects and organizations that use GNATS as their bug tracking tool include Juniper Networks and FreeBSD (*http://www.freebsd.org/support.html*). It was also used by the Apache community until March 2002, when it was replaced with Bugzilla. GCC has also moved from GNATS to Bugzilla.

Documentation for GNATS exists and mostly is correct, though not extensive. Reading the source really is the final documentation for GNATS. The mailing lists are all fairly low-volume as of early 2005.

GNATS interacts with the lowest common denominators of open source projects: email and browsers. It even works with text-based browsers, such as Lynx. Since many of the fields are simple text, regular expression queries work well. The latest version has made adding new fields easier and supports using separate database instances (for use by different projects, for example).

While GNATS does have an audit trail that can be configured to show the changes in different fields, this is not searchable by default. There is no explicit audit trail for changes to the configuration of the tool itself. Generating historical reports is complicated, though FreeBSD does have some Tcl scripts available to help do this.

GNATS is a project that seems to have grown by fits and starts, as each project using it fed their changes back into the GNATS source code. Even though Version 4.0 removed many of the valid concerns about the speed and index-corruption bugs of earlier versions, a number of projects had already stopped using GNATS, usually changing to Bugzilla, the other open source bug tracking system. Still, GNATS seems adequate for most projects and can be extended in many different ways without too much difficulty. If you like your tools to be Unix-based with a terse command line or to be purely email-oriented, GNATS may be worth further investigation.

FogBugz

FogBugz, from Fog Creek Software (*http://www.fogcreek.com/FogBUGZ*), was designed by Joel Spolsky, who also writes thought-provoking articles on development environments at *http://www.joelonsoftware.com*. Interaction with FogBugz is by web browser or email, and it uses the PHP scripting language and a web server (Apache or IIS) to interact with a database. FogBugz is licensed commercially but is released with source code for modification by system administrators. The cost is approximately $100 per user, with support wittily priced at five cents per day (which works out to be $18.25 per year, in case you were wondering) but available only in blocks of a year.

The whole design of FogBugz places a priority on usability over functionality. What this means in practice is that FogBugz is really easy for users to learn and will do 80% of what other, more complicated bug tracking tools will do. Adding new users and changing their preferences is straightforward. Changing the text used as labels for different fields is easy enough, since the PHP files are available. Adding a simple text field is apparently possible but not encouraged, since it leads to too many choices, which discourages people from entering bugs. Adding more complex fields that increase choices, or changing fields' default values or the interactions between fields, is definitely not recommended.

Limiting a tool's functionality takes some confidence in these days of bloated software. The following quote from the FogBugz web site demonstrates this confidence:

> FogBugz does not provide personal performance metrics for management, because in the real world, whenever people are measured based on the number of bugs they create (or fix, or report), every bug results in an argument. If you try to penalize programmers for writing buggy code, the only thing you can be certain of is that sooner or later, the number of *bugs* in the bug tracking database will approach zero, while the number of bugs in the software stays the same. FogBugz is not a crutch for your HR department. (*http://www.fogcreek.com/FogBugz/40FogBugzInDepth.html*)

Of course, you can still write SQL queries to produce any report you wish for, but FogBugz isn't going to make it easy for you to do so.

The different platforms supported for FogBugz servers are Windows, GNU/Linux, FreeBSD, and Mac OS X. Required software for Windows are some data access libraries and the Microsoft Jet, Microsoft SQL Server, or MySQL databases. Unix versions require Apache, MySQL, and PHP. Another alternative is to pay Fog Creek to host a FogBugz instance for you on one of its servers.

Documentation for FogBugz is clear, and the discussion groups are lively and mostly helpful. Support response is apparently excellent. There is one book about FogBugz so far: *Painless Project Management with Fogbugz*, by Mike Gunderloy (Apress).

Features of FogBugz beyond those usually found in simple bug tracking systems include the following:

- Integration with various SCM tools (including CVS, Subversion, Perforce, and Visual SourceSafe) is a core part of the product.

- Full-text searching with Boolean operators and prefix matches is available (though depending on the underlying database, this may only be for the title field).

- URLs are created automatically when the string http:// appears in text. XML content is unchanged in the fields.

- Spellchecking is available.

- There is support for estimating how long fixing a bug will take and how long it has already taken.

FogBugz provides robust and easy-to-use bug tracking, but by design does not have some common features. Whether these matter for your project is up to you to decide:

- The actions you can perform on each *case* (bug) are limited to the following: create a new bug, edit, assign, resolve (with a number of different reasons), close, and reactivate. Creating different states for bugs is not permitted, though renaming the existing ones should be possible.

- Text fields in the bug are for simple text only, since tab characters and long lines are filtered out. Presumably, formatted files should be treated as attachments, though this makes cutting and pasting text from log messages tedious.

- The history of a bug is recorded at the end of the bug, but historical reports are not available.

- Everyone can see and edit all bugs.

- The filters for reports are all single-valued fields, not multivalued, so searching for all bugs from User A or User B requires an SQL query.

NOTE

The version of FogBugz described here is 3.1.9. Version 4.0 was released early in 2005 and added more complex access controls; operations such as closing groups of bugs; spam filters on incoming bug reports; and the same discussion group software that hosts their own support forums.

FogBugz does a few things and does them well. It's simple to learn, doesn't scare customers away from submitting bugs, and is well supported. If this is enough for your project, then its very reasonable pricing may make it just what you want.

JIRA

JIRA (*http://www.atlassian.com/software/jira*) is a Java servlet–based bug tracking tool from Atlassian Software Systems. Interaction is by web browser or email. JIRA is licensed commercially, but the source code is also distributed to commerical users. Prices for commercial use range from $1,200 for the standard edition to $4,800 for the enterprise edition. Academic prices are half the commercial prices; open source and nonprofit use is free. These prices are one-off, per server; they include upgrades and a year's support. Version 3.0.2 was the version tested here.

JIRA provides a wide range of features, lets you change them in a number of ways, and then finally encourages you extend JIRA itself and integrate it with other tools. It is clearly very carefully designed to be easy to use. Administration is all performed through the web interface. Just as Bugzilla finds favor with system administrators who use Perl, JIRA fits well with system administrators who are already working with projects that use Java. For example, the build tool used for JIRA is Ant (see "Ant" in Chapter 5).

Features beyond those usually found in simple bug tracking systems include the following:

- JIRA has a clean and uncluttered UI.

- CVS integration is excellent right out of the box and can be configured from a simple UI.

- Integration with other tools such as SCM tools and mailers has a clear and documented API. The schema for the database is also freely provided, though subject to change with each version.

- URLs and emails are automatically made into links within text. XML text is not parsed. Long lines are not wrapped or truncated in text fields, which can sometimes lead to the layout looking stretched out.

- JIRA provides customizable notification by email and RSS feeds about all changes and about each bug.

- JIRA has a very useful default report called Recent History, showing which bugs you have recently visited.

- Voting for bugs is supported, and there are reports to show the most-requested bugs.

- Localization of JIRA is complete for at least three languages.

- There is support for timing different operations in the server, to provide some basic profiling.

- An integrity checker for the data is provided.

The requirements for JIRA are relatively platform independent. For the standalone version, only Java is required, since a pure-Java database and web server are provided. When the bug tracking system needs to grow larger, JIRA works with numerous versions of the OrionServer, Resin, Tomcat, JBoss, Weblogic, Jetty, and Oracle OC4J application servers.* The different databases that are supported include Oracle, DB2, MySQL, PostgreSQL, and Sybase. The web pages are said to work with Internet Explorer 5 and 6, Mozilla, Firefox, Opera, and Safari, and they work well with Opera 8.0 for me.

The user and administration documentation for JIRA is excellent, as is the documentation for how to modify it. The support is "legendary," and actually does have a rather good record. One of the reasons for this is that the project information for JIRA itself is publicly available at *http://jira.atlassian.com*. JIRA's list of customers is extensive and growing rapidly.

Features that aren't yet in JIRA that you might want are:

- A CLI for each supported platform, though a rudimentary Java API to write one is provided using SOAP or XML-RPC. More complex operations can also be performed using HTTP POST calls.

- The ability to change states for a group of bugs in one bulk operation (JIRA does let you reassign a group of bugs in one operation).

- Reports that include the history of each bug and groups of bugs.

JIRA is a good example of a highly configurable bug tracking system that also works well by default. Entering bugs is simple, but all the abilities for integration and fine-level control are also provided and documented. JIRA is particularly easy to install for a small-scale

---

* Application servers are a convenient way of making Java applications accessible remotely. J2EE™ (Java 2 Platform, Enterprise Edition) is one common standard for such applications.

standalone server. JIRA is a great choice for projects and organizations that want to be able to customize their bug tracking tool more than is permitted by tools such as FogBugz.

TestTrack

TestTrack (*http://www.seapine.com/ttpro.html*) is a commercial bug tracking system from Seapine Software, Inc. Pricing for TestTrack Pro begins at $295.00 for an individual license or $795 for a floating license that everyone in a project can use. Support typically costs 20% of the purchase price per year. The version tested here was TestTrack Pro 7.0. Seapine also sells Surround SCM, an SCM tool that integrates well with TestTrack.

TestTrack is highly customizable, but system administrators don't have to see the underlying details of the database to make the changes. Servers are available for Windows (in English and French), GNU/Linux, Solaris, and Mac OS X. The client is available only for Windows, though a Perl API is provided for remote access. Other platforms connect to the servers by using a browser. The backend database can be the default proprietary one (xBase), Oracle (natively for speed), or any other database with an ODBC connector.

Features beyond those usually found in simple bug tracking systems include the following:

- There is a standalone application for developers and customers to submit bugs using email or the Web, and there is good support for involving customers directly with the bug tracking system.

- TestTrack supports spellchecking of text fields.

- State transitions can be customized, and diagrams of the states are automatically created.

- Administrators can easily change the labels used for each field or users' names.

- Encryption of the data exchanged between client and server is supported, as is cryptographic signing of bugs.

- TestTrack has basic integration with Visual Studio, as does Surround SCM (which can be used to replace Visual SourceSafe). TestTrack also provides integration with other SCM tools including CVS, ClearCase, Perforce, and Visual SourceSafe.

- LDAP or Active Directory can be used for user authentication, and a fairly sophisticated set of administration options for users and their passwords is provided.

- Release notes can be automatically built from bugs that have been marked as part of a particular release.

- Import and export of all data—including bug data, reports, and user details—is in XML, which makes it somewhat easier to exchange data with other tools or future bug tracking systems.

The list of customers who use TestTrack is in the hundreds, with some good-sized companies listed. Seapine's documentation has received awards from a number of technical documentation societies, and TestTrack has also won Jolt awards from *Software Development* magazine. There is a moderated discussion site for TestTrack; it has lots of messages, but also plenty of unanswered questions.

Some of the drawbacks of TestTrack are:

No CLI

> While the data is all fairly easy to extract in XML, there is no out-of-the-box CLI. You can use Perl and SQL to access the database directly, or use the SOAP SDK add-on, but that's extra.

Lots of tabs

> The Windows client is faster and has a cleaner interface than most browser-based clients, but it's still hard to see all the information about a bug on one screen—there are seven horizontal tabs and four vertical ones to choose from! Not surprisingly, the web interface feels slower than the Windows client.

Separate license server

> TestTrack and Surround SCM use a license server, which is another potential central point of failure.

Two other aspects of TestTrack struck me as unusual, though they're not really problems:

Drop-down parentheses

> The Advanced Find screen has drop-down menus for selecting the number of parentheses in each part of complex queries with AND and OR. This looks a little odd at first, but actually works well enough for up to three or four levels of parentheses.

Separate registry editor

> There is a separate Windows application for modifying TestTrack-related values in the Windows registry, which made me wonder why the changes couldn't be made using the existing administration tools.

TestTrack is a flexible and reasonably powerful bug tracking system that is not too hard to administer. It's especially attractive if you can use the Windows client, which feels faster than any of the web-based clients.

Custom Bug Tracking Tools

When you're frustrated with a particular tool, sometimes it's tempting to oversimplify what the tool involves. For example: SCM is really just copying some files to a safe place; build tools really just run a series of commands; and bug tracking tools are really just a frontend to a database. Don't let yourself be deceived by this shallow thinking! One reason why there are so many bug tracking tools available is that lots of other people thought along these lines, and their tools really *are* just frontends to databases. These are not the tools you're looking for.

The requirements for a bug tracking tool that are listed in "Tool Requirements," earlier in this chapter, are much harder to achieve. If you feel you have tried all the different tools you can, and none of them do what you want, then why not modify one of the more substantial open source ones?

Bug Tracking Annoyances

There are a number of problems with using bug tracking systems that seem to occur regardless of which system is used. Some of these annoyances are discussed in this section.

Multiplying Products

Most of a bug's information has simple values: a string of text to describe the problem, the name (chosen from a list) of one person assigned to the bug, and so on. If a field holds only one value at a time, things are simple. Everything becomes more complicated when one field can have multiple values at the same time.

A good example of this is the field in a bug that is typically named something like Product, which is used to indicate which of a project's products are affected by the bug. A sensible default value for this field might be All, since that may well be true. However, when the bug affects just a few of the products, the obvious thing to do is to have the field contain multiple values. This could be a string with comma-delimited values, or it could be the input from an HTML form. Regardless of how the information is actually stored, the problem is that the number of choices that can be made in reports and other queries has just increased dramatically.

For instance, if there is a version of the product for Windows, GNU/Linux, and Macintosh, and bugs may affect one, two, or all three of these versions, then your reports show some subset of these choices. When another version for the next version of Windows is added, all the reports become out-of-date, because they don't include the new version.

Fields with multiple values always complicate the experience of using the tool, and the more fields that there are with multiple values, the more complex it all becomes. If possible, avoid fields with multiple values since they tend to make writing useful reports much harder.

In case the above seems overstated, imagine a bug tracking tool with just three fields in its bugs: Owner, Description, and Product. Owner is a single-value field (because only one person owns the bug at a time), Description is a text string, and Product is the multivalued field representing the different (but related) products that are affected by a bug. Each bug is actually a point in three dimensions: the Owner is along one axis, the Description along another, and the Product on the third. If the Owner and Description stay the same, and the Product value is All, then the bug has a definite point in space. The number of values the Owner coordinate can take is just the number of users, which only increases by one for each new user. The number of points that the Description can take is huge, being the number of ways to write a few paragraphs, so we ignore it except for keywords when trying to run reports. However, the number of different values that the Product coordinate can take with n products is 2^n (imagine a bitmap with a 1 for each affected product). Adding another product increases the number of choices by 2^n.

So if multivalued fields can complicate your bug tracking tool, what can make it simpler? Good pattern-matching capabilities and text fields are a start. Suppose you want to select all bugs found in a series of releases such as 3.1.1, 3.1.2, and 3.1.3. Using a pattern such as 3.1.* makes this easy. Having to select each value in turn is the hard way, and when 3.1.4 is released, the report becomes incorrect. A good bug tracking tool lets you use patterns and Boolean operators to create complex reports flexibly.

Cleaning Up

There are two parts to keeping a bug tracking system clean. The first part is the process as designed of adding new bugs, assigning them, fixing them, testing the changes, and marking the bugs as Closed. There may be some tendency to delay closing bugs while they are being tested more rigorously, but eventually most bugs that are marked as Fixed are marked as Closed, and that can be considered their final state. Some bugs will be marked as Deferred, meaning either that the effort to fix them is too great for the time and people available, or that no one understood the bug and more information needs to be gathered. (Or maybe the bug is actually a protest about some part of the product and closing it would be tantamount to telling someone their opinion is being ignored—see "Twisted Communications" in Chapter 12.)

The second kind of cleanup of a bug tracking system has to do with the available choices for each field. This is sometimes known as the bug tracking system's *metadata*. If there is a field for the build in which the bug was found, then every time a new build is created, the new build has to be added to the choices for that field. Doing this automatically as part of the build process is a good idea. The alternative is to require people to enter the build information by hand, which may well lead to more data-entry errors.

Using a small set of valid choices for a field on a screen makes life easier for people. However, as more builds occur, a small set of choices becomes a large set of choices, which is now not at all convenient for the user. More than a few dozen choices seems tedious to most people searching for an entry in a list. One solution is to keep only the last dozen values visible but still allow people to enter text (which can be validated separately). Maintaining the current list of values is something that needs to be done automatically, either as part of the build process or by a separate task that is run regularly. Reducing the number of choices also needs to be an automatic process, though some care is needed to retain the choices for any builds that have been released to customers.

When a developer leaves the project, what happens to the bugs she owned? If the developer is marked as somehow inactive, can you still search for her bugs and reassign them? How does the developer's name show up in historical reports? These questions are all part of cleaning up the data in a bug tracking system.

One last warning is about the effect that attaching large files to bugs can have. Many bug tracking tools allow people to attach files to a bug, which is useful for storing long text logs or screenshots. If no limit is even hinted at by the tool, then people start to treat this capability as some kind of magic filing system. Whole core dumps, CD or DVD images, and other enormous files are attached without a thought about the tool's underlying database or filesystem. The consequence is that the tool's performance becomes unacceptably slow. Regular automated checks of the sizes of attachments are a good idea. Some databases and filesystems may handle large datafiles better than others, but none of them are invulnerable to this particular problem.

One Bug, Multiple Releases

One of the more complicated pieces of information associated with a bug is the group of different releases that the bug exists in. For example, a bug might be discovered in Version 2.1 of the product, but Version 2.2 has already shipped and Version 3.0 is about to be released. Does the bug exist in all three versions? How should this be recorded in the bug tracking system? Notice that we're referring to releases here, not branches in an SCM tool, since a bug tracking system should not have to be aware of how a release was created.

The simplest way to handle this is to leave the information about the affected releases out of the bug tracking system. For each release, keep a spreadsheet of bugs that might be in the release and coordinate with the development team to confirm when the bug is fixed. This approach is tedious and is prone to error, but is not uncommon on smaller projects.

Another simple way to handle this problem is to make two extra copies of the original Version 2.1 bug and then change the value for the Release Found field in each of the two copies to 2.2 and 3.0, respectively. Each of the copies will have its own unique bug identifier. This approach has the advantage that the bug count for each release is more likely to be correct, and some bug tracking tools support duplicating bugs very well. One disadvantage is that information has to be added to the original and to each of the copies about their connections with each other; otherwise, information will invariably be added to just one copy and not the others. The main disadvantage is that developers, product managers, and customers find it hard to keep track of which bug was fixed in which release. If a customer has been told that the bug he reported is number 12345, then he expects to see that bug number in the release notes when his bug is fixed.

A different approach that is sometimes taken is to add multiple instances of the fields that are affected, and then use one instance per release. For instance, a bug might have fields named Release Fixed 1, Release Fixed 2, and Release Fixed 3, and then each field would be set to 2.1, 2.2, and 3.0 in our example bug. Other fields such as the status and who the bug is assigned to can also be treated in this way. This approach is equivalent to duplicating just the affected fields of a bug and can record the information correctly. The big drawback is that all the reports now have to use much more complicated queries—"Show me all my Open bugs" becomes "Show me all bugs that are Open in one or more of these fields." From experience, I recommend avoiding this approach.

Some bug tracking tools claim to support adding multiple releases to a bug, but then their support for reports using the multiple release values is often not as robust as might be expected. Generally, keeping track of bugs in multiple releases of a product is hard to do automatically and is not well supported by existing bug tracking tools.

Severity Inflation

Many bugs have fields to indicate how serious the bug is. One common series of values goes like this: Severity 1 means "The bug stops the product, and no workaround is possible"; Severity 2 means "The bug stops the product, but a workaround is possible." Severity 3 and 4 bugs are defined as meaning "The bug breaks a minor part of the product" and "The bug is cosmetic or an irritation," respectively. There may be one Severity field for the customer and a similar field for the engineering organization of a project.

In most companies and projects, limited resources mean that as the ship date for a release approaches, only bugs with Severity 1 and 2 get fixed; the others are closed or deferred. Over time this practice leads to *severity inflation*. Someone entering a bug knows that this bug won't stop the product, but she remembers that none of her Severity 3 bugs got fixed last time and she really wants this one fixed, so she makes it a Severity 2. In the extreme, by a process of induction, all bugs become Severity 1 bugs and the purpose of the field is lost.

One approach to avoiding such severity inflation is to have a small group of people who understand both the source of the product and the marketing and sales requirements assign the severity value for each bug. Of course, this kind of group has so many different outlooks that it is hard to make it work well. Along with having someone other than the originator of the bug decide on its severity, another approach is to use votes. Each developer or customer has some limited number of votes that can be cast for different bugs. This at least gives a sense of which bugs people care enough to vote for (not that software development is usually run as a democracy). It also goes some way to discouraging duplicate bugs that were entered just to add weight to an issue.

A Severity field for customers is even more prone to distortion than one for internal use. A Severity 1 bug may mean "I need an answer right now," "This bug is critical to our continued use of your product," or "I guess I have to keep making this bug more severe to get your attention!" That's altogether too much information squashed into one field. Having Urgency, Criticality, and Irritation fields might work ("Please indicate on a scale of 1 to 10 just how angry you are right now!"), but these may in effect just be knobs that do nothing but give you something to fiddle with (like the button to close the doors in an elevator).

One last thought: when you change the value of the customer's Severity field, it is always a problem. If you increase the severity, the customer worries whether the problem is part of a bigger issue. If you decrease the severity, you seem to be minimizing his distress. If you provide this kind of field for customers, let them change the values themselves.

Identifying the Right Area

Imagine entering a new bug on your first day at a new job. You have some idea of what the product you are using is called. Then there's a field in the bug named something like Area, Feature, Module, or Section and it has a dozen or more choices to indicate which part of the product the problem is in. If you're lucky, the choice is obvious, but these choices often seem vaguely named. Then it turns out that making a choice is a requirement for entering the bug. So you choose the catchall choice General, hoping that someone else will make a better choice than you for this bug later on. "There has to be a better way," you think.

There are some better ways. One way is simply to not require that the choice be made when submitting a bug. It's often wrong anyway, just a guess from some piece of text printed out in a logfile at around the same time that the bug occurred. Let the assigned engineer work out which part of the product it belongs to.

Another way is to eliminate the dreaded General and Miscellaneous choices, since they usually mean no choice at all. The most helpful thing is to have an easily accessible glossary of all the choices and their intended meanings available from where the bug is entered. An HTML link to such a page, or floating help text, or even just the local location of a glossary file are all better than guessing. Simple, concrete names and a small number of choices will also help everyone concerned.

Customizing the Bug Tracking System

The customizations discussed in this section are changes in the way a bug tracking system is configured. All these changes usually require some administrative privileges, and descriptions of any changes that were made should appear in audit logs.

One common customization is changing the states that a bug can be in, in order to make them better fit the project's existing workflow. The administrator should be able to add and remove states, and the tool should ask you how to deal with bugs in removed states. The transitions from state to state should also be customizable.

The administrator of the system should be able to change the name that users of the system see for each field. Here's a true story: in one company I worked at, we changed the name of the state where more information on a bug was required from Rejected to Returned, because people don't like feeling rejected. This was easy to do only because the text displayed was not the name of the field in the underlying database. An underlying database may have length and character restrictions on field names, and the name of a field (or the names of choices for values in a field) may change over time.

Adding a new choice for an existing field is a regular activity and should be possible from the command line, so that automated environments can do this as part of nightly builds. Adding a new field happens less frequently, but does occur as a project changes. What existing bugs show as values in the new field depends on the system. Some systems allow default values or have other ways to update the field's value in a bulk operation.

Removing values from a field or removing fields is harder. One approach for values is to make the values read-only and not selectable in a pop-up list. Deleted fields are usually not shown at all, even in historical reports. A more accurate bug tracking system would show how fields were added and removed when displaying the history of a bug. Merging

DEFINING YOUR STATES

A project's workflow is often hard to define clearly, usually because everyone seems to have different opinions about what should be a state, what should be entered in some other field or fields, and what is simply irrelevant. Some ideas to help when you're defining all the states that a bug can be in are:

- Think first about the reports that are most important for the project. Create examples of these reports. Then design the workflow and states so that the reports are easy to generate.

- Minimize the number of possible states. Open and Closed are two good ones to begin with. Many projects work well with only a few more states.

- Walk through not only the expected workflow, but also cases where bugs are moved to states by mistake. Make sure that users can recover from such mistakes without an administrator's help.

- Display a one-page diagram of the workflow's states and transitions somewhere that is easy to find when using the bug tracking system. Make sure that the diagram is updated when changes occur.

and splitting fields generally requires access to the underlying database and has all the same problems as a combination of adding or removing fields. In some systems, unpredicted things happen if you add a field, delete it, and then want to add it back with the same name. So don't do that.

Overloading Fields

One way in which bug tracking systems commonly grow is through the addition of new kinds of information. Say you want to record the name of the customer who reported a bug, but there is currently no specific field in the bug for this. The information often gets recorded anyway, often in an existing text field. If the bug tracking tool supports searching text for keywords, this is often good enough.

When this information becomes more important than having a vague sense that knowing which customer reported a bug might be useful, there is a temptation to keep adding the information just as before, maybe with some little separator characters to show that this information is different from the rest of the field. This is bad for your bug data in the long run. All sorts of data gets merged into a small number of fields. A common example is when severity inflation (see "Severity Inflation," earlier in this chapter) has occurred and someone needs to quickly identify the bugs to be fixed for the next release. He goes in, edits a convenient field such as the bug's description, and adds text such as "MUST!:" or "__VITAL__:" to the description. Very ugly.

Getting rid of this kind of quick workaround later on is often harder than it might seem. Many bug tracking tools support search but not search-and-replace in their text fields.

New bugs get added with misspellings of the text, and soon it's not clear to anyone when they should or should not add the cryptic message. The answer to this problem is simple: if your bug's fields don't do what you need them to do, modify the tool so that the fields do the right thing. Add a new field for new types of information, though if it's unlikely to be used by many others, you might want to put it far down on a screen where it won't distract from existing fields. If you are tempted to overload fields, first consider the time that someone will have to spend to remove that ugly workaround when the proper field is created later on.

Bug History

One of the marks of an adequate bug tracking system is the variety of reports that can be easily constructed with it. A good bug tracking system will let you generate such reports with the added dimension of time. Asking, "How many bugs are there?" is sometimes not as useful as asking, "Is the number of bugs increasing or decreasing?" or "How long do most bugs take from being reported to getting fixed?"

Some bug tracking systems do not support such historical reports; they can only recommend that you run your reports regularly, collect the information somewhere else (such as in a spreadsheet), and then create your own historical reports. This approach is particularly vulnerable to errors. Correcting something in the way the report is created can invalidate all the prior results. It's much better to be able to generate historical reports from within the bug tracking system itself.

Another important feature is the ability to see the history of a particular bug in full detail—what changed, when did it change, and who changed it? Different systems show the addition and removal of fields in different ways.

Bug Statistics

The state of software engineering being what it is, any means to measure progress toward a goal is eagerly seized upon. Bug tracking systems can provide a comforting sense of tangible data about a project. This is true only in a very general sense. There are generally no precise guidelines in a project about when a bug should or should not be created, and there are good reasons why developers aren't paid by the number of bugs they fix! Still, the science of statistics is designed to handle this kind of uncertainty, and statistical analysis can be applied to bug tracking systems.

Some examples of questions with statistical answers that people like to ask about bugs are:

- How long is a bug usually active?
- How long does it take to get bug fixes retested?
- How many bug fixes introduced new bugs?
- How many bugs were found in each area of the product?

These are all interesting statistics, and sometimes they may be useful for warning a project when something is going wrong with its development process. However, there are also a few good reasons to be wary of relying too much on statistics from bug tracking systems:

- "Bug sweeps" (meetings where many bugs are reassigned or deferred) can cause large discontinuities in statistical trends. There will be no more nice bell-shaped curves after one of these meetings.

- Bugs are subjective, so one tester might submit many more bugs than another tester. This may not mean that their respective areas really have any difference in the quality of source code.

- As noted in "Severity Inflation," earlier in this chapter, severity and priority values tend to become more urgent over time, even if the product's quality remains the same.

A still more theoretical approach is to create statistical models of the number of bugs in GNU/Linux and Mozilla, as a couple of Oxford physicists named Challet and Du did in their paper "Closed Source Versus Open Source in a Microscopic Model of Software Dynamics" (*http://tiago.com/doc/bug_dynamics.pdf*). Note that the appearance of this reference in a book that has the word *practical* in its title is meant only as a diversion from the business of doing useful things with your own bug tracking system.

Writing an Effective Bug Report

The three key points to bear in mind when creating a bug report should be:

- How to reproduce the bug, as precisely as possible, and how often this will make the bug appear

- What should have happened, at least in your opinion

- What actually happened, or at least as much information as you have recorded

Many applications can generate a textual description of how they have been installed and configured. If such a description is available, you should always add it to the bug. The application may also contain some tests to check that it is still configured correctly. If so, you should run the tests and attach their results too.

As well as providing correct and useful information in the bug, it's important to check that you behave as expected for the project. This is especially true for open source projects. Maybe you should ask questions first on a users' mailing list before escalating the issue to a developers' mailing list? Or you may mark a bug as maximum priority, because it's stopping your work, only to see it downgraded because no one else is blocked by that bug. Etiquette is important, and imperious commands to "fix this bug immediately" rarely help anything.

One common cause of frustration with bug tracking systems is related to how their information is added. Bugs are too often added with vague descriptions, missing information, premature conclusions, or a best guess at the real build label (see "Labeling Builds" in Chapter 3). A classic situation is when a complex program has a bug deep inside it, but the only error message that is visible is one from some unrelated area. That area often gets bugs from the deeper level assigned to it, much to the frustration of the developer responsible for it. Adding some good local documentation to wherever people add new bugs can go a long way to improving the quality of all the bugs.

Some useful documents with general advice about creating bugs include the Mozilla Project's "Bug Writing Guidelines" (*http://www.mozilla.org/quality/bug-writing-guidelines.html*) and Simon Tatham's "How to Report Bugs Effectively" (*http://www.chiark.greenend.org.uk/~sgtatham/bugs.html*).

There are also many examples of more site-specific documents about writing bug reports; these contain productspecific information such as descriptions of what each part of the product does. Two of these are Opera's "Guidelines for Filing Good Bug Reports" (*http://www.opera.com/support/bugs/guidelines*) and FreeBSD's "Writing FreeBSD Problem Reports" (*http://www.freebsd.org/doc/en_US.ISO8859-1/articles/problem-reports/article.html*). Slightly off-topic, but also useful, is Eric S. Raymond and Rick Moen's classic article "How to Ask Questions the Smart Way" (*http://www.catb.org/~esr/faqs/smart-questions.html*). This document has some excellent reminders and strong opinions about how to interact well with groups of technical volunteers.

> **NOTE**
> If you cut and paste text directly from some applications, you may find that non-ASCII characters appear in the bug's text. This can often be seen with text from Microsoft Word documents that use smart quotes. The end result looks ugly and is sometimes confusing, so it's worth checking what a new bug's text fields look like after you have submitted it.

Integrating with SCM Tools

A common question when working with a particular bug is which files were affected by fixing the bug. The answer can tell you which branches the fix was applied to, suggest areas for regression testing, and even guide developers who are fixing similar bugs in the future. Without any integration with the SCM tool, the usual way to find out this information is by looking at which files changed around the time when the bug was fixed. This method is obviously prone to error and is also rather tedious in practice.

There are usually other changes to source code that are not related to bugs; for example, a spelling mistake in a comment doesn't usually need to be reported as a bug before it can be fixed. One common way to integrate the SCM tool and the bug tracking tool is to mark a particular set of changes that are being committed as related to a particular bug. This may done by using some special string of text in a commit message such as `For bug 12345`, carefully designed to be detected by the SCM tool, which then uses the bug tracking tool's API to add more information to the indicated bug or bugs. The information that's added to the bug depends on the SCM tool, but the names and versions of the affected files, along with the differences between the files or the changeset identifier, are commonly used. The special text in the commit message can also be used to cause the SCM tool to change the state of a bug.

This approach works reasonably well most of the time. It fails when developers forget to add the special text to the commit message or mistype some keyword in the special text. The ability to go back and mark a set of changes as associated with a bug after they have been committed is a good idea. Another problem is if the bug tracking system is unavailable when the changes are being committed. In this case, the changes can either be discarded, which means that the information in the bug tracking system is imperfect, or saved for applying later.

An alternate approach is for the bug tracking system to regularly extract the commit messages and their associated data from the SCM tool, and to use this information to regenerate the SCM-related information in each affected bug. This is the approach taken by JIRA, and while it is somewhat less scalable than adding the information at commit time, it does have the advantages of being more robust and making it easier to correct mistakes.

Many bug tracking systems provide some support for integration with numerous SCM tools (for example, CVS, Perforce, and ClearCase). For detailed information about how CVS and Bugzilla can be integrated, see *http://www.einval.com/~steve/software/cvs-bugzilla* and *http://kered.org/article-2004.04.09-cvs_bugzilla_integration.html*.

Checklist

This section contains a short list of questions that you should feel comfortable answering about your current bug tracking system:

- How long does it take to enter a new bug? (More than a minute for a simple bug can seem like an awfully long time when you have do it over and over again.)
- Can you find the definitions of the reports that you regularly run?
- Can you make copies of these reports, edit the copies, or back up the definitions of the reports to somewhere outside the bug tracking system?
- How are bugs expected to progress through different states? Is there a diagram of this anywhere that users of the bug tracking system can easily find?
- How do you make sure that the correct people are aware of all changes to a bug?
- If you wanted to reassign 20 bugs to someone, would you have to do this one bug at a time, or is there an easier way?
- Can you change a comment field in a bug after the fact?
- How do you create historical reports using your bug tracking system?
- How do you add or remove values such as release names from a field?
- How do you modify the definition of a bug?

- When is the data in the bug tracking system backed up? When was the backup last tested by recovering it into a standby system?

- How big an attachment is deemed reasonable to add to a bug? 100KB? 1MB? 10MB?

- How regularly is your bug tracking system cleaned up?

- How will you move your current data to your next bug tracking system?

- Most importantly, does your current bug tracking system really help or hinder your project overall?

## CHAPTER EIGHT

Documentation Environments

THIS CHAPTER DISCUSSES WHAT DOCUMENTATION PROVIDES FOR A PRODUCT and who the customer is for the different kinds of documentation. This chapter also shows that development environments for documentation teams are similar to the development environments used by developers writing source code.

Some of the most commonly used file formats and the related tools for creating documentation are examined, and there is a discussion of how the different parts of creating the final versions of documentation can be automated. This chapter doesn't discuss writing style, different hyphenation schemes, or the flow of information in diagrams. I think that these topics are interesting, but they're outside the scope of this book.

Technical Documentation

The aim of technical documentation is to make a product easier for customers to use and, by doing so, to reduce the effort (and cost) of supporting a product.

Documentation, at least for this book, is an umbrella-like term that covers:

- All paper-based products with words and images
- Online documents in formats suitable for viewing and printing

- Videos and other recordings

- Interactive training applications

- Online community newsgroups, mailing lists, and weblogs

While interactive "wizards" in applications such as spreadsheets do make the product easier to use, such wizards are usually considered part of the product, not part of the product's documentation. Documentation can be for use by new or existing customers, for training sessions, consultants, executive briefings, press briefings, and exhibition and conference work. It can even take the form of books such as this one, which you may be reading in hardcopy, from a browser, or perhaps from some PDA-like device of the future.

Is Documentation a Separate Product?

Some products are unusable without their documentation, in which case the documentation is obviously a core piece of the product. (Some products are pretty unusable even with great documentation, but that's a discussion for another time.) Most projects find that the overall documentation of a product makes a large difference to the success of the product. In fact, if none of the documentation for a product is important enough to affect the product's release date, is it even worth the effort to ship the documentation with the product?

However, once an organization and its documentation group grows, the documentation is often treated like a separate product, complete with its own product numbers and identifiers. This may just be the same phenomenon as when different parts of the software become separated as the project grows. For closed software, the existence of separate price lists apart from the main product price list is one indicator of separated groups within a company.

To answer the question in the title of this section: most products need their documentation, and therefore the documentation is part of the product. To put it another way, documentation isn't a separate product, even if the group that produces it is separate from the group that writes the source code for the rest of the product. The opposite of this idea resurfaces later in this chapter as one of the Bad Ideas (see "Releasing the Documentation Separately").

Writing Documentation Is Like Writing Code

For whatever reasons, few technical writers are able (or choose) to write good source code. Likewise, few developers are able (or choose) to create good documentation. This situation has been known to lead to an unfortunate lack of interest within each group in the other's work. This is unfortunate because both groups are necessary for a product to succeed. The lack of interest is particularly ironic because the processes of writing code and writing documentation are more alike than not. Since both activities are similar, what is helpful in a developer's environment is also similar to what helps writers.

Table 8-1 shows how writing code and writing documentation relate to each other.

TABLE 8-1. Writing code versus documentation

Writing code	Writing documentation
Source code is written in an editor or IDE.	Text is written with an editor or word processor.
Compilers generate warnings and errors about incorrect source code.	Spelling and grammar checkers generate warnings and errors about incorrect text.
Machine-readable executables are generated from source code.	Human-readable formats are generated from other file formats.
Source code is ported to different platforms.	Different human-readable formats and languages are generated from the same raw text.
If you don't have a compiler for a platform, you can't port to that platform.	You may not be able to convert your document to a particular format.

Direct similarities between documentation and writing code include the following:

- Both have files that go through multiple versions, so both benefit from using an SCM tool.

- Both benefit from making changes in the source files, not in generated files.

- For both activities, the more steps there are between the source files and the final product, the harder it is to understand where an error was introduced.

- Debugging documents can be like debugging a product. Examples of questions asked during debugging are "Which source file lines make the product behave in this way?" and "What change in the documentation files made all these paragraphs narrower in the generated document?"

- Both benefit from usability testing—for example, whether a UI is easy to use and whether information can be readily retrieved from a document.

- Both products have errors, and their errors can usually be tracked using the same bug tracking tool. Documentation can be treated as just one more part of the product.

- Both need to track many different kinds of errors in their product. So both need tools to help analyze their text or source code in ways that change over time. This is work beyond the common spelling checks or compiler warnings; it can involve static analyzers (see "Static Code Analyzers" in Chapter 6) or tools that check cross-references.

- Both need to be packaged carefully for release as a product, and both benefit from automating the process of generating a release.

- Both groups often have a tendency to want to deviate from style guides, and they also avoid tools that weren't invented locally.

Documents and SCM

Anyone who has ever written even a small technical specification or article knows how useful it is to be able to look at earlier versions of the document. All the same reasons that developers keep track of source code changes with SCM tools apply to documentation: backing out unwanted changes and mistakes, coordinating your work with that done by other people, and recording the documentation as it was at the time of a release.

There are some SCM-related problems that occur more commonly when using an SCM tool to store documentation. First, the file format of many documents may be binary rather than text-based, and this makes merging from branches and integrating other people's changes more complex. Second, binary files are often much larger than text files, so the space demands on the SCM tool are larger.

Other issues are more psychological. For instance, documentation of a product's API is often generated from comments embedded in the source code. Javadoc (see "Internal Project Documentation," later in this chapter) is one example of a tool that uses this idea. The problem is that when the API documentation is reviewed, making the recommended changes to the documentation may involve editing large numbers of files, and these files are no doubt tightly controlled as the release date approaches. One way to avoid making accidental functional changes to the source code during these edits is to use a tool such as *diff* to confirm before the commit that all the changes are related to documentation. There are similar difference-checking tools for most documentation formats, either standalone or as part of the main editing tool.

Even if the file format for the documentation is binary and your SCM tool doesn't support showing the differences between two versions of a binary file, it's still worth using an SCM tool to track your documentation. First, the documentation files will be backed up with the rest of the source code for the product. Second, the SCM tool will let you recover the documentation as it was at any time in the past. This is another reason to avoid directories with names such as *version_1.0*, *version_1.1*, and *version_2.0*. Embedding the version name in an SCM-controlled filename or directory name is counter to the whole idea of using SCM.

For longer-lasting archives of your documentation, the files for each release to customers should be copied to CDs or DVDs, which should last for up to 10 years. If you want your documentation to last much longer than that, use a format-independent storage medium: print it out. With luck, those copies will make it to the next millennium, and the process of scanning printed text back into files will have advanced still further. "Maintaining an Environment" in Chapter 10 discusses how to archive your documentation environment in more detail.

File Formats for Documentation

This section describes some of the commonly used formats for documentation files and discusses the strengths and weaknesses of each file format. Some formats (such as XML) are more common as *source* formats—that is, the files where the raw content is added. Other formats (such as PostScript and PDF) are more often used as *release* formats—that is, the files that are available for customers to use. Only a few formats (such as raw text files) are used as both source and release file formats.

Some common requirements of a file format and the tools that support it are:

- Typeset printing, often using different file formats, sizes, and layouts

- Online viewing, often with hyperlinks

- Images interleaved with text

- Searching documents for text or formatting

- Support for non-English languages and characters

- Comments that can be mixed with text for reviews but that don't appear in the final product

- Joining and splitting files

- Generating lists of the differences between versions of the document, or *diffability**

Text-based source file formats such as XML are considerably easier to modify from the command line with simple tools that already exist. Modifying files in binary formats always requires more effort; usually you have to convert them to a text-based format, make the changes, and then convert the files back to the binary format.

Another aspect to consider carefully when choosing a file format is that of closed and open formats. If your documents are stored in a proprietary, closed format, then your ability to convert the documents to a different format is limited to the tools available from official vendors, or tools that use a reverse-engineered understanding of the file format. Microsoft Word is the most common closed file format; the other formats covered in this chapter are open formats. A strongly biased discussion of open and closed file formats can be found at *http://www.openformats.org*. A partial list of open file formats can be found at *http://directory.google.com/Top/Computers/Data_Formats/Open_Standards*.

File Formats for Customers

The file format for most released documentation is either HTML or PDF, with Word sometimes being used as well. PostScript is sometimes still used for academic papers. Raw text is

---

* The term *diffability* is used here to suggest how easy it is to run a command such as `diff` on files in a particular format. In another context, *diffability* also refers to people with different abilities, rather than disabilities.

used for small documents, and its advantages and disadvantages are discussed in "Raw Text," later in this chapter. This section briefly describes the HTML, PostScript, and PDF file formats.

HTML

Various file formats exist that are derived from the ISO-standardized SGML, notably any format whose name ends in "ML" (which stands for "markup language"). HTML is the best-known one. It consists of text with added structure in the form of elements such as `<h1>` for a header, `<p>` for a paragraph, and `<a href="index.html">` for a hypertext link.

HTML files are, of course, what web browsers can display for online viewing. Some browsers support vendor-specific extensions to basic HTML, but thankfully this seems to be increasingly rare. More common problems nowadays are partial implementations of the HTML specification (*http://www.w3.org/TR/html*) or issues with other technologies such as JavaScript or Flash.

Drawbacks of HTML, or sometimes of the way it is used, include the following:

- HTML is not designed for printing, so you may see text or images move around or trail off the edge of the paper.

- Different web browsers treat the same HTML files differently, so manual testing using multiple browsers is still a necessary part of releasing HTML documentation. Common problems are graphics with some nearby text overlapping them, too much whitespace before and after paragraphs or whole pages, or even pages that just won't display at all in some browsers.

- Books and manuals can be hard to read sequentially if you have to keep scrolling and then clicking links to go to the next paragraph. GNU manuals seem to be particularly prone to this, with a web page for each Info node.

- Support for mathematical equations in HTML is still limited; MathML (*http://www.w3.org/ Math*) is one effort to make this easier. The common solution of generating small images for each equation seems clumsy to me.

- HTML comments can't be nested, which makes commenting out sections of HTML awkward. Also, they can't have a double dash in them, which makes adding ASCII art to them hard. To be fair, HTML was designed to be simple to parse, at the expense of such infrequent uses of comments.

PostScript

PostScript is a language from Adobe for controlling printed output, the first to do so in a general way that worked well with printers from different manufacturers. Most printers still accept PostScript files directly, which was what made PostScript the default language for printed documents until PDF became more common toward the end of the 1990s.

The specification for the PostScript language is available at *http://partners.adobe.com/public/developer/en/ps/PLRM.pdf*, and a tutorial and cookbook are available at *http://www-cdf.fnal.gov/offline/PostScript/BLUEBOOK.PDF*.

PDF

PDF is a subset of PostScript, designed to avoid some of the problems of PostScript. Images and fonts can be embedded directly into PDF files, and some of the necessary processing of the PostScript has been already done for PDF files. PDF also has better support for links, searching, and accessibility. The Acrobat reader from Adobe is distributed at no cost for a large number of platforms, something that greatly encouraged the use of PDF after a slow start in the early 1990s. PDF is currently the most common format for distributing documents over the Internet that are intended for printing.

The specifications for PDF are available online at *http://partners.adobe.com/public/developer/pdf/index_reference.html*. There are tools from Adobe and other companies that can edit PDF directly, and there are also a few open source libraries for working with PDF files. More often, PDF is generated by an application, just as PostScript was generated. OpenOffice is one such application. One great place to start when looking for ideas for PDF tools is *PDF Hacks*, by Sid Steward (O'Reilly).

Documentation Environments

This section describes four of the most common file formats and associated documentation environments that are encountered in small to medium-sized software companies and in open source projects.

Raw Text

Text files are the most easily created and portable open document format, but they have many disadvantages. You can't change their formatting easily, since they usually have no formal structure beyond a title and some section headings. They have no hyperlinks, they don't include images (though ASCII art does have its own beauty), and non-ASCII characters are handled in different ways by different tools. Another disadvantage is that the end of a line is marked differently on Unix and Windows machines, though this is often well hidden from users. To improve the printed appearance of text documents, care has to be taken to keep line lengths below about 80 characters.

Many IBM platforms use EBCDIC instead of ASCII for representing raw text, but fortunately conversion of text files to and from ASCII is not difficult. Some text files handle non-English characters by using the Unicode encoding standard (*http://www.unicode.org*).

If you are writing the basic documentation for open source projects, then raw text is probably still the most common format, at least for small files such as *README* files, change logs, and release notes. There is even an artist mode for Emacs that lets you create ASCII art freehand within your text. However, raw text files are unlikely to provide what you want for the documentation of larger projects.

FrameMaker

FrameMaker (*http://www.adobe.com/products/framemaker*) is a well-established commercial document editor from Adobe that starts at $449 per user. FrameMaker has a choice of two native file formats: the default, binary format (*.fm* files) and a text-based format called MIF that allows you to modify the file via command-line scripts and also saves space with SCM tools. The MIF file format is openly available at *http://partners.adobe.com/public/developer/en/ framemaker/MIF_Reference.pdf*. Recent versions of FrameMaker (7.0 and later) also have built-in support for working with XML as a source file format.

FrameMaker is currently available only on Windows and Solaris. GNU/Linux is not supported, and Adobe discontinued FrameMaker for Macintosh in 2004. The Solaris version comes with a tool named *fmbatch* that allows you to manipulate *.fm* files from the command line, including converting to and from MIF, and printing documents to PostScript. There is a similar tool for Windows named DZbatcher available for download from *http:// www.datazone.com/english/overview/download.html*.

Conversion to PDF is commonly achieved by printing the FrameMaker book as PostScript and then using Adobe Distiller to produce PDF, which takes about one minute per hundred pages on an ordinary desktop machine. HTML can be produced dynamically by exporting the *.fm* file as XML and then using XSL transformations to produce the HTML for web server pages. Alternatively, tools such as "WebWorks Publisher Professional for FrameMaker" from Quadralay (*http://www.quadralay.com*) are commonly used to generate HTML, though some customization for your own templates will likely be necessary. The conversion process is illustrated in Figure 8-1.

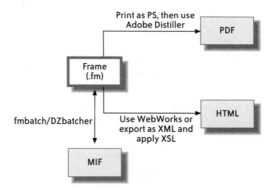

FIGURE 8-1. Conversion of a FrameMaker document from .fm to PDF and HTML

Apart from the official support web site and knowledge base, there is also a vocal FrameMaker community based around *http://www.freeframers.org*. Thanks to the FrameMaker Developer Kit, there are any number of plug-ins available for FrameMaker.

Though Adobe doesn't seem to be encouraging use of FrameMaker as strongly as in the past, knowledge of FrameMaker is still considered to be a primary requirement for many technical publication positions, and it's still the most common documentation tool for computer-related companies, including Microsoft for its own technical documentation.

XML: DocBook and OpenOffice

The advantages of editing text-based documentation are many, but text needs some structure to make it more useful. The most popular way to add structure has been to use one of the "markup" file formats such as HTML or XML. HTML is adequate for displaying pages in web browsers but doesn't contain enough markup for creating other kinds of documentation. Browsers are also very tolerant of incorrect HTML, so they shouldn't be the only thing used to test that your HTML is correct.

XML is more flexible, and a number of different ways to represent documents in XML now exist. These different ways are defined by the DTDs or schemas that describe which elements go where in an XML document. The big promise of XML is that because it has a well-defined structure, you should be able to transform XML files to other formats by using XSL scripts and other such tools. In practice, this really is true, but is rarely quite as easy as it first sounds. Using an XML-based documentation environment in 2005 requires a technical publications group whose members are willing to dig a little to resolve the inevitable teething problems of being early adopters.

DocBook

DocBook (*http://www.oasis-open.org/docbook*) is another markup language definition that uses XML (or less commonly, SGML, the big brother of XML). The XML DTD for DocBook is defined by OASIS, a nonprofit standards body, and was created in the early 1990s. Though it was originally created as a standard for computer documentation, DocBook can be used for any kind of documentation. DocBook's strengths are that it is an open file format, is text-based so multiple people can work on each file at once, and can be automatically converted to many different release formats. It is not usually used in WYSIWYG editors (though they do exist) and it takes more effort to set up than other documentation environments. DocBook is the primary source-file format for several large open source projects including FreeBSD, Apache, Samba, GNOME and KDE, and the Linux Documentation Project.

The official documentation for DocBook is *DocBook: The Definitive Guide*, by Norman Walsh (O'Reilly), which is also available online at *http://docbook.org/tdg*. Another useful book about DocBook and using XSL to transform it to other formats is *DocBook XSL: The Complete Guide*, by Bob Stayton (Sagehill), freely available online as HTML at *http://www.sagehill.net/docbookxsl*.

Generating simple HTML files directly from DocBook XML files works well enough for many web sites, but for finer control over the released files' appearance, many DocBook-based environments use XSL-FO (XSL Formatting Objects) as an intermediate file format. XSL-FO is XML that describes how a document should appear, as opposed to DocBook XML, which describes the purpose of each part of the document. Using stylesheets from *http://docbook.sourceforge.net*, the DocBook XML is transformed into XSL-FO XML. From there, an XSL-FO tool can create PostScript, PDF, or a number of other formats. The overall process is shown in Figure 8-2.

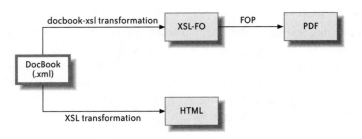

FIGURE 8-2. Conversion of a DocBook document from .xml to PDF and HTML

The best-known open source FO processor is FOP (*http://xml.apache.org/fop*), from the Apache Project. While it works fairly well, the current version of FOP does not implement some parts of the FO specification—for example, keeping titles and their text on the same page. The next version intends to correct many of these problems.

Two commercial tools for working with FO are XEP (*http://www.renderx.com*) and the XSL Formatter (*http://www.antennahouse.com*). There is a long comparison of which parts of the XSL-FO specification are supported by different processors at *http://www.antennahouse.com/xslfo/comparison-fo.htm*. There is also a book about this whole process, *XSL-FO: Making XML Look Good in Print*, by Dave Pawson (O'Reilly). I also found the DocBook FAQ that he maintains at *http://www.dpawson.co.uk/docbook* to be a good online resource.

The tools used to write this book

O'Reilly uses FrameMaker 5.5.6 as the common file format for almost all of its books, including this one. Authors write their text in one format, which is usually Microsoft Word or OpenOffice but can also be DocBook or POD (for the first three, see the sections "Microsoft Word," "OpenOffice," and "DocBook," respectively; POD is covered in "More File Formats," later in this chapter). The original is then converted to FrameMaker, either by importing the source files directly or by using scripts to convert the source files into XML that is suitable for importing by FrameMaker. The FrameMaker file is then copy-edited, figures are added, and an index is created; finally, the book is sent to the printing company as a set of PDF files with the necessary cutting marks on the page edges.

This book was written using DocBook Lite (*dblite*), which is an O'Reilly-defined subset of DocBook available from *ftp://ftp.ora.com/pub/dblite/dblite.tar.gz*. The text was added to the XML files using Emacs and its PSGML mode, with one file per chapter and a single file named *book.xml* to bring all the chapters together. The ability to tidy up a paragraph with fill-region-as-paragraph made reading large amounts of marked-up text much easier.

Generating HTML was simple using the Perl script *db2h* that comes with the *dblite* package. This script uses *xsltproc* (*http://xmlsoft.org*), a useful tool for running XSL scripts that is available for Unix, Windows, and Mac OS X. The XSL script generates the HTML, with one web page per chapter and a basic table of contents. Alternatively, a different XSL script can produce one HTML file per section. Generating the HTML for this book took around 30 seconds on an ordinary desktop machine.

Generating PDF was harder work. The original tool chain for DocBook XML to PDF was to convert the XML to L^AT_EX, then generate a *.dvi* file from that, and then convert the *.dvi* file to PDF. Instead I used FOP from the Apache Project, which is an open source tool to convert files from the XML format named FO to HTML or PDF. FOP hides this intermediate step nicely, and I was able to create a single PDF file, complete with bookmarks and internal hyperlinks, in under a minute on the same ordinary desktop machine. The precise steps for RedHat Linux 8.0 were:

1. Install a JVM and set your JAVA_HOME environment variable to it. I used Sun's J2SE 1.4.2.

2. Download and unpack the file *docbook-xsl-1.67.2* (*gzip*'d *.tar* or *.zip*, according to preference) from *http://docbook.sourceforge.net* into the same directory as your source DocBook XML files.

3. Create a file named *fo-stylesheet.xsl* in your source directory. This file is what you use to customize the PDF output. Mine started off looking like:

```
<xsl:stylesheet xmlns:xsl="http://www.w3.org/1999/XSL/Transform"
                xmlns:fo="http://www.w3.org/1999/XSL/Format"
                xmlns:exsl="http://exslt.org/common"
                extension-element-prefixes="exsl"
                exclude-result-prefixes="exsl"
                version='1.0'>
  <xsl:import href="docbook-xsl-1.67.2/fo/docbook.xsl"/>
  <xsl:param name="fop.extensions" select="1" />
  <xsl:param name="variablelist.as.blocks" select="1" />
</xsl:stylesheet>
```

4. Download and unpack the file *fop-0.20.5.bin* (*gzip*'d *.tar* or *.zip*) from *http://xml.apache.org/ fop/download.html#binary* into a convenient directory, which should be added to your PATH or otherwise made available at the command line.

5. In your source file directory, type:

```
fop.sh -xml book.xml -xsl fo-stylesheet.xsl -pdf book.pdf
```

You may get some warnings about things not yet implemented by FOP. These can be ignored. (I wish now that I'd sent a patch with a command-line argument to suppress such warnings.)

The generated PDF file is named *book.pdf* and includes bookmarks and a hyperlinked table of contents for books and manuals. If you need to change the locations of the various packages and files, use absolute names. There are a large number of parameters for the DocBook generation of an FO file, as documented at *http://docbook.sourceforge.net/release/xsl/current/doc/fo*.

Two things that I never got the FOP PDF generation to do well were keeping section headers and their text together with soft pagebreaks, and handling long URLs across linebreaks. The latter sometimes lead to ugly justification of the surrounding text, with the words padded out too far apart.

I found that the XML validation script *xwf* that came with *dblite* didn't give me enough information about which line my errors were on, so I used *xmllint* instead, which comes with *xsltproc*. *xmllint* can be run on the whole book or on individual chapters, which helps when tracking down things like a subtly missing closing slash. Overall, I didn't find any open source XML tool that made it really easy to find errors in a large document made up of multiple XML files.

OpenOffice

OpenOffice (*http://www.openoffice.org*) is a large open source office suite with a word processor, spreadsheet, and presentation editor, among other applications. It is intended to compete with Microsoft Office by running on not just Windows and Mac OS X, but also Linux and Solaris (and other Unixes are in progress). The two big advantages of OpenOffice are that it's available at no cost and it can read and write the file formats used by Microsoft Word, Excel, and PowerPoint, at least if their more complex features aren't used. The problems arise when you use complex Excel macros or newer features of Word. In this case, OpenOffice will usually ignore what it doesn't understand.

There is also a partly closed version of OpenOffice named StarOffice™, which has better support for Asian fonts, more clip art, and a database. StarOffice is available from Sun (*http://www.sun.com/software/star/staroffice*) for around $80 per user.

The native file format for OpenOffice is *gzip*'d XML files, but it uses a different set of DTDs and schemas than DocBook. The configuration of OpenOffice is also controlled by XML files, which has helped it to support many localized versions. Another of the strengths of OpenOffice is its ability to generate PDF directly from the source files, though without bookmarks and internal hyperlinks. Command-line tools are well supported by OpenOffice, but I recommend reading *OpenOffice.org Writer*, by Jean Hollis Weber (O'Reilly), if you intend to generate HTML and PDF automatically from OpenOffice as part of your documentation environment. There are a growing number of other OpenOffice books available; there's even one for dummies it seems.

If you're not generating complex documents and you really need to be able to edit the source files on both Windows and GNU/Linux machines, then OpenOffice may work very well for you. New features are still being added with each yearly release, so this tool is definitely one to watch for further improvements.

Microsoft Word

Microsoft Word (*http://www.microsoft.com/office/word*) is part of the Microsoft Office suite of programs. Microsoft Office runs on Windows and Macintosh and retails for $399 per user (though installation on two machines is permitted); Word can also be purchased separately for somewhat less. Word is the most common word processing tool in many companies today and is relatively easy to use, at least for simple tasks. What you see on the screen while editing a document is, for the most part, an accurate rendition of what you will see when you print the document. Editing simple images is built into Word, though if you want to convert the images to a different format, you have to cut and paste them to another application such as Microsoft Paint. If you need to view and edit Word documents on platforms other than Windows or Macintosh, then OpenOffice (see the previous section, "OpenOffice") or AbiWord (*http://www.abiword.org*) are both able to handle basic Word files.

The Microsoft Word file format, known casually as "doc" (from its default file extension, *.doc*) is a proprietary format that has changed substantially between major versions of Microsoft Word. Word files are large and quite complex since they can store macros, images, and previous versions of documents. Word provides its own tool for clearly showing different people's edits with change bars and color-coded lines below or through altered text.

There is a text-based, open file format named RTF (Rich Text Format) to which all Word files can be exported, though some formatting information is lost during this process. A better approach with more recent versions of Word is to use XML as a text-based export and import file format.

Each version of Word can import files from the previous major version, but this is not always true for versions that are older than that. With Word 2003, support for exporting files to XML is much improved, and if XML becomes a common choice for a source file format, then the upgrade problems may be more easily solved in the future. Other risks of using Word as a documentation environment are viruses disguised as Word macros and the fact that it is easy to accidentally leave information from previous versions inside a document where others may see it.

HTML files generated from Word have traditionally contained large amounts of Microsoft-specific HTML, along with a lot of directives to make the HTML resemble the printed page as closely as possible. More recent versions of Word have the option to generate "filtered" HTML, which is cleaner and smaller. Generating PDF from Word is possible with any number of small commercial converters, and there is also the open source GhostWord project (*http://ghostword.sourceforge.net*). The overall process is shown in Figure 8-3. For anyone putting together a documentation environment using Word, *Word Hacks*, by Andrew Savikas (O'Reilly), contains many of the mechanisms and scripts used by O'Reilly to produce PDF and HTML from the Word source files of most of its books.

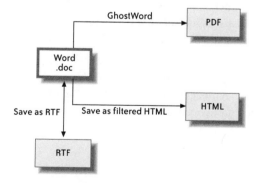

FIGURE 8-3. Conversion of a Word document from .doc to PDF and HTML

More File Formats

There are a number of other file formats and tools used for creating documentation. These formats and tools occupy odd niches; once they are established, the effort of converting to another format is seen as unnecessary work.

TeX

.tex files are structured text files for use by Donald Knuth's open source TeX program and extensions of it, such as L^AT_EX (*http://www.tug.org*). Not surprisingly (given its academic background), TeX has excellent support for mathematical formulas, and so is commonly used in universities for papers and theses. TeX-related tools usually produce *.dvi* output files, suitable for conversion to PostScript or PDF.

TeX produces documents that are typographically excellent, though too many documents start to resemble each other in appearance if the default templates are used. Various macros to produce simple images with TeX files exist, but PostScript images can be also be referred to in TeX documents.

Texinfo

Texinfo (*http://www.gnu.org/software/texinfo*) is the source documentation format for the GNU Project. Online manuals and manpages are generated from the text-based *.texi* files. Texinfo supports the idea of a tree of pages with links to other pages. With suitable macros, TeX can read Texinfo files and PostScript images, and can generate PDF. The other format that can be generated from Texinfo files using the *makeinfo* tool is *.info* files, which can then be viewed with the command-line Info tool or from within Emacs. *makeinfo* can also generate DocBook and XML output.

The move to Texinfo from *troff* (see the next item in this list) has meant, in some cases, that the GNU manpage for a given command has become a minimal summary, along with a suggestion to read the Info version of the file for that command. To avoid this two-step process, you can always try the Info version first. Other irritations with the HTML generated from Texinfo files are that some pages contain very little text, and the use of multiple HTML files means having to follow a link to load a new web page for each successive text page, which is a very slow way to read a lot of text (though you can generate a single output file by using *makeinfo*'s --no-split option). Luckily, most GNU manuals have other file formats, such as PDF, available as well.

troff

The original text markup language of the 1970s is *troff* (*http://www.troff.org*), and it's still found in the source files for manpages and some of the IETF RFC documents. There is a GNU version named *groff*, and this has even been used to produce book-sized documents. There are a number of specific macros defined for producing tables, figures, chemical diagrams, and so on.

POD

POD (Plain Old Documentation) is a simple markup language created by Larry Wall for Perl programs and other verbatim text, with default generators for HTML, manpages, TeX, and raw text. The special character for POD commands is =.

NOTE

The various file formats described in this chapter can often be identified by which characters need to be escaped in the text and by how the
tool commands are specified. = is POD, @ is Texinfo, . is *troff*, <> is XML
(so the document was probably created in OpenOffice or DocBook),
and \{ } is T_EX.

Automated Production of Documentation

Automation is just as useful when creating documentation as it is when writing source code.
Every manual step of the process is vulnerable to human error. So if there are fewer manual
steps, then the process becomes much more reliable—and probably a little faster too.

One major benefit of regularly producing the final format of the files for the documentation is that it reduces the pressure on the writers as the release date for a product
approaches. Each time the documentation is produced is a test of the production process,
so there should be fewer nasty surprises when the release is due.

Another benefit is that intermediate versions of the documentation can be distributed
more easily for reviews and beta releases. Just as with source code, regularly available
proofs of the documentation help you catch formatting errors when they creep in, not
weeks later when it's much harder to work out which particular change to the source files
resulted in the changes in the documentation.

WARNING

Some documentation requires so many manual modifications to an
intermediate file format during production that there can only ever be
one conversion from the input file format. A good example of this is creating a book from Word files, using FrameMaker as an intermediate file
format. There is no easy way to record all the hyphenations, soft linebreaks, text-flow changes, and moving of figures in the original Word
source files. I think that this effort is one of the great shortcomings of
documentation environments as they are now—no one would imagine
modifying generated assembly code by hand.

Even if they can do it more often, why is it that many projects generate their documentation only once or twice before creating a release? There are at least three reasons:

- Generation of the documentation requires some specific tools that are not available on
  every machine, and these tools are not cheap.

- Generation takes a long time, with lots of manual intervention to answer questions,
  enter values, and so on.

- The final formats of the documentation are so close to the format that the writers use
  that they see no need to view the documentation in its final formats.

Some responses to each of these problems are:

- Putting copies of the tools on more than one machine is an insurance against the possibility of that one vital machine failing just before the release is due. This insurance will cost something, but what's the cost of not shipping on time? How long will it take you to reinstall and reconfigure the required tools on a new machine?

  If the tools really must be used on just one machine, then there are a number of ways of running a tool remotely. Source files can be made available using shared filesystems or can even be copied from one machine to another. On Unix machines, *rsh* and *ssh* can be used to run processes remotely, and GUI screens can be made to appear locally if necessary. For Windows 2000 and later, there is the Remote Desktop tool, which makes it seem that you are directly logged in to the remote machine. There is a similar product named VNC (*http://www.realvnc.com*) for a larger number of platforms. Of course, with a single machine there is also the issue of how to avoid problems when multiple people want to use the machine at the same time. A simple lock file that is generated as part of using the tools can be used to notify other people that someone else is already using the tools.

- Every manual intervention will be done incorrectly by someone one day, which will make the whole thing take even longer when you have to start all over again.

  The number of interventions can be reduced in a number of ways. Some tools will let you use a text file to provide canned responses to their questions. Other tools will let you pass in values to a command-line version of the tool. Open source tools can have the local defaults hardcoded in their source code. In the worst case, UI test tools can be used to enter the required values at the appropriate times.

- What the writers see is close, but not *exactly* the same. Every difference between what writers see and what customers receive is a potential bug in the documentation. The analogous situation with source code is when developers never really use the product as it is shipped to customers, which is a surefire way to introduce bugs to a product.

Bad Ideas for Documentation

The Bad Ideas in this section are mainly related to pitfalls with using documentation tools.

Releasing the Documentation Separately

One situation that arises quite frequently is that the release of a product is running late, and the documentation for the release is running even later. The thought occurs to someone: "Perhaps we could release the documentation separately?" Yes, you can indeed release documentation on a different schedule from the product. Just as you could make a separate release of some binary library files used by a product. However, keeping track of all the different versions involved will make your release managers' work harder, and your customers' lives probably no better. Making sure that each version of the product will always refer to the correct documentation is not impossible, but it is fraught with potential errors. The long-term effect of releasing the documentation separately always seems to be increased confusion.

A variant on that not-so-cunning plan is to ship an early (i.e., unfinished) version of the documentation with the product, and then later on provide an updated version of the documentation on a public web site. The idea is that the customer can then check for updates. Sometimes you see a Help menu with View Documentation and View Latest Documentation. This idea is not a good one either, for a number of reasons. The customer may or may not be connected to the Internet when she wants to view the documentation. The customer may not be allowed to update the installed documentation. The busy system administrator who installed the product will not have time to check for updates and will likely disable automatic notification about available updates. Again, just say no, and release the correct documentation as an integral part of the product.

Ransom-Note Cut and Paste

The way that different fonts in a document are displayed can vary widely from one editor and platform to another. So long as all the glyphs (graphic symbols) for all the different characters are present, this doesn't usually affect how the document is read. But sometimes two fonts that are almost identical in appearance on one machine can appear quite different from each other on another machine, or when transformed into another file format. What happens then is that when changes are made in the document on one machine and the wrong font is used, maybe because "it looked close enough," the changes stand out on the other machine like the cut-out letters in a Hollywood-style ransom note.

For example, the original announcement document may have looked like this:

> Here at Tasteful Pets we look forward to a deep and meaningful relationship with Rabbits, Inc. and believe that their product FurWare is best of breed.

All the text is in one font. Then you decide to use this particular document as a template for your next announcement. You copy the name and product of your new partner, Foxes, Inc., from some other document and paste it into the announcement. To your surprise, you see:

> Here at Tasteful Pets we look forward to a deep and meaningful relationship with **Foxes, Inc.** and believe that their product **FoxyLadies** is best of breed.

In this case it's pretty obvious that a different font was used wherever the new name was cut and pasted from. But what if the fonts differed only by a single point size, or even worse, in some way that your text editor doesn't even show you? Then the difference may not be at all obvious until the document is viewed with a different editor or is converted to another file format such as HTML.

This can be especially embarrassing in press releases where company executives' names are changed. The obvious solution to this is to make sure that when you cut and paste text, the fonts match in name, not just by eye, and to preview the document on several different systems and file formats. Another slow-but-sure fix is to select each paragraph in turn and reset the font or formatting for the whole block. Remember: cut and paste is cool, but only if no one can tell you did it.

Old Versions That Never Die

Some tools such as Microsoft Word can save previous versions of a document as it is changed. This is useful for generating change bars and similar editing marks. It's also a lot faster to append recent changes internally when editing a document, rather than modifying the file in many places. However, if you forget to remove the previous versions before you publish the document, the different versions are all there for people to see.

This may be as harmless as people seeing your common spelling mistakes, or it may show changes in financial information that were never supposed to be disclosed. This is of particular concern if the document has been redacted (lines of text blacked out for reasons of security) and then the previous version of the document contains all the sensitive information anyway. This has happened a number of times in recent years, just because no one realized that the earlier versions were still present in the file format when it was released.

Funky Filenames

Different filesystems have different quirks about how their files and directories are named. Using the directory separator (/ on Unix, \ on Windows) in filenames is always a bad idea. Unix shells also use some other characters, such as ; * ? > < $ % | , so avoid these too. Macintosh filenames should not have colons in them. These rules are easy to follow by using only alphanumeric characters for filenames. There is also the problem of case: *File_A* and *file_a* refer to the same file in Windows, but they refer to two distinct files in Unix.

One common problem is that both Windows and Macintosh filesystems support spaces in filenames, whereas Unix filesystems do so only grudgingly. Some Unix tools such as shells and their commands will handle filenames with spaces by quoting the filename or preceding each space with a backslash (\ ); it varies by shell. Other common command-line tools such as *find* and *xargs* will take extra arguments to change how they use filenames, if you remember to add them. Older versions of CVS and related SCM tools didn't handle spaces very well either.

If you are expecting to use files across multiple platforms, keep these issues in mind when creating filenames. Renaming files later on is a tedious problem when the filenames have been used as part of links or images in a document.

Screenshots

Screenshots can be the bane of producing documentation on a tight schedule. They are tricky to capture, tend to change dramatically as the product develops, may need editing to remove sensitive information or spelling mistakes, and are often unreadable by the time a document is printed. A good screenshot at just the right point in a document can indeed be worth a thousand words, but you can describe many ideas better with just a few hundred well-chosen words. Far more helpful than an outdated screenshot with hard-to-read text and fuzzy images is a clear set of conventions throughout a document for describing the various prompts, the text that is entered, and any menu choices. If you have a long list of steps to follow, provide ways to check that the steps are working correctly as you go, rather than a screenshot of every other step.

If you must use screenshots (for example, in online help or tutorials), make sure that their file format and the resolution at which they are acquired is appropriate for all the release formats. It's very frustrating to click on a thumbnail image on a web site only to receive an image that is larger but still too small for you to see anything useful! You may also want to print the documentation regularly to make sure that the screenshots are still useful in black and white. Using links to screenshots rather than embedding them directly within the source document can help reduce the size of the files, but at the cost of more link checking as part of the production process.

Internal Project Documentation

Properly understanding a large amount of source code can take a long time, as described in "Understanding Code" in Chapter 10. One thing that can help is having documentation that describes how the different functions and methods in the code are supposed to be used.

The idea of documenting a function right where it's defined by adding comments to the source code is an old one. Just like raw text files, these comments need some structure to be more useful. Code documenters such as Javadoc and *doxygen* define special "tags" such as @return, which a method's comment uses to describe what is returned from the method. Others such as DocJet parse the comments as free text. Code documenter tools for languages that have classes are sometimes known as "class browsers."

Javadoc™ (*http://java.sun.com/j2se/javadoc*) is a tool that comes with the no-cost JDKs available from Sun. It's easy to use to document a large amount of Java source code, though if there aren't any comments, it becomes more of a class browser. It generates HTML reports by default, but is extensible and can be used as a basis for any tool that analyzes Java source code. As of JDK 1.4, you can define your own tags for the comments.

doxygen (*http://www.doxygen.org*) is an open source tool by Dimitri van Heesch that can analyze C, C++, IDL, and Java source code; it can then produce a L^ATEX reference manual, HTML files, or XML documents that describe the different elements of the program. *doxygen* has plenty of documentation, which is a good thing because it has a lot of configuration knobs to play with. You can create dependency diagrams, though this feature can take hours for projects with over 250,000 lines of C source code. As well as a *.tar* file of its source code, *doxygen* has binary releases for GNU/Linux, Windows, and Mac OS X.

One commercial code documenter is DocJet (*http://www.tall-tree.com*), which can analyze C, C++, Visual Basic, some versions of IDL, and Java. Prices are on a complex sliding scale starting at $300 per user. The reason that DocJet stands out is that it parses both the programming language that is being used and the natural language in the comments, so you don't have to add tags. It runs only on Windows.

A few questions that are useful when evaluating this kind of tool are:

- Can all the elements of a language be documented, not just functions and methods?

- Is the location of comments flexible? Or must comments come before and never after a variable or enum, for example.

- Can you exclude parts of the product not just by class or filename, but also by method or function name? Is this customizable—could you exclude all methods that started with my_get or my_set?

- Can you customize the reports generated by the tool—for localization or other customization, for example?

- Is the language that the tool accepts for comments checked for errors? For example, Javadoc allows HTML in its comments, but you have to use a different tool to check the generated report for incorrect HTML.

One benefit of using an IDE such as Visual Studio or NetBeans™ is that generated documentation can be added to the existing documentation. This also allows you to have real-time prompting for functions' names and parameters from within the IDE, so you don't have to change to a browser window to see the HTML report from a code documenting tool.

Checklist

Here are some questions you should feel comfortable answering about your current documentation system. For the first set of questions, imagine that you've found a serious technical error in the content of a document about your own product:

- How do you tell someone that this error exists? Do you file a bug? Send her email? Annotate a printout?

- Can you easily find out who is responsible for the particular document?

- Where do you find the version number of each document?

- How do you know when to check for a corrected version?

- Where would you go to find the corrected version?

Some more general questions to ask yourself about your documentation environment are:

- Can you view and print the released documents from all the environments you work in?

- When do updates to the documentation appear?

- How is feedback from reviewers incorporated into your documentation? What sort of information do you imagine is lost or garbled during this process?

- When you want to resolve conflicting input from different reviewers, is there a record of who approved each change to the document? This is often available either as part of the document itself or by using an SCM tool.

- What file formats do you deliver to customers, and why?

- How long does it take to convert all the source files for your documentation to the formats that are delivered to customers?

- How much of the time generating the documentation is spent doing things manually that have to be repeated every time the documentation is generated?

- On how many different machines can you create the released versions of the documentation?

## CHAPTER NINE

Releasing Products

THIS CHAPTER DISCUSSES WHAT IS INVOLVED WITH MAKING A PRODUCT WORK somewhere other than where it was created. The different areas are divided up into things that can be decided even before the first release of the product to customers; various issues that come up during a release; and some things to remember after a release has happened.

Overview

Releasing a product seems as though it should be the easy part after you've finally got your product working, tested it, and documented it. In fact, making a product work properly somewhere other than the environment in which it was developed is an area where many projects fall down. This is unfortunate, because no one can use software that they can't even install.

If a release is something out of the ordinary for a project, then the whole project can become distracted by the intensity associated with getting the release just right. People may have made changes that break the release process, but it's hard to remember when those changes happened because it's so long since the previous release. Finally, the product escapes. Everyone is exhausted, and their only consolation is that they won't have to do that again for a while.

Just as regular automated builds help debug the build process before a crucial build is necessary, so too does the regular, automated creation of releases greatly help debug the whole release process. Automated release processes also help you avoid the temptation to give customers "engineering specials" just because it takes too long to create an official release (see "Quick Fixes and Engineering Specials," later in this chapter). Finally, an automated release process can help you ship products faster, since human error is reduced.

Before the Release

Before the first release is even begun, you can make some decisions about how the product will appear to customers. It's well worth writing these decisions down and making sure that everyone in the project knows where to find the information. One key decision is how to decide when to ship a release. Is the date to be driven by features, by accumulated bug fixes for customers, by the elapsed time since the last release, by an approaching trade fair, or at the whim of someone in the project with a strong opinion? A mixture of all of these is not unusual, but it's good to be clear about it from early on, since many other decisions are driven by release dates.

Releasing a product is also where the differences between open and closed software become more apparent. For instance, license keys make sense only for closed software, and older releases of open source products are only ever maintained if there are sufficient people interested in doing so, since there are usually no legal contracts involved.

System Requirements

What is needed by customers must be very carefully documented. For instance, what platforms should the project's developers expect to support? Which browsers? Which versions of additional libraries and infrastructure code? If this sort of information is not readily available, then the environment used by each developer tends to diverge over time, and obscure bugs related to unsupported platforms can creep into the product.

These requirements need to be unambiguous and easily available from within the project. Customers need to be able to see this information before they begin to install your software; requirements are usually also put on a web page somewhere. The list of requirements for installing a product should include:

Hardware
    CPU type, CPU speed, disk capacity, video card, display resolution, and any other specific hardware.

Operating system
    Each version of each supported operating system needs to be listed. If specific versions of libraries or header files are shipped with an operating system and people may have upgraded these files, then the versions of such service packs or patches are worth noting. Any specific versions of drivers or firmware should also be noted.

Other software

Any other software such as libraries, *.jar* files, and small utilities should be listed, together with the supported versions.

License keys

If a customer needs a license key to use the product, provide information about how to obtain a key and whether the key is needed before installing the product or before using the product.

Legal

Make sure that the requirements clearly describe the product's legal status (e.g., commercial, GPL, or some other license). People need to know whether they are allowed to use what they are installing.

Effort

Some indication of how long a simple installation should take is useful. Similarly, tell customers whether installation of your product requires stopping other processes on the machine, or even rebooting the machine. This is all helpful for planning ahead when installing products.

For all these requirements, it is very helpful if you include links to where the files can be downloaded from or where to find more information about each requirement. If you can distribute any extra required software with your product, this makes the whole process of using your product easier for everyone (except maybe the release team).

Build Numbers

Build numbers are for internal use within a project, and a particular release number can have had many build numbers as the release was developed. The next section looks at release numbers, which are how customers distinguish between different released versions of your product.

The concept of build numbers is that each build that is used by people other than individual developers should have its own unique identifying number. The build number should increase over time, usually without gaps. There is no real need for customer releases to have build numbers (or at least to show them) since that's what release numbers are for.

If SCM branches are used for development, then the build number should follow the branch, as shown in Figure 9-1. This means that the build number on the main line always tells you the number of builds since the last major branch. Do record when the builds started using the branch, so that someone doesn't assume later on that all the builds for a particular release used that release's branch.

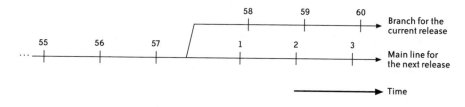

FIGURE 9-1. Build numbers following a branch

Release Numbering

The release number of a product is really part of marketing different versions of your product to customers. People want to be able to tell different versions apart, so each release number should be unique for all time, or at least for as long as the product is marketed under the same name. There's a general expectation that the release numbers should increase over time and that some release numbers are more significant than others. For instance, the first release of a product is usually suspected of having more bugs than it should. Developers should treat release numbers like project names (see "Choosing Project Names" in Chapter 3) and expect them to change for nontechnical reasons at any time. Within these guidelines, there are actually a number of widely used numbering schemes for releases.

A release number of the form *major.minor.patch* uses three separate integers; the major, minor, and patch release numbers. This scheme communicates something about the degree of change and maturity of each release. Version 1.0.0 is usually the first public release and bears the stigma of being a "dot zero" release. Note that 1.0.9 can be followed by a 1.0.10 release or a 1.1.0 release. Generally, the patch number is changed for bug-fix releases, the minor number is changed for releases with new features, and the major number is changed for releases that break compatibility with prior releases in some significant manner.

With this scheme, the question is what to call the releases prior to 2.0.0? One solution is to use 1.*x.y* and then a build number to distinguish between builds. However, sometimes it's important to know that this is going to be a 2.0 build for testing the upgrade process. In this case, the internal builds can all be named 2.0.0 and the first customer release can be named 2.0.1. Build numbers should always increase by one for simplicity, so try to avoid schemes such as starting customer releases at build 1000.

One drawback of this scheme is that the only information about the order of releases is for the patch releases; that is, you can assume that 1.1.2 was released after 1.1.1. We don't know from the release number whether 1.1.2 was released before or after 2.0, since the 1.1 release could be a very long-lived release. Figure 9-2 shows that a release number (1.1.0 in this case) can appear both on the main line if it is built from there, and then later on a release branch, which can sometimes seem counterintuitive. The build numbers and information about when the 1.1 release branch was created can help avoid any confusion.

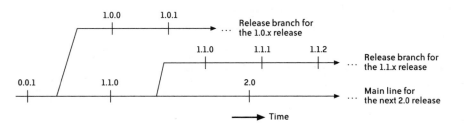

FIGURE 9-2. Release numbers and branches

Another scheme extends the *major.minor.patch* scheme by using *even* minor numbers to indicate which releases are considered stable and *odd* minor numbers to indicate which releases are still in development. GNU/Linux is the best known example of this scheme, where kernel Versions 2.3.*x* and 2.5.*x* are unstable, development versions and Versions 2.4 and 2.6 are the stable releases used by most GNU/Linux distributions. Linux is currently ensuring stability by allowing changes for only a one-week period after each release.

Another scheme uses numbers that asymptotically approach the intended release number. So after customer release 1.2 comes customer 1.3, but the releases leading closely up to 1.3 are numbered 1.2.99.1 to 1.2.99.999. This approach has logic to support it but seems confusing in practice to some people.

Yet another scheme you may see used is adding a suffix of *"rcn"* for "release candidate *n.*" For example, 4.0rc3 is the third candidate for the intended 4.0 release. When the final release candidate is promoted to be the actual release, it is repackaged with no changes. This scheme seems a little harder to parse algorithmically within an application, but its intent is clear.

Other, more creative release-numbering schemes include the one used by Donald Knuth for TeX, which has successive releases numbered as 3.1, 3.14, and 3.141, with each release adding the next digit from π. Another idea to minimize disagreements over what the next version number should be is to use complex numbers, with the real part assigned by one group (say, engineering), and the imaginary part assigned by another group (say, marketing). This is what has effectively happened in the past with large products such as Java and Windows. This is actually quite sensible: the real part can be a build label such as the project name and the build number, and the imaginary part can be the release number (or release numbers, for products on different platforms).

Whatever numbering scheme is chosen, the values must always be unique. For instance, periods are what makes 1.11.2 different from 1.1.12. An alternative approach is to add leading zeros to the numbers—for example, 01011002 instead of 1.11.2. Ideally, the release numbers should sort in a predictable manner, so they can be compared conveniently within the product and can easily be found in lists of releases in a bug tracking tool. Treating some version numbers purely as strings will lead to ASCII sorting and lists such as *release_1, …, release_101, release 2*. Maintaining major, minor, and patch numbers as integers accessible within a product's source code and other development environment tools can make the sorting order more useful.

All these numbers can become confusing, especially when spoken aloud: was that "three one two, build three" or "three one three, build two"? The numbers also begin to acquire deeper significance if APIs are allowed to change only in minor releases and not in patch releases, or when support for a release cannot be dropped until the major version number changes.

The internal engineering project name for the project is usually more useful than release numbers in SCM tags and bug tracking tools. The actual release number can be chosen later on, closer to the release date (Debian Linux does this). Some honesty should be encouraged here, though—a release shouldn't be declared a patch release just to reassure a customer that not too much changed, especially if it's really a barely tested rewrite of a core part of the product.

Release Information

Once you have decided on a build-numbering scheme and a release-numbering scheme, there is the question of what other information is needed about each build. Here are some suggestions for what to record with each official build:

Project name
> The internal project name for this build.

Build number
> The build number that makes each build unique for the same release number.

Build timestamps
> The times the build started and finished, including the time zone.

User
> The username of the account that was used for the build. If the build tool is configured correctly, the build should be independent of the user's particular environment, so this is a safety check.

Build type
> Was this build intended for internal testing or for customer use? Is it an official build by a release team, or an unofficial build? Is it for an alpha or a beta release, or some other kind of release-candidate build? Was it built with profiling, debugging, or optimizing enabled?

Build log
> A link or location for the commands used during this build.

SCM details
> The build label (see "Labeling Builds" in Chapter 3) used to tag the source files for this build, and the name of an SCM branch if used. If confirmation of the SCM tool is required, then a manifest or BOM that lists all the source files and their versions can be added.

Bugs
> Identifiers for any bugs that are related to this build.

Operating system and tools
> If some parts of a release, such as a compiler or the operating system, are not controlled using the SCM tool, then you can at least record information about them here. Most tools will generate a version number if prompted correctly, and this can be generated as part of the build tool's configuration stage, when it is making sure that it has the required tools for the build.

Size
> Recording the size of a build is useful for tracking changes over time or checking that a build seems superficially complete.

Test results

The versions and results of all automated tests that have been run on this build should be easily available given a particular build label.

Once you have decided what information to record with a build (be generous here), you also need an easy way to find that information. A simple text or XML file that is created with each build is one way. If the information is embedded in the product, there should be some way to display the information (for example, an About box for a UI, or a -version argument for a CLI). Note that this is entirely separate from information gathered at runtime about a customer's environment. However the information is accessed, it needs to be easy to use from a wide variety of tools.

Another useful idea is to create and document a standard way of referring to releases in the SCM tool, in the bug tracking tool, and for other purposes such as coverage and profiling reports. When you're trying to rebuild a release from source, it's irritating to have to wonder whether the tag was 1-2-3, 1.2.3, or 1_2_3. Yes, you can probably look it up somewhere, but a common way of doing things avoids even this effort. Some tools will have restrictions on the format of names. For instance, CVS tags cannot start with a digit or have periods in them. "Labeling Builds" in Chapter 3 discusses this idea of build labels in more detail.

Upgrading

Deciding how customers will upgrade to a newer release of your product is something you should do before the first release. There are two aspects to upgrading: the political and the practical. The political side is how to convince your customers to upgrade, whether it is for features, bug fixes, or because you no longer want to provide support for an older release. Upgrades are extra work for customers and always carry a risk. The risk for them is that the upgrade may not work; the risk for you is that they may choose to use someone else's product instead of yours. Some customers and some products can never be upgraded— think of the software in a household appliance such as a toaster.

Setting expectations early on about how long a release will be supported can prevent some nasty arguments years later. If the customer is a large company, its influence may be enough to force a release to live forever, a sort of "living dead" horror film for those who have to maintain it. One common way to write the expectations into a contract is to declare that a release will be supported for one calendar year after the next major release (that is, any release where the major release number changes).

Another question is whether patch releases are independent of each other, or whether they are cumulative. That is, does release 2.0.8 also include all the bug fixes in releases 2.0.1 to 2.0.7? Most customers assume that patch releases are cumulative, but if this is not the case, then a separate numbering scheme for patches is necessary. The advantage of independent patches is that there is less risk of destabilizing a large product when applying a patch. However, keeping track of which patches have been applied can become very tedious for the customer and for your support team.

On the practical side of upgrades, there is the question of how to deprecate public APIs if they are part of your product.* Deprecating part of an API tells customers not to use that piece of the API, but that it should still work. If it doesn't work properly anymore, then you shouldn't continue to make it available. Many compilers can generate warnings about using deprecated code, which is a great way to make sure that customers using the API are aware of the changes, so long as the warnings can be suppressed when not wanted. API changes should be marked as deprecated in one release and then removed in a later release, giving customers time to update their code. Within the source code, the old, deprecated methods should call the new methods to avoid code duplication. Old classes should inherit from new classes, if possible.

Another question is the file format of upgrade packages. Generally, using the same package format as the original release makes things seem simpler to the customer. Some installation programs are written to require you to uninstall the product first before you upgrade, which always seems heavy-handed to me. Of course, a customer's data and configuration information should never be lost due to an upgrade.

Upgrades can fail after they have been installed, for a number of reasons. The converted customer data for the new version may be larger than the installer estimated, causing a lack of disk space to halt the product. The licensing scheme may have changed, and the upgrade was installed without this having been noted. The previous version of the product may have been modified in ways that the installer program knew nothing about, and those changes were lost in the upgrade. These are all problems to consider carefully when designing an upgrade for a product.

Products that can have multiple versions of themselves running side by side can make testing upgrades much easier for everyone. This is particularly important for large applications that take a long time to move from evaluation to production. For instance, certifying upgrades of software products in large telecommunication networks often takes many months.

Downgrading to a previous version is rarely supported well by most products. Database schemas or configuration file formats may have changed, and there always is the question of what to do with data that doesn't make sense in the older version. Unless the ability to downgrade is noted explicitly in a product, it is wise to assume that only upgrades are supported.

Legal Licenses

"Open and Closed Software Development" in Chapter 1 covers some of the different legal approaches to distributing both types of software. Deciding on the legal ownership of your product before it is ever released has many advantages. First, changing legal text can affect a large number of source code files, though the source code can usually be updated by a

---

* There seems to be frequent confusion between the words *deprecate* and *depreciate*. Deprecation is what happens to APIs when you stop supporting parts of them. Depreciation is what happens when you drive a new car home and it's suddenly worth only three-quarters of what you just paid for it.

straightforward automated search and replace of copyright notices. Second, installation programs often display license agreements; these too can be changed in their source form.

The largest problem with changing the license of your product is the unwanted publicity that can arise. Changing a commercial End User License Agreement (EULA)—for instance, to stop competitors from using your product to improve their own product—may go unnoticed. Converting an open source product to a closed license will usually draw some ire and lead to a few forked versions of the code. Oddly enough, even changing a license from closed to open source seems to generate lots of speculation about the business reasons behind the decision.

Some informed discussion before your product is released, together with clear and documented decisions about why a particular license was chosen, will help make your legal status clear to customers.

License Keys

This section is about how you allow people to use your product—in the practical sense, not just in the legal sense of the previous section. The kind of issues here are how to enable and disable different parts of your product, usually according to how much someone has paid you.

Creating software that requires licenses is often frustrating for developers and customers. Developers want to use it without generating licenses, so workarounds and back doors get built into the source code. Customers are frustrated when a license server fails and stops them from using the product they have paid for. So the first thing to consider is whether your product needs license keys at all. If you want people to pay to use it, it probably does, though revenues can also come from installation, configuration, and support consultancy on many open source products. If your product can be decompiled or even run in a debugger, then whatever license scheme you use can be broken eventually, given enough time and effort.

If licenses are required, then you need to decide whether they are per user, per machine, per OS, or sitewide. Per-user licenses require some local administration; per-machine licenses will often break if the IP address, network card, or other parts of the machine are changed. If the licenses are time based (maybe because they are evaluation licenses), it's hard to guarantee that the clock on a machine will always be accurate. Some licenses contact a central license server within the customer's network or out on the Internet. Given time, such exchanges can be reverse engineered using network sniffers, as Microsoft has found with Windows XP.

However you decide to restrict usage of the program, be careful about how the product operates without the license. Make sure that any transaction or feature is atomic, so that it either works fully or stops working entirely, but nothing in between. Menu choices may be grayed out or, more usefully, they could bring up windows with text about what license is needed, how to obtain the required license, and how to install it to make the software work. The same applies to command-line tools. Hiding license information away in logfiles makes it harder for the customer to understand why your software seems to be broken. A better mechanism to inform customers about when licenses will expire and how to renew them is vital. For cheaper products, allowing the user to purchase a license over the Internet with a credit card and to receive the license by email is one solution that can get the product working quickly.

One of the hardest things to decide about products that do use license keys is which features a customer needs to evaluate the product and which features a customer will pay for. It's even harder if there are different levels of licenses. Changing these requirements can result in much tedious development work.

One suggestion is to implement licensing in your product in two layers. The lower layer is simply an API for checking whether an operation is permitted. This can be used throughout the code as the product is developed and new features are added. This way, features can be enabled or disabled consistently at design time and can be checked for at many different locations in the software. The higher layer is where a particular licensing scheme is implemented, by checking for different license keys and then enabling or disabling the different pieces of functionality. When a different licensing scheme is decided on, only the higher layer should need to change.

Developers using interpreted languages (such as JavaScript or Perl) or languages that use a virtual machine (such as Java) should be particularly careful about decompilation, which will leave the licensing scheme wide open to abuse. There are a number of obfuscation tools that can change the symbols used in your product to make it harder to understand (e.g., by using short variable names and confusing method names). For Java, DashO is one of the better commercial offerings, but the battle between decompilers and obfuscators is a fast-moving one, so you should search for recent evaluation reports before choosing an obfuscator.

Other ways to make a licensing scheme more robust are to avoid the string license in any variable that is actually used for licensing; to store any vital secret strings as many smaller strings in different parts of the product; and to check for valid licenses in different ways in many different locations. Creating different releases of the product with the same release number but different ways of checking for licenses means that a crack for one version won't work for every copy of that version. One financial program detected that it was running without the appropriate license but stopped working only about a month before various annual taxes were due, forcing people to purchase legal licenses so that they could submit their paperwork.

Securing Your Releases

If your product is distributed over the Internet, then your customers need to have confidence that what they download is the same package that you released. There have been numerous cases of web sites being compromised and modified software being left for customers to download. Once installed, the modified software can be used in turn to compromise even more machines.

One common way to increase confidence is to provide customers with checksums of the packages they download, preferably through a separate channel such as an email message. The customer can generate a checksum for the package that she downloaded and compare that checksum with the one that she obtained from you in the email message. An even more secure option is to cryptographically sign the release using a private key and then let customers use the associated public key to decrypt the signature. PGP is a popular way of doing this, and a description of how to confirm releases of the Apache web server can be found at *http://httpd.apache.org/dev/verification.html*. Another useful resource is the "Strong Distribution HOWTO" article at *http://www.cryptnet.net/fdp/crypto/strong_distro.html*. Java's JAR files (described in the "Windows" section, later in this chapter) and Windows executables can also be signed for security.

Quick Fixes and Engineering Specials

Among the things that plague software products as they grow are special releases. If they are not carefully controlled, products have ways of getting released that make them practically impossible to support.

One way this can happen with closed source products is when you are working with a customer to debug a problem and it's too much overhead to generate a patch release for the customer, so you give the customer the executables from a private build. Once the problem is fixed, the customer may well not want to make any more changes, and so the engineering special becomes a de facto release.

Oddly enough, specials happen with open source software too. The usual symptom is someone complaining that something in the product doesn't work as expected, and then you notice some output text included in his bug report that doesn't exist in the product as it was released. It turns out that you are trying to help him debug his modified version of the product, without knowing about the changes he'd made. If such source code changes are necessary to fix a popular piece of functionality, then they should be merged back into the project's source code; otherwise, the project will have effectively forked, and unintentionally at that.

The best solution for closed source projects is to track every file given to customers as part of a release and to define a process for unsupported releases. If this process is defined and well known before engineering specials escape to customers, then most developers will be willing to follow it, especially if its turnaround time is quick enough to help with debugging on-site problems.

One such minimal procedure for unsupported releases has the following requirements:

- You should explain to the customer that this release is unsupported and what that means. Documenting the agreement in writing will help everyone later on.

- All source files involved in an unsupported release must be checked into the SCM tool and labeled before release. This is an appropriate case for using a suitably named private branch of just a small number of files.

- The labels for each unsupported release should be recorded somewhere, along with the customer's name, the date, and any related bug numbers.

- The build information associated with the unsupported release should show who built it. This is useful for finding holes in the process if an unaccounted-for release turns up later on in the field.

- Once the customer is satisfied, you should tell her which official release will include the changes that she helped to test.

> **WARNING**
>
> Sometimes it's tempting to build *time bombs* (code to stop your product working after a certain time) into unsupported releases, to make sure that customers really do upgrade to an official release. This idea is not a good one, since you never want to deliberately stop a paying customer from using your software. It may also backfire and force you to ship an official release before it is ready.

There is also the question of what to do when the source code is taken to a customer's site and unsupported releases are created on the spot, perhaps for debugging a problem that can be reproduced only at the customer's site. The same procedure can be followed. Ideally, the SCM tool can work while disconnected from the main server. If not, then a local copy of the affected files can be checked into a local SCM tool on the developer's laptop and then merged back into the original versions back home each night. Having all the benefits of SCM while you are developing on-site is very helpful anyway.

Creating the Release

Ideally, system testing should be performed on releases, rather than on builds without the final packaging steps of a release. That way, when a particular release is deemed worthy of shipping to customers, the release process can use a known set of files to build the release. This also ensures that the installation software is tested, at least in the most common way that testers install the software.

When a build is converted to a release for internal testing, or an internal release is converted into a customer release, the following steps are commonly followed:

1. Obtain virgin copies of the correct files using the local SCM tool. The version of the product that uses these files has already been built and tested.

2. Set the release number and other build information, either in a file, a database, or on the command line.

3. Build the product for each platform.

4. Build the packages that are released to customers.

5. Update the release notes as part of the packages.

6. Retest the different packages prior to releasing them. Don't just check that the installer works—run as many of the unit and system tests as possible against the installed product.

7. Use the SCM tool to tag all of the files that are part of the release, including all automated tests and test results.

8. Archive all customer releases and any other important builds.

Automated Releases

Automating the process of creating a release will reduce human error and speed up both regular customer releases and emergency fixes. There are some common tasks that are awkward to automate, so here are some ideas. Some of these ideas are also discussed in the context of how to choose an automation environment (see "Automation Environments" in Chapter 3).

First, use your build tool to create as much of the release as possible. Debugging a mixture of different build and release tools only makes getting a process right much harder, and using one good tool will save confusion. For instance, a single set of makefiles is much easier to work with than shell scripts that call *make* and Perl scripts. Newer build tools including SCons and Ant have built-in support for using various SCM tools to obtain the correct source files, for tagging the source files after a build, and for creating different kinds of packages.

The version number for a release is often set by hand (in one central location), and then a build number is automatically incremented. Incrementing the build number requires storing the current build number, as shown in Example 9-1. If a single build machine is used, then a simple text file may suffice. A better scheme is to store the build number in a file that is controlled by the SCM tool. Just to be sure, add checks to make sure that contents of the file storing the build number always correspond to the build label used when tagging that file.

EXAMPLE 9-1. Updating the release number using a shell script

```
#!/bin/bash
# An example shell script to store the build number in a file.

# The file where the current build number is stored between builds
CBN_FILE=/home/build/current_build_number
.
.
.
PREVIOUS_BUILD_NUMBER=`cat ${CBN_FILE}`
BUILD_NUMBER=`expr $PREVIOUS_BUILD_NUMBER + 1`
.
.
# Build the product.
.
.
# Make sure that you can work out whether the build number was updated
# just by looking at the build log.
echo ${BUILD_NUMBER} > ${CBN_FILE}
echo "Build number ${BUILD_NUMBER} was recorded in ${CBN_FILE}"
```

If an IDE is being used to develop the product, take the time to find out whether the IDE can be called by a build tool, or whether you have to export a build file from the IDE before you can build from the command line. Some IDEs provide fewer ways to build products from the command line than when using the GUI, which is frustrating to discover later on in a new project.

> **NOTE**
>
> In older versions of Visual Studio, adding a /Y3 argument to msdev on the command line is an undocumented way to display the time spent in each part of the build.

Some tools used during a build require input from the user. If these inputs are textual, are consistently in the same order, and consist of answers that are known ahead of time, then redirecting the input to a file containing the required text can work. For example, if a *configure* file requires some input, generate a suitable input file and pass it to *configure* with `./configure < configure.input`.

Some of the visual tools used as part of a build may not provide any command-line interaction or may have pop-up windows with choices that appear occasionally. GUI testing tools can sometimes help you here, or the underlying API of the tool may be available for scripting, but maybe this tool really isn't designed to be part of a build and release process?

When an automated build finishes, it's useful to tell people about it. If it failed, then project leaders and developers should be told, particularly those who have committed changes to the source since the last successful build. If it succeeded, then people such as the testers waiting for an internal build should be informed. Email is one convenient way to do this, though changing who receives the email requires aliases or some other minor email list management. Email can also be used later on for working out when releases should have been available, but for one reason or another were late. Another approach is to use RSS feeds, which each interested person can subscribe to. Some people like to receive a brief text message about broken builds on their mobile phone, so they can track down the cause of the breakage quickly.

Sometimes a build may hang, and no notification at all will appear. To make sure you are made aware of this, a separate *watchdog* process can be started at the same time as the build. Assuming that you can predict how long the longest build should take, the watchdog process can monitor the build and look for some evidence that indicates that the build finished. One good piece of evidence is the text of the email notification sent when the build is finished. If no such text or file appears after the given time, then the watchdog should send out a "failed build" notification instead.

Automating Release Information

There are various kinds of information that can be generated automatically for a release, as discussed in "Release Information," earlier in this chapter. A common request from testers is for a list of the bugs that are supposed to have been fixed in this particular release, along with the test reports from any automated tests that were run as part of the build. This list of bugs can then be used for testing and confirming that the bugs are indeed fixed. Producing this list automatically depends on whether the bug tracking system has an API that can be queried from within an automated build process. If it doesn't, then a file can be manually updated by developers, though of course this is prone to error.

If the bug tracking system can be queried from within a build, there are usually two approaches that are used. If the current release number already exists in the bug tracking system, then a simple query for the associated bugs is all that is necessary. Alternatively, if fixed bugs are in a state named something like "Fixed but Not Yet Available," then the current release number needs to be added to the bug tracking system metadata so that when the state of such a bug is changed to Fix Available, a field such as "Fixed in Release" is filled in with the current release number.

Another common request is for a list of all bugs fixed since the a particular customer release. This is often provided in release notes. When creating the names of releases within the bug tracking system, make sure that the tool supports searching for bugs both using an exact release number and using a pattern such as 1.3.* to find all bugs related to the 1.3 releases.

Other useful information for developers and testers is a change log, showing all the files that were changed since the previous release and what those changes were. Since this can be a large amount of information, an HTML change log with links to a graphical browser for the SCM tool is helpful. Change logs are discussed further in "A Typical Day's Work with SCM" in Chapter 4.

Another action that can be automated is the assembly of release notes from fragments of text associated with each bug or associated with a particular target release inside the bug tracking system. This helps to make sure that lots of small pieces of information are put together in an organized manner and none are accidentally left out.

Developers as Customers

The version of a product with the fewest bugs is usually the one that runs on the same platform that the product was developed on. This makes sense, because some bugs are only found by long-term use. Similarly, a product behaves best when it is used in the same way that the developers and testers used it when they created it.

One good idea is to make the released product resemble the versions that are used during development as much as possible. For instance, if the product is run as a service under Windows, build the product the same way for developers too. Make it easy for developers to build a release package and install it on their machines.

Another good idea is to avoid using #ifdef RELEASE and the related compiler -D arguments to change the build for a release. If system tests and other utilities have to be built for testing, then build them separately from the main product. If there are still unavoidable differences between the development and release builds, then try to capture all of them in a very small number of files, and then use the build tool to choose which files to build. Debugging later on will also be easier when customers' environments can be reproduced by developers.

Packaging Formats

A released product usually consists of many files, all of which need to be carefully installed in different places on each customer's machine. An appropriate file format for this collection of files has to be chosen for the released package of a product. Sometimes simply unpacking a collection of files is enough for the customer to use the product. For instance, when a product is distributed as source code, a customer unpacks the source files and then follows the build and installation instructions that are part of the package. This section describes some of the packaging formats used to release software.

For most products, simply extracting the files from a package is not nearly enough for a complete installation. Other steps in a successful installation may include running other programs, running tests on the customers' machines, and preserving existing data and configuration settings. The unpacking of files and each of the other steps could be done, one at a time, by the customer. However, it's often more convenient to run a single installation program and have it perform all of the different steps. "Installation Tools," later in this chapter, describes some tools that can produce such installation programs, or *installers*.

> **NOTE**
>
> How an installation program actually packages a product's files is mostly irrelevant to the customer, though many installers do use one of the packaging formats described in this section. When you click on *setup.exe* for a Windows installer, you neither know nor really care how the files are actually packaged and compressed within the installer. However, if there is no separate installation program, then you will need to know how to extract the product's files from a particular packaging format.

The first guideline to follow when choosing a packaging format for your product is to use the most common format for each platform and language. Windows packages commonly use WinZip, Unix packages often use *tar* and then *gzip* or *bzip2*, and Java products are often distributed as JAR files. Red Hat Linux uses *rpm* files, Debian uses *deb* files, and some other GNU/Linux distributions have their own packaging formats. Since many products are downloaded rather than read from a CD or DVD, compressing the package before releasing it is a normal part of releasing a product.* Quite often, a build tool that is favored for a particular language will also support the most common packaging format for that language. For example, Ant is used to build many Java products and can also generate JAR files.

Unix

The original packaging format is the one used by *tar*, a tape archive program that dates back to the early days of Unix. To create an archive, or *tarball*, each file has an ASCII

---

* The days of using 1.44MB floppy disks for installers have passed at last. Creating installers that would fit on those disks—often breaking them up into a dozen or more disk images—was a pain for everyone concerned. "Please insert disk 14 of 20," indeed.

header with information about the file prefixed to it, and each header refers to the next file in the archive. Each header also includes a CRC (cyclic redundancy check) to ensure that corrupted headers are detected. If all the files in an archive are ASCII, then the whole *tar* archive is also ASCII.

Older *tar* files had limits on filename length (Solaris *tar* still does, apparently), but newer versions do not. *tar* is most commonly used with a compression program such as *gzip* or *bzip2* to produce compressed *.tar.gz* (alternatively, *.tgz*) or *.tar.bz2* files, respectively. These compression programs are often fully integrated with *tar* nowadays, so creating a compressed *tar* file is done with a single command. By default, a *tar* file preserves the directory hierarchy and the permissions of the files inside it. However, there is no support in *tar* itself for cryptographically signing the generated *tar* files. Another problem with the *tar* format is that extracting individual files is slow, since all the links in the file headers have to be followed until the correct file is found. Although *tar* was originally Unix-based, some Windows tools such as WinZip can now also unpack *tar* archives.

> **NOTE**
> When *tar* and *bzip2* fail, the most common reason is an incomplete
> download or a lack of space to decompress the files, not corrupted files
> in the archive. Obvious, but well worth remembering.

Two other packaging formats are also encountered on Unix systems: *cpio* and *pax*. *cpio* (*http://www.gnu.org/software/cpio/manual*) is intended more for system backups. *pax* (which may stand for "portable archive exchange") is designed to combine the strengths of *tar* and *cpio*. A good introduction to *pax* can be found at *http://www.onlamp.com/pub/a/bsd/2002/08/22/FreeBSD_Basics.html*. Both *cpio* and *pax* can read *tar* archives. Though they are almost unheard of nowadays, you may come across *shar* archives, perhaps in old postings to USENET. These are simply shell scripts that unpack the files embedded within them.

Other common packaging formats for GNU/Linux are Red Hat's *rpm* (*http://rpm.org*) and Debian's *deb* (*http://www.debian.org/doc/FAQ/ch-pkg_basics.en.html*), which both add more information to the package formats so that the installers that use them can track which files were installed from various packages by using a local database. Internally, *rpm* uses *cpio* archives and *deb* uses *gzip*-compressed *tar* archives. Both formats can contain the binary executables or the source files for a package. An extensive comparison of the differences between *rpm*, *deb*, and *gzip*'d *tar* files can be found at *http://kitenet.net/~joey/pkg-comp*. A handy tool for checking that *rpm*s are correctly constructed is *rpmlint*, which used to be found at *http://people.mandrakesoft.com/~flepied/projects/rpmlint*.

Windows

While there are versions of *tar* for most platforms, the most common packaging format for Windows is *zip*, a freely documented format from PKWARE (*http://www.pkware.com*), which also sells applications such as PKZip to create *zip* archives. Other Windows tools such as WinZip (*http://www.winzip.com*) and 7-Zip (*http://www.7-zip.org*) also work with the *zip* format. Some of these tools can extract files from many other packaging formats as well. Info-ZIP (*http://www.info-zip.org*) is an open source, highly portable *zip* tool that runs on both Windows and Unix. Note that *zip* is not related to the compression utility *gzip*.

WARNING
By default, unzipping an archive with WinZip converts any directory names that are entirely uppercase to all lowercase, though there is an option for disabling this overhelpful behavior.

JAR, the standard packaging format for Java products, is an extension of the *zip* format, with optional signing and versioning abilities. Some of these extensions were later added to the *zip* format after JAR was defined. You can also use *jar* to zip and unzip *zip* files.

Installation Tools

The previous section described the various file formats that can be used to release a collection of files (i.e., a *package*). This section describes *installation tools*, which are the tools that create *installers*, which are the programs (and their datafiles) that actually run on the customers' machines. Installers not only unpack and decompress the files from whatever package file format was used; they also perform all the other steps necessary to make the product work on each machine. Table 9-1 shows some of the different ways to install software, along with examples.

TABLE 9-1. Different ways to install software

Package contents	Installation tool	Installer
Source code	Packaging tool such as *tar* or WinZip	Run a build tool such as *make* (e.g., many open source projects).
		Run a custom build script (e.g., some Perl applications).
Compiled files		Unpack the executables (e.g., *.exe* files in a self-extracting *zip* archive).
	Packaging tool such as *rpm*	Unpack the files and execute other commands, using an already installed application (e.g., *rpm*).
	Specialized installation tool such as InstallShield	Run the programs that were shipped with the compiled files (e.g., most commercial software).
Platform-independent compiled files	Packaging tool such as *jar*	Unpack the files and execute other commands, using an already installed application (e.g., JVM).

NOTE
Installation tools can be thought of as specialized build tools: both kinds of tools take a description of what needs to be built, including where to find the files for the build, and both can produce executable programs. Both kinds of tools need to show you what they did, and you need to be able to debug both the tool and whatever is finally produced by the tool.

In the same way that each different kind of machine requires a different set of actions to install software on it, so too do different installation tools exist for building installers for each platform. One installation tool builds Windows executables, while another builds *rpm* packages for a GNU/Linux distribution. The Java-based tool InstallAnywhere generates multiplatform installers from a single specification, but this tool seems to be used mostly for creating installers for products written in Java.

Requirements

When evaluating an installation tool, be careful to distinguish between what the installation tool should do and what the installers that it produces should be able to do. For instance, you may want to produce installers that have Japanese text, but do you also need the installation tool to be localized for Japanese?

Just as some projects choose to write their own build tool, some projects create their own installation tools. This does have the advantage that the source code for the tool can be reviewed and tested as exhaustively as the rest of the product. However, this approach is a substantial amount of overhead for most projects, so carefully consider the existing tools first.

Tools

Some desirable characteristics of installation tools are:

Small, fast, repeatable
Just like a compiler, an installation tool should not produce overly large installers; it should run as fast as possible; and the resulting files should be the same each time the tool is used.

Portable
The configuration files for the installation tool should be portable to other machines, and ideally to other platforms. Absolute pathnames should not be part of the description of an installer. If the description of the installers are in a text-based format, this makes comparison easier.

Debuggable
Debugging how an installation tool creates an installer and debugging what an installer did when it ran are both tasks to consider when deciding how easy it is to work with each installation tool. The ability to simulate running an installer can also ease its development effort. Installer debugging logfiles should contain line numbers, timing information, and other descriptions of each part of the installation tool as it was executed.

Automated
Integrating the installation tool with an automated build process should be possible, by using a command-line version of the tool, for example. This includes signing packages.

Multilingual
An installation tool should be able to produce installers that are localized for different languages while running on a nonlocalized machine. In other words, you could use a

machine with an English operating system to produce Japanese and German installers, as well as producing English installers.

Produces installers for updates

The installation tool should be able to produce installers to update products that have already been installed. Making customers uninstall a previous version of your product is ugly, and once they've uninstalled your product, they might install someone else's product instead. Some installation tools can produce installers that can be used to check periodically for updates over the Internet.

Supports different media

You should be able to create an installer suitable for download from a web site, as well as an installer for releasing on CDs or DVDs. The installation tool should be able to put the different files onto multiple CDs or DVDs in such an order that the most common installation sequences never require the customer to reinsert a disk.

Flexible

A good installation tool can be extended to do things during an install that no one imagined when the tool was designed. Sometimes this is done with a scripting language.

Stable

Beware of the ability to automatically update the installation tool; such updates can make it hard to be sure which version was used for each product. You should update only when you have chosen to, not just because the tool prompts you to update. This feels like an installation tool just demonstrating that it can create an installer for itself that checks for updates.

Installers

Some characteristics to look for in installers and uninstallers, no matter which platform or packaging format is used, are:

Simple

The main purpose of an installer is to make a product work correctly on a customer's machine and to do this as simply as possible. This means that wherever possible, the installer should run tests (rather than asking the user questions) and then copy the product's files to the right places on the machine. Anything other than major product configuration can be done by the user after the install has finished, including entering license keys.

Atomic

A failed installation should remove all traces that it was ever there. Leftover files can make subsequent installations fail in obscure and hard-to-debug ways.

Provides an installation summary

Before making any changes to the machine, the installer should show at least the product's name and version, where it will be installed, how much space it will take up, and any other useful configuration details.

Supports unattended installs

System administrators installing your product on numerous machines will want two things: the ability to install it with no input, and the ability to customize the installer (for instance, by adding other, unrelated packages). The first can be supported by reading responses from a text file or even by using Expect (*http://expect.nist.gov*). For silent installs, the user should also be able to redirect all output from the installer to a file. Many installation tools are able to create installers for this kind of unattended install, but customization is less commonly supported.

Some smaller, but helpful ideas for graphical installers are:

- A map of where you are in the install, and some indication of how much longer the installation should take

- Go Back buttons, to let you return to previous screens and change the choices that you made there

- An option to restore the default choices on a screen

Unix

Installer programs for Unix have become more common since the 1990s, with the rise of GNU/Linux and CPAN for Perl modules. The lack of standard locations for key files on a Unix machine means that you always have to be aware of how each machine is configured, and so installation using source code is more common in Unix than on Windows machines. I'd like to report that Unix configurations have become more standard and that there was an obvious installation manager to choose, but I can't. I recommend using the default installation tools that already exist on your machine and then trying others if and when they fail. Using packages from a single source may help your installations to succeed more often.

Source code and binaries

The source code to your product can be distributed using one of the packaged formats discussed in "Packaging Formats," earlier in this chapter. They're easy to create and, if the customer has the right tool, easy to unpack. The packaged files may contain ready-built binaries for each platform or, more commonly in the case of open source products, the actual source code itself.

There are de facto standards for files to help customers complete the installation of the product after unpacking it. There are files such as *README* (start here first), *LICENSE* or *COPYING* (legal stuff), *HACKING* (how to change the source code), and the vital *INSTALL* file, which usually tells you how to actually use the product. Build tools such as GNU Autotools (see "GNU Autotools" in Chapter 5) provide help with creating such files. Another, much more formal standard is the Linux Standard Base (LSB; see *http://www.linuxbase.org*), which describes what to expect from a standard GNU/Linux machine.

Installing products from their source files is probably the most portable way to install software onto a wide variety of Unix platforms. When the more convenient *rpm* or *deb* packages fail to work, or when you want to know why the product isn't supported on your platform, it's time to "use the source, Luke."

RPM package manager

The Red Hat distribution of GNU/Linux is responsible for creating the *rpm* format and its companion installation tool (also named *rpm*), which now ships with each copy of Red Hat Linux. Various products were repackaged in the *rpm* format for Red Hat, and web sites such as *rpmfind* (*http://rpmfind.net*) grew up to help find RPMs for each package. *rpm* maintains a database on the local machine to track every package that has been installed, and it's relatively easy to use. However, if an installation fails because other packages have to be installed first, *rpm* simply leaves you with the name of the missing packages, and it's back to *rpmfind* you go—there is no automatic downloading of other required packages.

In an attempt to make the whole process of installing and upgrading packages a little easier, Red Hat created *up2date*, an application with both command-line and graphical interfaces, to download and install not only packages you specify, but also those required by your specified packages. However, *up2date* requires that you sign up on the Red Hat Network and register your machine and its current configuration.

Other choices for *rpm*-based installation managers are Yum (*http://linux.duke.edu/projects/yum*), which is becoming the de facto standard for RedHat, and *apt4rpm* (*http://apt4rpm.sourceforge.net*), which is a version of *apt* for *rpm*s by Conectiva, the Brazilian GNU/Linux distribution (now part of Mandrakesoft). Both of these installers can create their own package databases from the local *rpm* one, use signatures, and download any other necessary packages. One installation manager that claims to handle conflicts better than all others is the Python-based Smart Project Manager (*http://smartpm.org*), developed by Gustavo Niemeyer, who was part of the team that created *apt4rpm*.

> **NOTE**
> To unpack the contents of the *rpm* file *myproject-1.0.0-i586.rpm* into a fresh directory, simply type:
>
> ```
> rpm2cpio project-1.0.0-i586.rpm | cpio -i --make-directories
> ```

apt

Debian Linux's *deb* packaging format also has its companion installation tool named *dpkg*, but the installer tool that is more frequently used is *apt* (Advanced Packaging Tool), which has always supported downloading the dependent packages needed to make an install succeed. *apt*'s other advantage over *rpm* is that it uses benchmark systems to determine which versions of software should work best on your system. One GUI for *apt* is *synaptic*, but there are a number of others available.

apt has also been made to work with *rpm*s in a few different ways. The tool *apt4rpm* (*http://apt4rpm.sourceforge.net*) is a version of *apt* for *rpm*s. There is also *alien* (*http://www.kitenet.net/programs/alien*), which is a package converter that can convert between *rpm, deb*, and several other package formats, allowing you to use *deb* packages like *rpm* packages, and *rpm* packages like *deb* packages.

CPAN

CPAN (Comprehensive Perl Archive Network) is a good example of a successful installer, though only for products in one language: Perl. The command-line interface for using CPAN is straightforward, and there are plenty of graphical interfaces available too. The modules are downloaded as *gzip*'d tarballs of source code and built locally using *make*. Any other missing modules can also be automatically downloaded. CPAN uses a worldwide collection of mirror sites, all containing the same packages.

The strengths of CPAN are that the range of modules is enormous and that it is a focal point for the Perl community. It has scaled well with a large number of users and is one reason for the popularity of Perl. The main weakness is that all of the modules are developed independently, so you may end up with long installation chains (see "Installation Irritations—Ship Happens!" later in this chapter) or with two different modules needing different versions of another module.

Windows

Some good resources for lists of mainly Windows-related installation tools are the Open Directory category at *http://dmoz.org/Computers/Software/System_Management/Installers* and InstallSite (*http://www.installsite.org/pages/en/msi/authoring.htm*), which is a web site dedicated to Windows installers and to InstallShield in particular.

Windows Installer

Windows Installer is the name of the installation toolset that has been released with all Windows releases since Windows ME. Now at Version 3.0, Windows Installer produces MSI files that can be executed to behave as an installer. The benefits of Windows Installer include atomic installs, add/remove program integration, checking for files in use, and full support for automatic reboots. If you want your product to be compliant with the Microsoft Windows Logo program (*http://www.microsoft.com/winlogo*), then it has to be released as an MSI installer. This is one good reason why all the commercial installation tools now support MSI.

The main drawbacks of Windows Installer are its complexity and the size of the generated installers. Many of the restrictions imposed by earlier versions of the MSI SDK seem to have been fixed in the latest version.

One interesting installation tool is WiX (*http://sourceforge.net/projects/wix*), which is used by Microsoft internally to create MSI files. WiX uses XML for its configuration files. There is an overview available at *http://www.ondotnet.com/pub/a/dotnet/2004/04/19/wix.html*.

InstallShield

InstallShield from Macrovision (*http://www.installshield.com*) is probably the most commonly used commercial installation tool. InstallShield is also one of the oldest such tools. It costs $2,499 for the top-level edition. Earlier configurations were not stored in XML, but they were mostly in text files. You can build installers for a number of different platforms, but most InstallShield installers appear to be for Windows. Available in English, German, and Japanese, InstallShield can produce installers in over 30 different languages. It has integrated support for Visual SourceSafe and a huge range of other features, which explains the large number of choices on every screen of the UI.

Simple projects are easy enough to create using the wizards that come with the tool, but larger ones can require some time to get right. The installer debugger and the binary install logs in *C:\Program Files\InstallShield Installation Information* can help you greatly with this. There is a list of rather overpriced InstallShield books at InstallSite (*http://www.installsite.org/pages/en/books.htm*), along with a good community of users.

InstallAnywhere

InstallAnywhere from ZeroG (*http://www.zerog.com*), now also owned by Macrovision, is a good example of a newer type of installation tool, one that uses the platform-independent nature of Java for its installers. The cost for the top-level edition is $2,999. InstallAnywhere installers are specified using XML configuration files created by a nicely uncluttered UI. Almost any platform that has a JRE (Java Runtime Environment) is supported, both for the installation tool and for the installers that it creates, so creating installers for many platforms is faster than usual. InstallAnywhere is focused on releasing Java applications; it has a documented API so you can call it from other Java applications and it even has an Ant task for creating installers. The tool is available in English, German, French, and Japanese.

When you run an InstallAnywhere installer, it communicates very clearly what it is doing. There is a list of steps to show you what stage the install is in, and there are thoughtful buttons to restore choices on a page after you have messed around with them and forgotten what their original values were. The summary page that is shown after the installer has gathered all the information it needs, but before the install begins, is quite thorough.

> **NOTE**
>
> To enable extensive logging in debug mode when you run an installer, press and hold Ctrl on Windows or set the environmental variable LAX_DEBUG to true.

The disadvantage of all this portability is that the customer has to have a JRE on his machine to use the installers that are generated by InstallAnywhere. This is hardly unlikely if the final application is a Java application, but it can be a hindrance to installation. InstallAnywhere does let you bundle a JRE together with the installer, but of course this makes the installer much larger.

Wise for Windows

Wise for Windows from Altiris (*http://www.wise.com*) is the other commercial installation tool that seems to be most commonly used. The top-level edition retails for $1,999. There is a comparison of Wise for Windows and InstallShield at *http://www.installsite.org/pages/en/msi/comparison.htm*, and there are some more technical tips at *http://www.ewall.org/ContentExpress-display-ceid-8.html*. Most reviews comparing InstallShield and Wise for Windows seem to feel that the two tools are roughly comparable in what you get (both good and bad) for your money.

InnoSetup

InnoSetup (*http://www.jrsoftware.org/isinfo.php*) is an open source installation tool by Jordan Russell. It has an active community and some enthusiastic users. However, InnoSetup runs only on Windows, produces installers only for Windows, and does not use the MSI installer format provided by Windows. There is good support for installers in languages other than English, and indeed a single installer can be run using many different languages. Since the tool is written in Delphi, Pascal is used to write any scripts that are executed by installers, but the UI is clear and a script debugger is nicely integrated into it. The documentation is concise, and there are a number of third-party tools built on top of InnoSetup. One well-known project that uses InnoSetup for its Windows releases is Subversion (see "Subversion" in Chapter 4).

NSIS

NSIS (Nullsoft Scriptable Install System) from *http://nsis.sourceforge.net* is another open source installation tool that runs only on Windows and produces installers only for Windows. Originally developed by Joost Verburg for the WinAmp music player, its claim to fame is that it adds only 34KB of overhead, so its installers are almost as small as possible. Like InnoSetup, it doesn't use MSI, so you can't create installers that are Windows Logo–compliant. NSIS is used by a number of low-cost products, including Google's Gmail Notifier (*http://toolbar.google.com/gmail-helper*).

Installation Irritations—Ship Happens!

Some common issues with installations from the project's point of view are:

Testing installs
> Testing installs is hard since a single installer can change the entire environment of the machine on which it was run, and can do this in ways that are hard to revert. One approach that can help is to use Norton Ghost, *g4u* (Ghost for Unix), or VMware to create copies of the system software, and to restore the machine's original state after each test install.
>
> Automating the process of testing installs is also hard because many products' installers are GUI driven, and it's also complicated to determine whether an install really succeeded or failed.

Testing localization

Ideally, you want to test every localized installer on an appropriately localized machine. This problem grows linearly as you support your product in more languages, and automating this is hard.

Automating installer creation

Automation of the installation tool as part of a release process, to create the installers for the product, is also tricky. Command-line use of installation tools often doesn't seem to have had the same amount of testing as the GUI versions of the same tools.

Installing third-party products

Bundling other products with your own product in the same installer is a common requirement, since it makes installations simpler for customers. Simply invoking other installers from within your installer is not very elegant, since the same questions may be asked of the customer over and over again. Catching broken installs and uninstalling other products is also hard. Some of Microsoft's products provide versions of themselves ("merge modules") that other installation tools can integrate into their own installers.

Some irritations that customers often find with products' installers are:

Installation chains

If you know what other software is already on the machine that the installer was created for, then you can bundle everything that your product needs into one installer. This is often the case for products for Windows. For products for Unix, especially open source products, the chain of other software that also has to be installed is daunting to many customers. Sometimes the chains turn into circles, or fail frustratingly when you are six levels deep.

Inappropriate privileges

Why should a user have to be root to install a package to her own Unix home directory? Why should your child need to have Windows administrator privileges just to install a simple game? Too many products assume they have to be installed as the superuser on a machine when they don't really need to be.

Corrupted installers

Adding a virus or trojan horse to a publicly available installer is a classic approach for infecting other machines. Consequently, making sure the installer you released is what customers actually download and run is going to become even more important. I think that signed packages and installers will become a requirement for all platforms, just as they are now for embedded Windows devices.

Uninstallers

How does a customer know that uninstalling your product won't damage some other vital part of his system? Just as installers describe what they are going to do before they do it, thus giving customers a chance to cancel the installation if they're not comfortable about something, so uninstallers should provide detailed information about what they are going to change. Cryptic messages like "Couldn't remove all the files" are really irritating—they could at least say which files, and why they couldn't be removed!

Lost data

No data generated by someone using your product should ever be deleted, even if she unwisely stored it in the same directory where the product was installed; all customer data is sacred. This data includes how the customer configured your product.

Multiple versions

Make it very clear before an installer actually changes anything whether two versions of the same product can coexist on the same machine. If not, then explain how the customer would be able to restore the previous version if there are problems with the version currently being installed. If this can't be done, then the customer may need two machines, one for production use and one for development and testing new versions of various tools.

After the Release

Once a release has shipped and the project team has celebrated and been given suitable mementos, stock options, cash bonuses, and vacations in Hawaii, what comes next? If it was Version 1.0 and all goes well, then more people will be using the release than any beta version, so they will probably be finding more bugs. You may want to plan early for a 1.1 patch release soon after your 1.0 release date—such are the vicissitudes of producing software.

Even if you have confidence that you have recorded everything necessary using an SCM tool, most people still prefer to preserve the actual source tree that was used to produce the release. This is partly a defensive move in case the SCM tool fails in some way, but it also helps you cope with unforeseen questions about the build later on (for example, "Was file *A* built before file *B*?").

The first step in preserving the build is to make the files read-only. One way to do this is to change the file permissions. Another way is to copy the files to a CD or DVD and then make that copy available online when requested. *rsync* is a standard Unix tool that can create a mirror image of the files on another machine for backups. Norton Ghost or the open source *g4u* are useful for preserving the entire contents of a hard disk when parts of the environment are not being managed by an SCM tool.

It's a good idea to create a build-preservation policy, clearly summarized somewhere public. This will avoid making one up on the spot when you start to run out of space to store the releases. (This is also discussed in "Cleaning Up Your Environment" in Chapter 10.) I recommend keeping all customer releases and internal releases that had bugs filed against them available, and deleting all other releases older than a few weeks or months. The reasoning for removing internal releases that have no bugs is that it's unlikely that they will ever have any bugs. Enough generated files should be kept with each release to permit the use of debuggers. If non-debug versions are released to customers, then keeping both the non-debug and debug versions of the build is helpful for this.

Another task that may be necessary after a release is to prepare the source code and development environment to be placed in escrow. This is to protect customers in the event that your company goes out of business, in which case the source code to the product is released to them so that they can maintain it as they feel the need to.

Checklist

This section contains a short list of questions that you should feel comfortable answering about your own release process:

- What's the next version number that your product will use? Who decides when it's time to make a change to each part of the version number?

- Where do you go to find the latest public release of your product?

- How large is the latest release of your product? Which part of the product creates most of the files that you deliver to your customers?

- What other software does your product depend on, and which versions?

- If your product needs license keys, where do you obtain these? How do customers obtain them? How long does it take for a customer to obtain a new license key?

- What kinds of changes are allowed in a patch release? In a minor release? In a major release?

- Which versions of your product will operate correctly with each previous version of your product? How does a customer know this?

- Are a customer's data and configuration choices preserved when she upgrades your product?

- Can a customer downgrade your product to an earlier version?

- What's different between how developers run the product, how testers run the product, and how customers actually install and use the product? Have these differences been the root cause of any recent bugs?

- If your product is available on the Internet, how does a customer prove that his downloaded package contains the same bits that you released?

- What help do you have in your product for supporting it once it has been released? Can a customer easily display installation and configuration information, along with the results of any diagnostic tests? Can you use this as part of a phone call or in email?

- How many releases can your group really work on at the same time?

## CHAPTER TEN

Maintenance

In the long run every program becomes rococo, and then rubble.

—*Alan Perlis*
"Epigrams in Programming"
ACM SIGPLAN, September 1982

THIS CHAPTER DESCRIBES HOW TO MAINTAIN A DEVELOPMENT ENVIRONMENT and what causes development environments to change. Maintenance of software products is then discussed, along with some typical maintenance tasks and how maintaining a product is affected by each part of a development environment. The final section examines planned removal of things such as files and SCM tags that have been generated while creating products.

Maintaining an Environment

The useful life of the tools that make up a development environment is generally much longer than the life of the products that were created using the environment. No one wants to have to use a different bug tracking tool or a new build tool for every different release of the product. However, environments and their tools do age with time, and as tools are replaced with other tools, the environment gradually changes. The environment that you wrote code in 10 years ago is not the same one that you use now—even Emacs and *vi* have changed in that time. It's also probably faster now than it was back then.

What's important is that older tools and their environment still have to be maintained until all the products that were developed with them are no longer supported. It's very frustrating to spend time learning about an older version of a product and making changes to the source code, only to find that you're unable to build and test that version, or that something else has changed in the environment and now you have to spend time working out what it was.

Part of maintaining an environment is checking that the versions of the tools that you use are still supported. Using the latest version of any tool is somewhat risky, but is acceptable if the tool does just what you need it to. However, beware of the total amount of time that can be spent upgrading to every new version of a tool.

WHY DO TOOLS ROT?

Code rot is a casual way of describing what happens when a piece of source code is not regularly maintained. As the source code around it gradually changes, that piece of code eventually stops working or, even more annoyingly, causes bugs to spontaneously appear in the product. A similar kind of decay called *tool rot* occurs with development environments when tools are not used for a while and then don't work when you want to use them.

There are at least five common reasons why tools stop working properly when development environments change:

Operating system changes
> A tool may work with only certain versions of an operating system. If a developer's machine is upgraded to a newer version of the operating system, then this may prevent older versions of the product that still use the tool from being built.

Command-line argument and API changes
> If the arguments passed to a tool change in number or order, or the API to the tool changes in some other way, then the tool may not work properly in older environments.

Data format changes
> If the format of the data given to a tool for input (or expected from a tool as output) is changed, then the tool may stop working properly, or may create hard-to-detect errors in the data when used in older environments.

Licenses
> You may simply not realize that a license key for a tool has expired, especially if the tool is part of an infrequently used older version of your environment.

Mergers and acquisitions
> When companies or projects join forces, their development environments usually undergo large changes. The best tools should win, but sometimes the survivors are those that are used by the largest number of people, or that it would take the most effort to migrate data from.

The remedy for tool rot is to regularly use the older environment. Changing either the environment and tools or the product's use of the tools, but not both at the same time, will also help you avoid tool rot.

The more common case is environments that are set up but never maintained until some key tool stops working. Then the pressure to solve the problem, along with the ensuing discussions about fixing or replacing the tool, can greatly distract people from developing the actual product. Instead, it's far better to regularly monitor all the tools that are used, and to maintain a sense of the effort and cost to make particular changes to your environment. You can then decide whether to postpone upgrades and deal with the inevitable crises, or to spend the time to gradually upgrade tools before they break. Also, mistakes happen and priorities change in a project. If you have a good understanding of the costs of changing the environment's tools, then you're better placed to deal with these unplanned changes.

Some estimated life spans of different kinds of tools in a typical small to medium-sized project are shown in Table 10-1. These are the times before the tool is replaced with an entirely new tool, not just the intervals between upgrades. The values are subjective, based on my own experience and observations about when the larger open source projects have changed the tools in their development environments over the past 15 years.

TABLE 10-1. Typical tool life spans

Tool	Life span (years)
SCM tool	5–10
Build tool	8–15
Test environment	3–6
Bug tracking system	3–5
Documentation environment	5–10

Ideally, a development environment's own SCM tool should be able to track all the changes in the development environment, including changes to the SCM tool itself. In practice, many of the tools used in an environment are inconveniently large for tracking with existing SCM tools. Operating systems can be checked in to SCM tools but they rarely are, for just this reason. In this case, making copies of the important disks, CDs, and DVDs is appropriate. Another approach that's quicker when you want to reproduce an environment later on is to use Norton Ghost, *g4u*, or VMware to create copies of key machines, and then to store those copies elsewhere.

Even if the original files for the tools themselves are too large for your SCM tool, you can use files that describe the environment, and these files can be controlled using your SCM tool. One approach is to use a collection of files named the *environment documents*. Some of these files are updated by hand (for example, when processes and policies change). Other files can be automatically updated—for instance, if the build tool generates a list of tools used and their versions. This is also a good place to record the location of copies of large tools.

Another aspect of a development environment that needs to be regularly maintained is the test environment, since making changes in an older environment is doubly hard if you don't have the same test environment that was originally used. Just as with the current environment, it's important to be able to use both development and production machines in an older environment.

Migrating Your Data

The purpose of many tools such as SCM tools and bug tracking systems is to make stored information easily accessible. Part of maintaining an environment is migrating data from one tool to another as you change which tools are in active use.

Good practice with data is to use well-defined and open (i.e., license-free) file formats. Structured ASCII text, XML, and Ogg Vorbis for audio are all examples of open formats.

Before adding data in whatever format a specific tool uses, you should ask yourself how you could extract the data in the future. Many tools such as Microsoft Word use proprietary formats that only tools from the creator can fully understand. This is, of course, part of the sales strategy for such tools: if you can't extract your files and data from the tool, you are locked in to the tool and can be forced to pay for upgrades, generating more income for the product. The simple test of how easy it will be to migrate away from a tool is to search the tool's documentation for "export" and "Save As." Count the number of different formats that are supported and compare this to the number of different data formats that the tool can import. The numbers should be about equal.

Data migration is one part of defining an exit strategy for the tools in your environment. You can't define the tools that you will use five years from now, but you can make it easier to change to those tools when you have to.

What Is Product Maintenance?

One simple definition is that it's everything that comes after the first release, whether adding new functionality or fixing bugs. It's certainly true that for many products much of the code is written for that first release and then never drastically changed, unless it's eventually discarded for a completely different set of files. Another way to define maintenance is that for many companies and projects, all releases except the next one—the one that is still to come—are in maintenance mode. This includes any version of the product that is actually in use by customers.

Being in maintenance mode usually means that fewer people and resources are assigned to that version of the product, and sometimes these are the less experienced or less expensive people and resources. There are fewer and less-frequent changes committed to the source code, and there are quite likely fewer builds. Less effort is spent testing, so fewer bugs are found, at least by the developers and official testers. In the maintenance phase, bugs are reported mostly by customers.

Figure 10-1 shows some estimated life spans of typical software products; note that products spend most of their life in maintenance. For example, if a short-lived product has one major release each year, and each major release is expected to have a useful life of at least three years by the time everyone has upgraded from it, then two-thirds of its life span is spent in maintenance. The amount is about the same for long-lived products.

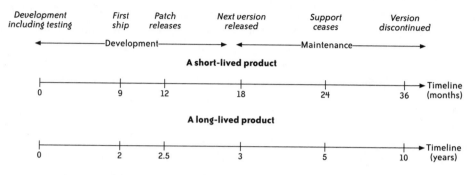

FIGURE 10-1. Life spans of typical products

Since so much of a product's lifetime is spent being maintained, it's worthwhile seeing how a development environment can help with it.

Developing for Easier Maintenance

How to write code is not the main focus of this book, but here are a few suggestions for making your source code easier to maintain. The next section, "Product Maintenance Tasks," also discusses tools and books that can help when it comes to understanding code.

- Remember that source code is a communication from human to human, as well as from human to machine.

- The less code there is, the less there is to maintain. Eliminate all commented-out code and code surrounded with the ugly `#ifdef NOTDEF` directive. It's still in the SCM tool if you need it later. If it's code for logging or debugging, use a proper framework for these, not ad hoc commented-out code.

- Avoid or clearly document functions and methods that need to be called in a certain order or that should not be called more than once. Treat functions with side effects with great caution; avoid writing them if at all possible.

- Describe the current implementation before you change it. This helps to make the changes clear for you, and it's useful as a reminder later on of how it all used to work.

Finally, consider why code rot occurs in your project. Perhaps it is due to particular changes that occur regularly or to individual practices by certain people. If you can see a pattern, then you may be able to change it.

Product Maintenance Tasks

This section describes some typical tasks that occur for products in maintenance mode and how the tools in the development environment can help with each task.

Understanding Code

Whether you wrote it or not, there's always a certain amount of time spent coming back up to speed on any piece of code. A good description of the key classes and methods or functions, or even a UML diagram, can go a long way here. Comments on how each class or header file is expected to be used, together with comments for each method or function and descriptions of their expected arguments, will also speed up your understanding.

There are some tools that can help with understanding legacy code. After *grep*, the simplest of these are *etags* and *cscope*, both of which generate information about source files that editors such as Emacs and *vi* can use to locate definitions and uses of keywords. Some editors, code browsers, and class navigators will analyze the structure of the product's source code and allow you to jump from one area to other connected areas. This is something that you should expect from any decent IDE.

Some of the more interesting tools are those that can help with *refactoring* a product. Refactoring is reorganizing source code so that it is easier to understand but behaves exactly as it did before being refactored. These tools often have a deeper understanding of programming languages than ordinary text editors, so they can do things such as rename a variable throughout a product; create a method from a section of code and insert a call to the new method; or add a new parameter to a method and also to all the places where the method is used. However, just as when you use a calculator instead of mental arithmetic, it's still important to know what the tool is really doing and to understand which cases it doesn't handle well. Currently, Java and .NET are the languages with the largest number of refactoring tools.

Tools such as Javadoc and *doxygen*, which are both described further in "Internal Project Documentation" in Chapter 8, can produce documentation about each part of the source code. *doxygen* is particularly useful for showing the call graphs—that is, which methods call which other methods. Schema analysis for relational databases is another area where automated tools can help you understand what an existing product does.

In the end, however, understanding a complex system is a subjective thing. I've even seen people tape printouts of code to a large wall and color-code different lines by hand. There are a number of other approaches to and ideas about reading code on the Wiki page at *http://c2.com/cgi/wiki?TipsForReadingCode*. One book with an extensive pattern-based approach to understanding source code is *Object Oriented Reengineering Patterns*, by Serge Demeyer, Stephane Ducasse, and Oscar Nierstrasz (Morgan Kaufmann). Another book, which has excellent step-by-step descriptions of how to understand and change existing products, is *Working Effectively with Legacy Code*, by Michael Feathers (Prentice Hall). A book with a much less formal approach, but still with many practical observations, is *Software Exorcism: A Handbook for Debugging and Optimizing Legacy Code*, by "Reverend" Bill Blunden (APress).

Reproducing a Build

Often the first thing to be done when maintaining a product is to reproduce a particular build, whether for debugging or for adding functionality. Actually, if you are just trying to understand a particular bug or debug a core file, you may well be able to use the read-only version of the build's source files and its generated files, if they have been kept (see "After the Release" in Chapter 9). Still, if the bug involves anything more than changing a configuration, you will probably need to be able to reproduce the build yourself to fix it.

This is when you get to discover whether your toolsmith really did save everything that you needed, either with your SCM tool or by copying it elsewhere. Comparing the files generated by your own build to those from a known build is a useful technique for finding out what changed and whether the changes were expected. Of course, dates and usernames may have changed, but sometimes it's worth using tools such as *diff* and *od* (a Unix tool for octal dumps) to compare the generated files at the bit level. Once you know that you have accurately reproduced the build, you can make your changes with a much greater level of confidence.

Handling Product Name Changes

> After the product hath been released once or twice, a new marketing direction shall arise and require a different name for the product. And lo, Engineering shall wail and gnash their teeth, for they did hardcode that name in many, many places.
>
> *—Book of Lessons Learned the Hard Way*

Product name changes are something to expect right from the moment when you are first developing the product. An internal project name chosen by engineering, not by marketing, should be used for things such as directories, filenames, documentation, and any other aspect of a project that is tedious to change. Ideally, the product name should be stored in one location in the source code, for just this sort of situation. This is doubly true for products that are localized for many languages. "Choosing Project Names" in Chapter 3 has some guidelines on choosing project names.

However, even with the wisest forethought, changing the name of a product can still be a tedious task. The first step is to make a global search, ignoring case, for the offending text in all the source code and configuration files. GUIs are particularly hard hit by such changes if their screen layouts are changed by the size of the product name. The actual global replacement of the name is usually straightforward enough using flexible tools such as Perl scripts. I strongly recommend doing a test run somewhere that you will be able to create a list of all the changes, for careful inspection. The easiest way to do this is to use the project's SCM tool.

Of course, product names creep into more than just source code. SCM labels, the names of build targets, bug tracking metadata, and documentation are all affected. Some of these will be easy enough to change, but others such as database field names are much more work. Images, such as screenshots used in documentation, will probably have to be inspected manaually. In general, each time you use a product name anywhere in the environment, consider what it would take to change that name later on.

Handling Company Name Changes

If your product is produced for a company, don't use the company name throughout the source code, except in boilerplate copyright text. Company names are part of marketing and do change over time with different marketing approaches. Company names also change when companies are bought or sold. This kind of change is particularly hard on Java applications because they tend to use the company's domain name as part of their Java package names (e.g., *example.com* and `com.example.myproduct`, respectively).

A more subtle form of company name change occurs when your company has a contract to produce a special version of your software for someone else, who is misleadingly known as the original equipment manufacturer (OEM). Depending on the agreement, you may have to remove your company's name from anything that the OEM's customers will see, including configuration files. So it's a good idea to define the current name of your company and the name of the vendor of the product as separate strings in your source code.

The mechanics of changing a company name are essentially the same as changing a product name (see the previous secton, "Handling Product Name Changes"). There may be more versions of the name—for instance, with "Ltd." and without "Ltd."—and there may be other variations on abbreviations such as "Inc" and "Inc." to deal with. Also, if the company name appears in copyright notices in source code, a new line with the new company name and the current date needs to be added, leaving the lines with the old company name and dates in place.

Handling Copyright Date Changes

Copyright law varies widely from country to country, and each software license has its own quirks, but a common requirement seems to be recording when it was that source code files were changed. SCM tools will readily tell you this information, but it seems that the years themselves have to be embedded in the source files. So most source files now have lines of text at the top of each file with comments such as:

```
Copyright © 2000-2005. Acme Corporation, Inc.
```

Whether or not this copyright notice is actually necessary (and I've heard different legal opinions), it persists. Then someone notices that the ending year (say 2005) is last year and she wants to update all instances of 2005 to 2006. A simple global replacement is fine, if you make sure that only actual copyright lines are changed and that no copyrights in third-party source code are modified. Usually someone else in the project then points out that only the files that really were changed in 2006 should be updated, which means that someone has to create a list of all files that have been modified in the last year. At least an SCM tool makes this relatively easy. To list all the files that were changed in a CVS repository in 2005, change to a top-level directory and type:

```
cvs -q log -NRS -d "01 Jan 2005 00:00:00<31 Dec 2005 23:59:59" .
```

If your machine is in a different time zone from the CVS server, then you may need to adjust the times to account for the difference between the time zones. Newer versions of CVS allow you to specify the time zone to be used with the log command.

Product Maintenance and Development Environments

This section discusses how maintaining a product is helped by each part of a development environment. The next section discusses the process of deleting things such as SCM tags, files from builds, test results, and documents.

SCM

The different parts of an SCM tool that particularly help with maintaining an existing product are:

Change logs
Change logs will show you exactly what has changed in a given version since it was last released. They're also good for finding the right people to talk to about the changes in that version, and deciding which areas of the product ought to be retested.

ACLs
Limiting who is permitted to make changes to a release branch should mean that the amount of change to it is limited, which should in turn reduce the amount of manual retesting that is needed later on.

Annotation
The ability to know who changed each line, and in which revision, makes it easier to understand the purpose of specific changes. This is a major feature for large open source projects, where the developers may never have actually met each other.

Removing unused files
Periodic sweeps through the source code to remove files that are entirely unused is safer when SCM tools are used.

What do you do if you find you didn't add everything that you needed to reproduce a build into the SCM tool? Perhaps some patches were applied to the operating system but not noted anywhere. Perhaps the compiler used was a particular version that's no longer available? The first thing to do is add the missing requirement to your environment documents (as introduced in "Maintaining an Environment," earlier in this chapter) and keep those documents under SCM control.

The second thing to do is revisit the precise checked-out source files that were used for the build, if they are still available (see "After the Release" in Chapter 9). Can you narrow down the effects of the unrecorded change? If you rebuild using a copy of these files and the current environment, which files are unchanged and which files are totally different? The next thing to do is find a machine that is unchanged since the time that the original build was created. Maybe the environment on that machine will give you some clues about what changed? Good luck, and remember to add the information that you do discover to your environment documents.

Building

After you've made changes as part of maintaining an older version of a product, automated builds for all the product's supported platforms can help to catch platform-specific errors quickly, before the changes become too distant in the collective memory of the group.

Automated builds also help to detect when changes to your development environment have broken your ability to recreate older builds. For instance, imagine that you make a change in the current version of your product and that the changed source code doesn't compile with the older version of the compiler used for a previous release. An automated build using the older environment can tell you about this explicitly, possibly even before you try to port the change back to the earlier version of the product. This gives you a clear understanding of which changes to the product make an older environment unusable.

Testing

Large numbers of automated unit and system tests are what most people want when they are maintaining a program. Tests for the new functionality are good, but knowing that you haven't just introduced bugs into a shipping product is even better. Of course, no test suite has 100% coverage or accuracy, so just because the automated tests pass cleanly doesn't mean you don't need to review the code changes and have other people confirm the test results and run manual tests.

The drawback of having large numbers of automated tests is that they increase the number of tests that have to be maintained. At least if you maintain the source code for the product and the tests that go with it at the same time, then the whole product gets changed at the same time. This is also a good argument for why unit tests should be built every time the product is built.

Bug Tracking

One of the most frustrating parts of maintaining a product is when a bug has to be fixed in multiple releases of a product. This is one place where a bug tracking system can help or hinder the maintenance effort. Sadly, tracking one bug in multiple releases is rarely done well by current bug tracking systems, as discussed in "One Bug, Multiple Releases" in Chapter 7.

Even if tracking a bug in different releases is not as clear as it could be, if your bug tracking system is integrated with your SCM tool, then you may be able to tell which releases a bug has been fixed in by looking at the precise file changes that are associated with the bug.

During maintenance, assigning priorities to bugs often seems to become harder—egos outside the project are now involved. On the other hand, there may be fewer bugs to deal with now that the release is in maintenance mode. Historical reports are just as useful with maintenance releases as with cutting-edge releases, especially if you can track how long it takes for bugs to get fixed. You may even be able to use this as a selling point for your product.

Documentation

Many different aspects of documentation need to be considered during maintenance. The original requirements documents may need to be updated if a change is not simply for a bug fix. Any major changes to the source code should be reflected in the source code's comments, especially comments that are no longer accurate after the change. The customer documentation for the product may also need to change as part of the maintenance change. Internal documentation may need to be regenerated after a change, though this is usually something done by the automation environment.

A bug that is associated with a particular change may contain text to appear in the release notes for the next release. It's helpful if all of these pieces of text can be assembled automatically from the bug tracking system into a release notes document. Many open source projects contain a file named *CHANGES* or *ChangeLog* that describes the changes made to a product in each release. There is a GNU standard for change logs as part of the coding standards at *http://www.gnu.org/prep/standards/standards.html#Change-Logs*.

People and Politics

People who write software are often neophiliacs ("lovers of the new") by nature, so getting their attention to help fix older bugs is hard. You may hear them say, "But that's already fixed in the latest version," which often implies, "You should upgrade to it and live with the possible presence of other, different bugs." Sadly, such a reply may also imply, "Fixing that bug in your version is a low priority for us because we don't make any money by fixing old versions of our software."

This tendency to neophilism can also lead to maintenance tasks being considered less prestigous within a project. To avoid this slur, some projects assign maintenance tasks to all members of the project, which makes particular sense if the original authors of the code are still present. Other long-standing projects have two teams that leapfrog over each other, with the team that maintains the oldest version of the product also developing the newest version when work on it begins.

Cleaning Up Your Environment

Part of maintaining a development environment is deciding when to throw things away. Taking out the trash isn't anyone's favorite chore; it usually gets ignored for as long as possible, and the bigger the trashcan, the worse it smells when you do finally take it out. This section discusses how you can make this chore less tedious by carefully planning it beforehand and then automating it as much as possible.

NOTE

Before deleting *any* file that took longer than an hour to generate, it's a good idea to compress and archive such files to CDs, DVDs, or backup tapes. If possible, do this yourself so that it's not a burden on an IT department. Then keep these archives in folders or boxes with something like "Discard after 2006" written on them.

SCM

The purpose of SCM tools is to store as much information about their contents as possible, so in some sense it's ironic that we have to clean them up. Storage space is finite, though this is rarely a problem unless you have many copies of binary files, or large files that differ greatly from each other. Backups are harder and take longer as repositories become very large, but that too can be dealt with as necessary. The real clutter in an SCM repository is actually dead branches and hundreds of dusty tags on files. This clutter can make it hard for people to see the changes of interest to them.

For a medium-sized project producing a few builds per week for testing purposes, some guidelines for removing tags and branches are:

- Most importantly, never remove a tag for a released version of the product, or a branch for a released version of the product.

- Remove tags for internal builds older than six builds (or two weeks) that have no bugs filed against them. If no one has used a particular build by then, they probably aren't ever going to.

- Lock private branches a month after the last change to them, or when their users have finally merged them into another branch.

- Archive and then delete private branches after two more releases of the product—if the changes on the branches haven't been used by then, the product has probably changed too much for those changes to still be useful.

There are projects that periodically remove all revisions of files except for the versions of files that are tagged. This seems extreme to me, since sometimes changes in developing source code are where the mistakes to be avoided in the future are recorded.

Builds

For internal builds, the ones that are used only for testing, keep the entire build directory with all its object files for the last two or three builds, if space permits. For builds older than that, you can most likely just keep the generated packages or executables and delete the object files and the source code used to produce the build.

If an internal build is older than six builds (or two weeks) and has no bugs filed against it, then that build can be removed entirely.

Testing

Just deleting the actual files related to the build doesn't mean that the build is gone, of course; it still exists as a tag in the SCM tool. Once the tag for a build has been removed, then the test results for that build can also be deleted.

Full-time testers quite often have personal storage space or databases allocated to them, and they may well create very large amounts of data while they run tests. The temptation is to keep everything because "the bug might reappear" or "a similar bug might reappear." One useful guideline here is to ask how long it would take to recreate the data if it were needed, and then to delete the largest files that are easiest to reproduce.

Bug tracking systems

"Cleaning Up" in Chapter 7 also discusses cleaning up bug tracking systems, but the most common kind of clutter is the labels for all the builds that different bugs appear in. Removing a choice from a drop-down box of builds should not change any bugs that already exist, though it may make it harder to modify existing bugs later on. Periodic scans of bug tracking systems for overly large attachments are also part of maintaining the tool.

Documentation

Documentation directories seem to be traditional areas where things are never thrown away. Consequently, they come to contain layer upon layer of unusable documents. One way to avoid this quagmire is to keep documents in formats that work well with your SCM tool, and to then store different versions of the documents using the SCM tool. Too many "documentation" files turn out to be copies of other documents, and then the copies diverge and neither can be deleted.

"Avoiding Content Rot" in Chapter 11 contains some ideas about how to avoid content rot on project web sites, and many of these ideas are applicable to the rest of a project's documentation.

Releases

The obvious rule for releases is never to delete anything that has ever been distributed to customers. Very old releases should certainly be archived; they should also be made unavailable, or harder to find, on your web site or FTP server. The download statistics for each release package come in handy for checking what is still used. "After the Release" in Chapter 9 has more suggestions about what to keep and what to discard from releases.

Something else that can take up a great deal of storage is files from customers, especially if the files include core dumps from crashed programs. Even text-based logfiles can be quite large sometimes. The most important thing is to be able to identify a bug or customer issue related to each file. Otherwise, you'll never know whether you can delete these files.

Files from customers can also contain sensitive information, so make sure you know who is allowed to access them, or scramble the sensitive parts without affecting the issue. This is another good reason to delete these files and their backed-up copies after a certain time.

People

Removing a person from a project doesn't mean rewriting history to make it seem that he never existed. Disabling his accounts, stopping access to the various tools in a development environment, removing him from email aliases, and redirecting his email should all be as automated as possible. The details of changes to source files, bugs, test results, and documentation should all keep the person's name, but all uses of his name as a contact within the project should be changed. If it isn't possible to remove the person's account without all references to him being removed too, perhaps his account can be renamed in some consistent way? Be careful to avoid reusing a username, though; for example, if two people named John Smith work on the same project at different times, use different usernames for each of them.

Documents, source code, and test definitions that contain the name of their current owner should be updated. Another place to make sure that the person's name is removed is any part of the project web site that refers to him as a contact for something. This can be avoided in the future by using email aliases such as *scm-admin*, *bug-admin*, and *build-admin* for different areas of the environment.

One subject that is rarely discussed is what to do when someone working on the source code dies, and you're the one who has to take over her code. All of the above guidelines for removing someone from a project still apply, but you may feel awkward when you come to change or delete her work. My suggestion is to put a memorial comment block in the code with an injunction to future developers not to remove it, ponder your own mortality for a while, and then move forward.

Checklist

This section contains a short list of questions to ask yourself about how your own development environment is maintained and also how your project's products are maintained:

- Who is responsible for deciding when tools or operating systems need to be upgraded or replaced?

- Who makes sure that new licenses are acquired for tools before the existing licenses expire or are exceeded?

- How much of your development environment can be controlled using your SCM tool? Can your SCM tool track changes to itself?

- How long does each release of your product last? How long is it supported by your project or company, and how long is it actually used by customers?

- Which areas of your product are the hardest ones to work on? Why? What could make them easier to maintain?

- Which parts of your product would you most like to refactor or rewrite? How do you know whether the time spent refactoring or rewriting them would actually make them easier for anyone else to maintain?

- What finite resources are used by your development environment? How long could you use your environment if nothing were ever discarded?

- Do you know who is permitted to make changes in product releases that are in maintenance mode?

- How confident are you that your unit and system tests let you know if your maintenance changes have broken something unexpectedly?

- How do you decide what to test in a maintenance release of your product?

- How do you know who to contact about each part of the product in earlier releases?

- Do you have processes defined for removing files, SCM tags, builds, test definitions and results, bug tracking information, and releases from your project?

## CHAPTER ELEVEN

Project Communication

**The speed of the project is proportional to the speed at which
information moves between people's heads.**

—Alistair Cockburn
The End of Software Engineering

THIS CHAPTER DISCUSSES HOW COMMUNICATION CAN BE IMPROVED WITHIN A PROJECT by using a
range of different tools, including web pages.

Imagine if all builds took no time at all and we all wrote perfect code. Then the limiting
factor in how long software takes to write would probably be how well the people in a
project communicated ideas with each other. Even back in the real world, where we all
have to wait for our builds and where bugs somehow spontaneously appear in our code,
poor communication in a project still wastes enormous amounts of everyone's time. Many
cases of poor communication are for complicated and emotional reasons, and when a
group of people don't want to communicate with each other about something, no mere
tool can make it happen. However, providing a group with different communication tools
can encourage them to communicate better.

Tools for Communication

Some of the most helpful tools for project communication have common characteristics. These characteristics are:

Easy to use
> If a tool is hard to use, people will use other tools instead. Obvious, but often overlooked.

Context
> Who is speaking? When did they speak? Who were they talking to? Without this kind of context, all communication becomes harder to understand.

Active and passive modes
> Sometimes you want to find information or actively seek someone out. Other times you want the information to be sent to you, with no action needed on your part. A good environment can provide both kinds of communication.

Archives
> Communications that can be stored, printed out, and searched are more useful than those that are ephemeral or just a mass of data.

Some communication tools that are commonly used in software projects are:

Web sites
> Web sites, Wikis (which are web sites that anyone can edit, with the editing being done via a web page) and weblogs (online diaries, also known as *blogs*). These are all simple to browse actively (though they are not always easy to follow) and they can sometimes be searched.

Email
> Email, mailing lists, web-based groups such as Yahoo! Groups, and newsgroups. Email is the common denominator, and everyone on the project already uses it. It's easy to be a "lurker" and passively receive information. Messages are often archived, and following a conversation by subject or thread usually works well enough.

RSS feeds
> RSS feeds are places that RSS reader applications can regularly poll for information. Most weblogs and many news sites already have RSS feeds. Some automation environments can provide RSS feeds about the state of the build. Many web browsers also have RSS readers already built in.

Messaging
> Instant messaging (IM) and SMS text messages on mobile telephones are used by some groups for short conversations. Some IM conversations are archived for later reference.

Telephone
> Telephones are easy enough to use, but they actively interrupt other people, and voice-mail messages are tedious to search through. "Twisted Communications" in Chapter 12 discusses other problems with telephones in a development environment.

Office navigation aids

> The basics for finding people in an office are a list of telephone numbers that is regularly updated and name tags on cubicles and offices. A map of where people sit and a web page with photographs of people's faces are even better.

Wise users of each of these tools know when it's time to put the tools aside and to try to talk to the other people face to face. All the tools listed above deliver compressed forms of communication, and some information is inevitably lost in the compression. Subtle tones of voice, quick facial expressions, and body posture are all part of complete communication. If you are in a company, find the people involved and find a good-sized conference room; corridor communication is only good for short conversations and it can disturb other people who are working.

A Project Web Site

The best idea that I know of for helping a group to communicate clearly is a good set of web pages. Even the best web page won't replace other forms of communication, but it can be a central place to store many of the results of using the other tools to communicate. A web site can be useful both for relatively static information (such as how to build the product) and also for more dynamic information (such as the latest commits to the project or the current state of the automated builds).

Some general suggestions for a project's web pages include:

- Host the web site on a server with enough resources to run other jobs, as well as serving up web pages. There are always periodic jobs that are more convenient to run on the same machine as the active collection of web pages. Larger jobs can always be run elsewhere and their results can be copied over to the web server.

- Create an email alias for each area of the web site and make this address prominent on each area's web page. Example addresses are *scm-admin* for SCM-related questions, *build-admin* for build-related questions, and *bug-admin* for questions about bug tracking in the development environment.

- When someone leaves the project, wait a month and then scan the web pages for references to him, then update the pages with the relevant contacts or remove the references. The information is still there in the SCM tool. Updating the web pages doesn't mean erasing his name as though he never existed; you're just removing him from the current contacts.

Access Control

One issue that is part of making the project's information available on a web site is how to restrict access to it. In an open source project, this is usually a question of who is allowed to change the information, which then comes down to commit rights (see "Commit Rights" in Chapter 12). Still, in some open source projects, some bugs are marked as private if they are related to security risks.

In a closed source development environment, the web site should be accessible only from within the private network. In some companies, the engineering group doesn't want salespeople selling features they may have seen being added to the source code, since the features may never be released. Many companies consider the list of bugs in a product to be sensitive information.

The simplest way to restrict access to sensitive areas of the web site is to configure your web server to request a username and password for certain locations. There is a good tutorial about authentication, authorization, and access control for Apache at *http://httpd.apache.org/docs/howto/auth.html*. You can also use *.htaccess* files on a per-directory basis, but this is less efficient. If the information on sensitive web pages is going to go over a public network, or any part of the network contains a wireless link, or the physical security of the network is in doubt, then make sure that URLs use *https://* rather than *http://*.

Different Areas for the Project Web Site

This section contains some of the information that I've found useful on the project web pages that I have created. There is very little about web page design in this section; basically, the web pages should be as clear as possible, with as few clicks as necessary to get from any page to any other page. For medium-sized projects, most of the key information for each area should be able to fit on a single web page. The web pages should also work on every browser used by anyone in the project, including text-based browsers such as Lynx running over slow connections.

Much of the information can be described using simple HTML, which makes retrieving it faster than having to open PDF or Word files. Many automated tools that generate reports already generate HTML. If not, then tools exist to convert the report to a format more suitable for browsing.

Home Page

The home page is the default page for the web server. It should have links (often in a menu on the lefthand side) to the main page for each of the other areas. Other useful information for the home page could include:

- Messages about server outages and other current project-related news. When news items become old, move them to a separate location; don't delete them.
- A link to FAQs.
- The current status of various important builds.
- A search box for different parts of the web site.

Adding some RSS newsfeeds can also encourage people to revisit the page throughout the day. The feeds can even be project-related ones.

Getting Started

One use of a project's web site is to help people to get started with the project. One document is the "I'm New Here" document. Other documents can be the "New Developer," "New Tester," "New Writer," and "New Toolsmith" documents. In theory, you should be able to give a new member of the project the URL of the home page and leave her alone for a few hours. Good information for the "I'm New Here" document includes:

- Names, email addresses, and locations of IT people and toolsmiths
- A step-by-step guide to setting up an account on a machine and accessing email
- Names of important servers, what accounts or permissions to ask for, and a basic overview of the local network
- Which directories and files are backed up, and when
- How to find a list of contacts for each project
- A link to a map of where people are located, with their time zones if the project is global

Once the new project member has a working environment, she can use the "New *X*" documents for information that is more specific about what she will be doing. An important part of these documents is a step-by-step guide to the basics of the job. For developers, this would be how to check out source code, how to build the product, and how to run it. For testers, the document would include where to get internal releases, how to install them, and how to run the automated tests.

This is a good time to ask people to write down what they didn't understand or felt was missing from these documents. Every question you answer in these "Getting Started" documents is a question that you or someone else won't have to answer later many times. (Actually, what you'll have to say many times is, "Let me show you where that question is answered," but that beats having to explain something or other that you've just forgotten the details of because you haven't done it yourself for three or four months.)

Specifications

The specifications web page is similar to any library, helping you to both find and read different kinds of documents. Grouping the documents into functional and implementation specifications and providing a place for developers' written notes about each feature in the product can help other readers later. A clear separation between speculative specifications and ones that describe what actually exists in the product is also helpful.

One very useful document that can be automatically generated is a list of the available documents sorted by when they where first created and when they were last modified. Most documents that are wanted by people are recently written or recently updated documents.

A good search tool is particularly important for this part of the web site. "Indexing and Searching," later in this chapter, discusses this in more detail. The formats allowed for specification documents should be indexable by search engines and should be convenient for all members of the project to read and modify. PDF files are great for printing, but unless you have the right tools to modify them, people will have to create other files for comments on them. Plain text, Word, and HTML are some file formats commonly used for project specifications. Chapter 8 has more details about these and other file formats for documentation.

SCM

Useful information about the local SCM environment includes:

Files

Graphical browsing of the hierarchy of files managed by the SCM tool. You should be able to locate any single file and inspect and compare different versions of the file. It is also very convenient to be able to search for text in both past and present versions of files, and to be able to restrict the view of files to a particular branch. Tools that do this include ViewCVS (written in Python), CVSWeb (older, in Perl), Bonsai (Perl), and FishEye (a Java servlet). Some commercial SCM tools such as BitKeeper and Perforce have their own UI for browsing directories.

Change logs

Change logs for the mainline and other branches, also arranged by project, showing the names, versions, commit messages, and usernames, grouped and sorted by time. Tools that do this include *cvs2cl* for CVS and FishEye.

Branches

A list of major branches, their names, purpose, and creation dates. If a branch is unavailable for commits, then a message about who to contact to change this is a good idea.

SCM tool

More information about the SCM tool, including details about how to configure it for each project. Providing some contact names or an *scm-admin* email alias for further questions about the tool is very useful.

Building

Information about builds for the projects includes:

Current state

If automated builds are running, a web page is a great place to display the results, especially if there are many different platforms and products being built continuously. The reports should include links to build logs and change logs. If there were any warnings or errors generated by a build, then another useful idea is links to the files and line numbers that generated them. LXR (*http://lxr.sourceforge.net*) is an open source tool that can create versions of source files that can be browsed, complete with cross-references to each file.

Another useful page is a description of all failures of automated builds that were intended for other people, including the root cause of the failures. Documenting this is painstaking work, but it pays off when people begin to mutter that "there seem to have been lots of broken builds recently." The information on this page can show whether they are really right, or this is just a vague impression.

"How Not to Break the Build"

A document describing the minimal process to follow when committing changes to the source code. When a build does break, check whether the root cause was a failure to follow this document; if not, add sufficient details to the document to stop whatever the actual cause was from happening again.

"How to Fix the Build"

The counterpart of "How Not to Break the Build," this document describes where to find information about when the build broke, which files or tools changed since the build last succeeded, and who made those changes. This document should also describe how to rerun the unit tests.

Supported environments

A single, authoritative place for project members to find out which machines, operating systems, and tools, and their versions, are supported for the project. Reports of other unsupported versions that have been found to work, or not work, can also go here.

Build tool

More information about the build tool and the specific details about how it is used in various projects goes here. Providing some contact names or a *build-admin* email alias for further questions about the tool is very useful.

Historical information

Tracking the size of the product and how long builds take can be useful information for finding out what's making the product so large, or why builds take so long now.

Testing

Useful information for testers and other people includes:

Current state

The latest results of running the system tests on different releases, including releases internal to the project and releases for customers. Test reports should include links to the definition of each test.

"How to Fix a Test"

This document describes the processes for confirming that a test is failing and for escalating the problem appropriately.

Test tools

A description of the tools used for testing, along with more information about using and modifying the tools. Providing some contact names for further questions about each different tool is helpful.

Bug Tracking

Almost all bug tracking systems now have interfaces that can be used through a web browser. This allows you to refer to the following information from your project web site:

Bugs
> Access to the bug tracking system. To help infrequent users, include a way to get a reminder of the username and password.

Common reports
> Links to common reports for developers, testers, writers, and managers.

Submitting a bug
> Some guidelines for how to submit a bug for each project. A useful document here would include a summary of each area of the product and guidelines for choosing an area for a new bug.

Bug tracking system
> More information about the bug tracking system and how it is configured locally for your projects. Providing some contact names or a *bug-admin* email alias for further questions about the tool is useful.

Documentation

Useful information about a project's documentation environment includes:

Documents
> Links to both released and latest versions of the product documentation. The release process should automatically update the links to the latest versions.

Review process
> A description of how the project usually reviews documents and provides feedback.

Building the documentation
> The tools required and the process to create the documentation as it is distributed to reviewers and customers.

Documentation tools
> More information about the documentation tools themselves. Contacts within the project for each tool are also useful here.

Releases

Information about releases can include:

Releases
> Instructions for finding and downloading internal and external releases, often using their build labels (see "Labeling Builds" in Chapter 3). The release process should automatically update this page as releases appear and are approved.

Creating a release
> A step-by-step description of the process of creating a release. This is a good place for further details about what each step does in the automated parts of the release process.

Roadmap

A link to a description of the features planned for each future release. This could also appear in the specifications web page.

Release tools

More information about the release tools themselves. Names to contact for each tool are also useful here, as is a *rel-admin* email alias.

Maintenance

Useful information about maintaining a product includes:

Design

A description of the architecture of the product, ideally including both the original design and subsequent modifications.

Implementation

Notes about the intentions of various developers who have worked on each part of the product. Previous maintainers may have kept notes about their understanding of each part, too. A good description of the directory hierarchy for the source code and the intended use of each directory.

Coding standards

Coding standards for the project, to be followed by future maintainers.

Deprecation

A document describing how to deprecate parts of a product's public API.

Support

The support group will want information such as:

Support tools

Links to the main tools used for tracking customer issues, such as ticket systems, knowledge bases, and other informative articles. Also links to tools developed by support for their own use when diagnosing customer problems.

Customer information

A document describing what information to gather from a customer with a problem and, more importantly, why the information is useful and to whom.

Privacy

A document about the privacy guidelines for customer information and data.

Triage

A description of the basic steps for investigating a problem with the product. For example, how to debug a core file from a crash of the product and how to copy logfiles and core files to developers and testers.

Project Management

Useful information about the people involved in a project includes:

Projects
> A list of all the projects, past and present, and email aliases for contacting the members of that project. A list of the names of the products for each project, including internal project names and older names, is also a good starting point for understanding what is going on.

People
> The people in each project and contact information for them. Charts showing the structure of different groups and people's roles in each project can help guide others when trying to decide whom to contact. If the group is part of a company, then a map of the offices (i.e., a floor plan labeled with who sits where) is great. Of course, someone has to update the map when people change where they are working.

Resources
> A list of the key machines used in the project. For each machine, list its purpose, location, owner, maintainer, backup strategy, and an estimate of the time it would take to recreate it from scratch. This can really help when assessing the largest physical risks to a project.

Email archives
> An interface for browsing and searching a centralized archive of the messages to email aliases for each project. Creating such an archive saves multiple people from doing the same thing within their own mail clients.

Statistics
> Project statistics can include the number of lines of source code, the top ten committers, the complexity of the code, and the estimated value of the code (e.g., using SLOCCount; see "Performance Tools" in Chapter 6). These values are often inaccurate, but are at least entertaining. Historical trends are more useful than absolute values here.

About the Web Site

All the other web pages discussed so far contain information about projects and their products. This web page is about the project web site itself:

Sitemap
> What information is available on the web site. This page should be automatically generated.

Changing pages
> The instructions for how to modify a page. These have to be simple, ideally simple enough to add as a footer to the bottom of every page on the web site.

Changing the web site

A description of how the web site is structured and how to modify the structure of the web site.

Usage statistics

Statistics about how the web site is used. For example, the most popular pages, the pages no one ever uses, and pages that produce "404 Page Not Found" errors. A list of recently changed pages is also helpful if you are an administrator for the web site trying to monitor what information people most want. The changes to the static parts of the web site can often be tracked using change logs, assuming that these static parts are stored using an SCM tool.

Web tools

Information about how to run a link checker for the web site and about other web-related tools such as HTML Tidy (*http://tidy.sourceforge.net*).

Contact details

An email alias for contacting the people responsible for running the project web site. *webmaster* or *web-admin* seem popular. I know of at least one church that uses *websexton* for this alias.

Creating the Web Site

This section discusses the process of creating a web site for a project. As with many parts of a development environment, the simplest possible solutions are often the best. There are thousands of complicated web sites that describe how to design and build complicated web sites. To me, this seems like too much hard work for a site whose aim in life is to help communication between project members.

Let's assume that you know how to write basic HTML and already have a web server such as Apache (*http://www.apache.org*) running on a machine. The web server reads files from a group of directories and returns them to the visitors to the web site. You will also want to be able to run some other tasks on the same machine, mostly for generating dynamic web pages.

The first thing to make sure of is that you have a process for updating web pages in a controlled fashion. To make this easy, I suggest using an already familiar tool such as your SCM tool to control your HTML files. Some writers may be more comfortable with HTML editors that have built-in support for copying files to and from a web server. Even so, they should keep versioned copies of the sources to their web pages using an SCM tool.

Static Web Pages

The simplest solution that I have found for web pages that don't change very often starts with a small number of HTML files. Static files make life easy for a web server: they take less work to return to visitors and they can be mirrored on multiple web servers for redundancy and to spread the load. To update the web pages that people see when they are browsing, you can simply arrange for commits to these files to also check them out to whatever location the web server reads them from.

To do this with CVS, check out the HTML pages just once to get started, and add the line:

```
^html/*            $CVSROOT/CVSROOT/update_web_site
```

to your *CVSROOT/commitinfo* file. Then add an executable shell script named *update_web_site* to your *CVSROOT* directory and also name it in the *checkoutlist* file. Now whenever files in the *html* top-level directory in the repository are committed, the script *update_web_site* will be run. If the web server's pages are in */var/www/html*, then the script should contain:

```
#!/bin/bash

cd /var/www/html
sleep 1
cvs -q update -dP &
```

The -q argument causes CVS to show only the filenames that are updated, and -dP will make sure that directories appear properly. The sleep 1 and & are necessary so that CVS doesn't interfere with its own system of locks on files in the repository. The disadvantage of this approach is that as the number of HTML files grows, it takes longer to update them all, and thus longer to commit a change to just one file.

Another approach for simple content is to use SCM browsing tools (such as ViewCVS and CVSWeb) and instead of using simple filenames in the web site's <a> links, use links that download and display the pages directly from the SCM browsing tool. For instance, a link from the home page to a page about builds might usually look like:

```
<a href="builds.html">Builds page</a>
```

but if you want to use ViewCVS to always return to the latest version of the file, you would change the link to look like:

```
<a href="http://cvs.example.com/cgi-bin/viewcvs.cgi/*checkout*/
builds.html?rev=HEAD&content-type=text/html">Builds page</a>
```

Of course, this approach does increase network traffic and the load on the SCM tool, in this case the CVS server at *cvs.example.com*. For moderately busy web sites, this approach seems to be responsive enough that most people can't tell when ViewCVS is being used.

For convenience, use CSS stylesheets to define the appearance of your web pages. This makes it easy to change the appearance of the whole web site from a single location.

If possible, avoid JavaScript and HTML frames for this kind of simple page: JavaScript is not always enabled in people's browsers and doesn't work at all with text browsers; frames make me feel like I'm reading a web page through a keyhole.

NOTE

You can produce the illusion of menus expanding when clicked to show further choices, while using only HTML. First create an HTML fragment for each page that shows the menu for that page already expanded. Then include the HTML fragment in the page, so when that page is selected in the menu, the menu appears to expand as the HTML fragment shows all the other choices.

Dynamic Web Pages

Dynamic web pages are pages that are regenerated each time someone visits them. If you are using Apache as a web server, then Server Side Includes (SSIs) can work well for small amounts of dynamic information. SSIs are described in the Apache tutorial "Introduction to Server Side Includes" (*http://httpd.apache.org/docs/howto/ssi.html*); basically, you write HTML comments that tell the web server to insert some text or other content in place of the comment. For instance, the HTML text:

```
Today is <!--#echo var="DATE_LOCAL" -->
```

will be appear on the visited web page as:

Today is Fri Jan 28 20:59:54 PST 2005

There are all sorts of SSI commands available; they can be used to run a command and insert the command's output or to include other fragments of HTML. Web pages that use SSIs often have a filename with an *.shtml* suffix to distinguish them from HTML pages that don't have dynamic content.

If SSIs don't meet your needs, then it's time to investigate CGI (Common Gateway Interface) scripts. These are executables placed in designated locations on the web server. These scripts are typically written in Perl, Python, or PHP, but can in fact be ordinary shell scripts or any other executable file. When the script is visited, it is executed on the server and the HTML that it generates is returned to the visitor. Since these scripts are running on your web server and use arguments passed in by the visitor, security becomes a significant problem. You may also want to limit how often a script can be run, and checking for this within every CGI script can become tedious.

For those who feel that CGI scripts are overkill for a simple project web site, there is another approach. Using *crontab* or a scheduled task in Windows, arrange for the dynamic pages to be regenerated every minute or two. Say you want to include some news headlines in the home page of the web site. You can periodically run a script that will download the headlines, massage them into appropriate HTML for your page, and add a header and footer to the page. So long as people are aware of when the information on the page was last generated and when it will be regenerated, this approach seems to work well enough for small to medium-sized projects.

Indexing and Searching

Before you can search for anything on a web site, you will need to run an indexing program on the files. This may take some time and effort to get right, so when adding search capability to your project web site, decide carefully about:

- Which files and documents you want to index and which ones you don't.

- How you want to group files so that visitors can search in specific areas of the web site or exclude other areas from a search.

- How much support for complex searching you want. Different indexing and search programs support different search patterns and syntaxes.

For an extensive collection of search tools, see *http://www.searchtools.com/tools*. One of the better open source search tools is *ht://Dig* (*http://www.htdig.org*). *ht://Dig* is a *spider* search engine, which means that it follows all the links within your web site. It can use external programs to index a wide variety of file types and it supports a good range of search patterns through the use of Boolean expressions and wildcards.

The higher-end approach to searching and indexing is to purchase a Google Search Appliance (*http://www.google.com/enterprise/gsa*), which is a piece of hardware that you connect to your network and allow to "crawl," indexing everything that it can reach. As of early 2005, these appliances start at $4,995 for the Google Mini. If your web site is public and paid advertisements are acceptable, you can have Google WebSearch index your site and provide your search interface for you.

Avoiding Content Rot

> Nothing endures but change.
>
> *—Heraclitus of Ephesus (c.535–475 BC)*

Creating simple web pages and making some of them dynamic and searchable is actually the easier part of setting up a good web site for a project. The harder part is making sure that the information stays correct. As soon as someone has written down the steps to do something, the process may change and make the web page incorrect. Such "content rot" may seem at times to be as inevitable as the second law of thermodynamics. The key ideas of this section are how to help project members remember to update the information, one piece at a time. Ideas to help keep the information on the web pages accurate are:

A designated librarian
Someone has to want to have accurate information on the web site. This person is acting as the librarian for the project. It could be a manager, a writer, or even the toolsmith. This person should monitor the content changes in the web site to make sure that links work and page formatting is consistent. If he is involved in the development and testing of the project, then he may know who to ask for updates to pages. When email is sent to the team about some change, the librarian can be the person to send back a request or reminder to update the related information on the web site.

Easy updates

The process to change a page has to be as easy as possible. This is the advantage of Wiki-based web pages, where the Edit button is right next to the content. Failing that, you can add text to the bottom of every page containing the name of the file for the current web page and the commands to check it out using the SCM tool.

Timestamps

Sometimes just knowing when a page was last changed is enough to decide whether its contents should be updated. The date can be found from your SCM tool, rather than relying on people to change a date by hand. Copyright dates are usually unhelpful for this purpose. Extracting the name of the person who made the last change from the SCM tool can provide a good starting contact for making future changes.

Templates

A small set of template files for web pages helps people add new information to the web site in a consistent manner. The templates can also contain comments about the steps to follow to add a new page to the web site.

Another approach is to add empty web pages for people, but only if they let you identify them on such pages in a large font stating who is responsible for adding content.

Link checking

A sure sign of a decaying web site is when all the interesting links don't work. You can use one of the open source link-checking tools, such as *linklint* (*http://www.linklint.org*) or *checklint* from W3C (*http://validator.w3.org/checklink*), to check that the URLs referenced on your web site aren't broken. These tools can also be run as part of your automation environment.

Web logs

Many web servers can tell you from their logs which files are most visited, from which you can create your own list of the files that are almost never visited. These files are often the ones that have become useless and need to be updated or discarded. Note that this doesn't refer to those cheesy counters that appear on some dusty home pages.

## CHAPTER TWELVE

Politics and People

THIS CHAPTER CONCLUDES THIS BOOK WITH A LOOK AT WHAT A TOOLSMITH CAN DO FOR A PROJECT, what a toolsmith shouldn't do, and what to look for on a résumé for a toolsmith. The chapter finishes with some of the most complex issues that can affect projects. These issues involve people more than process and are sometimes referred to with a grimace as "political problems." These sections are included in a book with a practical focus because it's good to be forewarned (or reminded) about some of the people-related problems that arise so often in projects. Some of the ideas mentioned along with the problems might even help ease your pain.

First, for anyone who wants to understand more about the kind of person who enjoys writing software, there are some classic books on the subject. Good places to start are *The Psychology of Computer Programming*, by Gerald M. Weinberg (Dorset House), and *Computer Power and Human Reason*, by Joseph Weizenbaum (Freeman), particularly Chapter 4, "Science and the Compulsive Programmer." Another way of seeing how people think about writing software is to look at the phrases in "The Jargon File" (*http://catb.org/~esr/jargon*), which is maintained by Eric S. Raymond and was also published as *The New Hackers Dictionary* (MIT Press).

The Role of the Toolsmith

In traditional factories (that is, factories that produce things you can actually pick up and drop on your toes), there is often a tools department. This department is responsible for producing and maintaining the tools used by the other workers. The members of the tools department are called *toolsmiths*. Much of this book has been about choosing and using different tools to provide a satisfying software development environment. The people who do this are acting as toolsmiths for their software projects. However, in many projects the position of a toolsmith is not properly filled, and each worker just uses whatever tools are familiar and comfortable. Interestingly, this is the same situation that small-scale craftsmen were in before the Industrial Revolution.

THE APPRENTICE

A traditional introduction of an apprentice to the toolsmiths in a factory:

> SENIOR WORKER TO APPRENTICE: Go down to Tools and tell 'em you need a long weight.
> *(Later on...)*
> APPRENTICE TO TOOLSMITH: I need a long weight!
> TOOLSMITH: Fair enough, you just wait right there and I'll be with you in a while.

And indeed the apprentice had a long wait ahead of him.

(More of these "sleeveless errands" can be found at *http://www.museumofhoaxes.com/af_1700s.html*.)

Some smarter companies and projects do have people who are specifically designated toolsmiths for the software. These organizations believe that, just as a product works better when it has been designed (rather than being allowed to just grow irregularly over time), a well-thought-out environment produces better products than does an environment that is a haphazard collection of whatever tools seemed useful at some point. For instance, this book was produced with the assistance of the Production Tools group at O'Reilly, which supports the production editors who shepherd a book from the author's source files to the printed copy and online version.

I'm not aware of any hard financial or organizational results to justify employing a toolsmith for your project, but the idea of a tools department seems to have generally done good things for the Industrial Revolution, so I recommend it.

So, what is the role of a toolsmith? Each of the chapters in this book describes a part of what a toolsmith can be expected to be involved in. To recap, these areas are: SCM, builds, testing, tracking bugs, documentation, release, and maintenance. Any and all of these areas are good places for toolsmiths to contribute to a project. In the wide-ranging paper "The

Computer Scientist as Toolsmith II" (*http://www.cs.unc.edu/~brooks/Toolsmith-CACM.pdf*), Fred Brooks (author of *The Mythical Man-Month*) wrote:

> If the computer scientist is a toolsmith, and if our delight is to fashion power tools and amplifiers for minds, we must partner with those who will use our tools, those whose intelligences we hope to amplify.

A good question is "What does a toolsmith usually *not* do?" The toolsmith should not try to be an architect or designer for the project. The toolsmith should also not be a long-term developer for the project. The thought behind both of these opinions is that anything long-term that distracts the toolsmith from the development environment means that the environment stops being maintained, and then the rest of the group will suffer as a consequence. However, as discussed below, a few weeks spent developing, testing, and documenting by a toolsmith can produce a crystal-clear understanding of the real problems faced by those groups.

Since a toolsmith is a service provider, some customer-service types of activities are often helpful:

- Gather feedback from the group regularly. What are the top three irritations? What solutions can they suggest? If they aren't too vague, you can file bugs on these problems and update the bugs as changes are made.

- Don't let fires burn out of control. As soon as there are whispers of discontent about some aspect of the environment, create a document about how it's supposed to be used, print copies of the document to give out to project members, and offer to give a short talk about it. If there really is a problem, then create a bug about it and refer people to the bug to add comments. If possible, schedule a time when the problem can be fixed.

- Providing regular updates about the status of the environment (what's working, what's broken, and when will it be fixed) to the group and to management will also help manage their perceptions of the environment's status.

- Keep a clear trail of decisions and feedback from all parties. Sign all your email cryptographically, print out key documents, and store them securely off site. Keep records not just of license files, but also who was responsible for choosing each tool.

Another valuable form of feedback for the toolsmith is to have to use the environment he has created, also known as "eating your own dog food." Though I don't recommend this as a long-term practice (since it distracts from the maintenance of the environment), this is a good idea in the short term. For instance, try entering six bugs in one session—which is the slowest part of the whole process? Debug a problem in a file that is used by large numbers of other files and see how slow the rebuilds really are. Try to fix a broken unit test and then rerun the test suite by hand. I guarantee that the results of these activities will bring a clearer understanding of a group's complaints to any working toolsmith.

A toolsmith should also try to avoid making off-the-cuff policy decisions about subjects such as who has access to different parts of the source code, when SCM branches are created, or whether a particular bug really is a critical show-stopper. The toolsmith provides mechanisms to support policies and may well make strong recommendations about how to use the tools, but policy decisions really ought to come from the project leaders and managers.

A good toolsmith also has to be nonpartisan about tools that she does not control. The classic example here is the choice of file editors for Unix: Emacs or *vi*. Both editors are in common use, and the arguments about which is better, and better for what, have raged for decades now. A toolsmith cannot dismiss one editor or the other, no matter her personal preferences (even mine are considered secret). However, it is fair for a toolsmith to restrict official support to a limited number of tools, in order to be able to provide adequate time for each one.

How to Choose a Toolsmith

While there is rarely a clear career path for software toolsmiths (most of us seem to be developers who have come to specialize in tools), here are some ideas for what to look for on a résumé or to ask for in a job description for a toolsmith:

- Experience with at least two different SCM tools, two different build tools, and two different bug tracking systems.

- Both administrative and user experience with tools. There is a world of difference between using a tool and administering the same tool for a large group of people.

- Demonstrated ability to identify the causes of problems in a development environment in a systematic way.

- Ability to summarize problems in an environment, to propose and evaluate solutions for the problems, and then to implement the solutions in a reasonable amount of time.

- For each of the projects he has been involved with, can he identify the most significant mistakes that he personally made? If he says there were no mistakes, either hire him immediately or treat the rest of his comments as highly suspect!

- What books, magazines, newsgroups, mailing lists, web sites, or weblogs that discuss tools and development environments does she read on a regular basis? Appendix B contains suggestions about some appropriate ones you should expect to hear.

It's interesting to note that while many of these abilities are very similar to those required for developers writing code, it is not essential (though it is definitely helpful) for a toolsmith to be able to write source code. In a few projects, the managers are the toolsmiths for the project.

When Good Projects Go Bad

What are the signs that an environment or a whole project is in trouble? One major red flag for project rot is when the documentation, tools, or platforms are never updated. Another clue is when a product depends on old, unsupported versions of compilers and operating systems, since eventually the product will become unwanted or unusable by customers. If the documentation is never updated, it's often more confusing than not having it there at all. These changes occur over a period of years, so they are long-term indicators of trouble.

Specific signs to look for in a project are web sites full of outdated documents, and too many of the web site's pages left blank, to be filled in later, which really means never. In companies, outdated organization charts with too many unfamiliar names are a warning, as are mythical team meetings that never, ever happen.

Another clear sign of a project losing momentum is when people within the project can no longer say who owns each part of the project. As people leave and their areas are not passed on to others, those parts become stale, scary places where the rest of the group fears to make changes. Just to be safe, they will often not apply even small changes being made throughout the rest of the product to these areas. Even in projects that claim to practice "egoless programming," where any developer can make changes in any part of the code, people still know who to ask about each area.

Other obvious signs of a project in trouble are bored developers and the consequent high turnover as they leave for more interesting projects. One cause of such boredom can be lack of vision for the project, so that there are not enough new ideas to keep anyone interested. "Us and them" ways of talking about different groups in a company, or treating another group as though they are competitors, or communication failures due to personal animosity between developers—these are all signs that a project is having difficulties. Boredom and unowned code will also lead to increased numbers of broken builds and bugs that reappear after they were supposedly fixed.

On a more positive note, one sign of a project turning around is when people get around to doing things that they could have done a long time ago. Deleting old source code is a good example of this (it's still safe in the SCM repository if you need it).

Awkward People

It's a stereotype with a strong basis in fact: people who write code for a living or for pleasure are often more introverted than people who sell things or teach other people all day. As with every stereotype, you can think of exceptions, but it's a good place to start making some more generalizations about people in projects. The descriptions below can apply to any group of people, but it's cheap entertainment to place people you know into the categories. You can even make up some more categories of your own:

The Great Leader
> One of the people who came up with the ideas for the project in the first place. Usually overwhelmed with requests for information or meetings, and this makes her terse. Prone to venting about other people's code and rewriting it overnight.

The Quiet Hacker
> Doesn't bother talking much, just writes the code. Email exchanges with him can be cryptic as he assumes that you have recently read all the same source code that he has immersed himself in.

The Whiner
> Everyone else's interfaces don't work well for what she wants to do. Everyone's else's documentation is unhelpful. The project is out to get in her way.

Standards Guy

Has a touching belief that following published standards is always the Right Thing for the project. Horrified by interoperability tests where software fails to interoperate despite being standards-compliant.

Ms. Inflexible

Doesn't see why she should change her code when you can change yours. When you do change your code to work with hers, she fails to let you know that she changed her code in an entirely different way.

Mothman

He flitters from tool to tool, project to project, drawn to the bright lights, justifying this with the belief that he will surely pass on fruitful ideas to each one. Everybody remembers him, but people often have difficulty remembering exactly what he did for the project.

Afraid-to-Code

It all seems so overwhelming—where should she start? Daunted by the fear of breaking something, she does nothing.

When-I-Wrote-Code

Used to be a developer, but is now a manager frustrated by developers. "When I wrote code, I didn't make any mistakes" is one of his thoughts, but he's not foolish enough to voice it aloud.

Just don't forget to notice how people don't really fit in a single category, because we are all a mixture of these types, and still more.

Twisted Communications

As soon as a project has more than one person working on it, communication within the group becomes vital. By default, communication seems to occur in the slowest, most error-prone ways that it can. If there is some choice between two things, then *both* choices will usually be made within a project, sometimes at the same time!

Everyone who has been frustrated by the bugs and extra work due to lack of common knowledge in a group suspects that improving communication within a project will improve the product. They're usually correct, but it's quite hard to improve poor communication right when it is happening. Some instances of twisted and tangled communication include:

Email arguments

Email is fine for short discussions without interrupting the whole group, but it's very hard to resolve disagreements using only email. After a couple of back-and-forth emails, it can help if you reduce the number of recipients to the minimum and, if possible, go and talk to each other face to face, and then write the resulting decision down and send it out to tie up the email exchange. If you're getting annoyed by someone's email, don't use email to reply—or at least wait five minutes before sending the mail. What you intended as a witty retort may seem like provocative noise when reread later.

Bug thrashing

Changing the state of a bug from Open to Closed to Open to Closed because there's a disagreement about the bug, or when there is managerial pressure to resolve it, is no way to solve anything. It only demonstrates that the group is not communicating properly. One helpful resolution that is sometimes possible is to reclassify the bug as a feature request. Otherwise, talk and listen to each other.

Noise in commit messages

"Fixed Paul's ugly code." "I hate this parser!" "Stupid customer request implemented against my better judgment." Such commit messages seem funny at the time or may temporarily relieve some frustration, but remember that the purpose of SCM tools is to store information for a *long* time. None of these messages will tell someone looking at the code two years from now why you bothered to change it at all; it's just noise to be ignored. Take a breath and write a message that you might want to find yourself reading a few months from now. Huge messages rarely get fully read either. If the message is that large, then add it to the project documentation elsewhere and refer to that file in the commit message.

Overly terse sentences

Just as too much content can hinder communication, so can too little. Concise and clear is good; overly terse or silent is just incomplete and frustrating to the listeners. It can also, correctly or incorrectly, give the impression that you are not really participating in a group.

Offensive code comments

Opinions are part of communication, and everyone expresses their opinions in different ways. Comments that seem fine in the context of a few beers can seem overly harsh when written down and read later by someone without the same alcoholic context. Making offensive comments about other companies can bite you when you want to sell the source code to someone else. Expletives are usually just noise in code comments, but if they reach customers (for example, in log messages), then extra work may be required of everyone to remove them later on. Just stick to the facts in your source code comments.

The Linux kernel "swear count" graphs at *http://www.vidarholen.net/contents/wordcount* show how this phenomenon has decreased as GNU/Linux has matured.

Telephones

Telephones at work are a terrible way for developers to communicate! They interrupt the focus that is necessary for writing good code, and they don't help you communicate particularly clearly with the other person. They interrupt everyone else around them with their noise, and there's not even a record of the conversation after you're done. People who listen to their messages on speakerphone still amaze me. Caller ID can help somewhat, as do turning down the ringer volume and making sure that your voicemail greeting suggests that the caller use email instead. Even with all the drawbacks of email, I think that it is far preferable to telephones in a development environment.

Paging systems

I once worked in a company that used an overhead paging system with loudspeakers in the corridor ceilings to find people, to announce meetings, and for anything else that was considered sufficiently interesting to someone. These pages interrupted the useful work of an entire company dozens of times per day, truly a net loss to that company. The only interesting pages came when the CEO was annoyed at someone and snarled at them publicly to come to his office.

Those are plenty of reminders of what can go wrong with communicating with other people. Chapter 11 contains many ideas for how to improve the communication within a project.

Commit Rights

The question of commit rights—that is, who gets to change the source files of a project—is a common ground for disagreement. Numerous open source projects have split over this. This is hardly surprising, since the source code is what defines what the product does, and whoever is granted sufficient access to a centralized SCM tool gets to define the source code. All product design and management is just wishful thinking until it becomes committed source code. Since commit rights are a sensitive issue, it is politically wise to make sure that changes to them have at least an agreed-on policy and a plausible audit trail.

In software companies, the usual procedure for deciding who has commit rights is quite simple: if you are paid to write code, then you have to able to commit that code. Non-technical managers may sometimes also acquire commit rights, but their changes will be scrutinized carefully. Some methodologies declare that anyone in the project can modify any source file, but wise developers respect each other's work and make major modifications to source code written by other developers only after some discussion, or to fix a broken build. Occasionally, a truly irritating developer may be prevented from changing all files outside her given area, but this is a very strong sign of distrust.

In open source projects, the decision to grant commit rights is usually based on whose code the project leaders trust. Most projects have a personal email address or a mailing list to send requests for commit rights to. Most projects expect that the requester has previously submitted a number of useful bugs and patches to the source code for the project. When commit rights are denied, frustration tends to make the requester either give up on making contributions or flame the entire project and all the leaders. For this reason, it is helpful if open source projects describe what is expected of developers with commit rights and how to request commit rights; they should also clearly communicate the reasons for denying someone commit rights.

> **NOTE**
> It's also helpful with open source projects if there is a document describing how to submit patches in a suitable format for project members to commit. Some projects have very specific requirements about how patches should be generated and what is needed in a patch (e.g., does documentation have to be updated too?)—even the format of the subject of an email message is sometimes minutely specified. If you are dealing with hundreds of different patches, you will want to optimize how they are presented.

A related question is "Who gets read rights?" In closed source projects, this is often just the developers and their managers. Well-meaning sales and marketing people have inferred (and sold) features from the current, buggy source code of the next release too often to make it wise to give everyone in the company access. Open source projects give read rights to everyone, by definition; but again, just because there is functionality in the source code doesn't mean that it works yet.

Automation Discipline

The theme of automation has been mentioned numerous times throughout this book. Perhaps the best thing about automation for most people is that it is impersonal in nature. Imagine yourself as a developer who has committed code that has broken the build and stopped other developers from making progress. You'd want to know about this mistake as soon as possible, but you don't really want other people moaning at you, or your manager hovering over you. A machine-generated email is a pleasant way to become aware of your errors. Your manager and colleagues can expect you to act on the email without having to come and hound you; this in turn builds trust over time.

That said, some form of Pavlovian training may be necessary to reach such a state of trust within the group. Effective forms of carrot and stick are numerous. Free lunch can be provided at the end of a week with no broken builds (or whatever the current problem is). Glowing lava lamps and traffic signals have been used to proclaim the state of the build (*http://www.onjava.com/pub/a/onjava/2004/11/10/automation.html*). Those who hinder others can make small payments into a group fund, with proceeds to be spent on something for the group. I have an *ugly* picture of a cat with tearful eyes painted on black velvet that people who break the build have to hang in their cube for a day. A public summary of the state of the group can also do some good, just like the signs you see in factories proclaiming "42 accident-free days."

I find the most useful encouragement is to make sure that the expected process to avoid problems has been documented (e.g., "How Not to Break the Build"), and then to ask precise and detailed questions when there is a problem until everyone understands which part of the process was not followed and why. The process may really need amending, in which case everyone wins. If not, the business of being quizzed may dissuade future offenders.

What Do Developers Really Want?

The ideas in this section are taken from informal polls of colleagues at different companies and from my own observations of any number of small frustrations that have become larger problems in various projects that I have worked on. You may object that chairs and coffeemakers are *expected* parts of a work environment, not rewards, but there's a world of difference between the basic and the exceptional versions of both of them. Every one of the ideas here helps people feel happier about working on a project and, in my opinion, they're all much better rewards than boring coffee mugs and T-shirts:

Not too many interruptions

The actions of writing code, tests, and some kinds of documentation have a startup effort associated with remembering how the different pieces work together. Every interruption means that time has to be spent getting back into the task. Too many meetings, noisy telephone calls, long hallway conversations, or mobile phones left on desks can all interrupt developers. Interruptions may not always be from other people: this also applies when builds take long enough for a developer to become distracted by the latest news on Slashdot.

Fast connections

Finding examples of how to use a subtle language construct, other peoples' diagnoses of the error messages that you're seeing, documentation for installing and using a new tool—all these activities are greatly enhanced with a good Internet connection. A slow connection also allows people to get distracted.

Ergonomic peripherals

The amount of painful damage to peoples' wrists in the software industry from using poor and badly placed keyboards is absolutely incredible. The cost of a good keyboard tray, one that can be moved up and down (in and out is really just for convenience), is under $200. There are also numerous ergonomic keyboards available for under $200.

Good monitors

Flickering or dim monitors are distracting and tiring for people's eyes. Flat-screen monitors are no longer as expensive as they once were, and they take up less desktop space, too. Small screen sizes mean that more time is spent closing and opening windows or moving them around, and it feels like you're working through a keyhole.

As an aside, it's just basic politeness not to touch other people's monitors—just as you wouldn't smear someone's glasses or their car's rearview mirror.

Good chairs

Good back support is essential, as is adjustable height. Surfaces and material should be just soft enough and breathable. Some people find armrests on chairs interfere with using a mouse, so armrests should be detachable. Chairs should not be covered with any material that generates large amounts of static electricity, such as nylon.

No drafts

Air conditioning vents should not blow cold air down onto people, because drafts are distracting.

Personal disk space

Many people listen to music while they work and need a place to keep their MP3 files. Space on a server can let them listen to music from different machines. The backup policy on this disk space can be different from that on other servers, and disk quotas can be imposed.

Many developers find that being allowed time and disk space to work on personal projects for a few hours a week helps keep them stimulated about their main project.

Kitchen

Soda machines, coffeemakers, microwaves, and refrigerators are all useful for finding the energy to focus on developing code. Kitchens are also places where people talk, so a whiteboard is a good addition to the kitchen.

Low effort for background tasks

There are things that project members just shouldn't have to waste their time on. Filling in forms for office supplies is one. Repeated issues with basic office cleaning and maintenance is another. Small frustrations can become focal points for irritation about other aspects of a project, and then they become regular distractions.

An Upbeat Ending

My advice to those finding themselves becoming toolsmiths is to make it clear to everyone that this is what you are doing, to ask regularly for feedback about tools and the local environment, not to speak your mind too quickly, and to wait a couple of minutes before sending email, especially mail that you think is witty. With a good attitude, being a toolsmith can be a very satisfying way to use your time.

How Tools Scale

**If you change the order of magnitude of a problem, then it
becomes a different problem.**

—Anonymous

THIS APPENDIX DISCUSSES HOW TOOLS SCALE AS A PROJECT GROWS. When a project grows, there
are a number of ways it can grow:

- More files and directories, which demands more from the underlying filesystem. The
  subjective experience of working with 100 files in a single directory is quite different
  from that of working with 1,000 files.

- Longer files, with more functions, methods, and classes in those files. A 1,000-line file
  can often be edited much more easily than a 100,000-line one. Generated source files
  can reach such sizes.

- More generated files that need to be combined. Linking 100 object files into a library is
  much faster than linking 1,000 such files together. Creating a *.jar* file from 1,000 *.class*
  files is quite different from creating one with 10,000 *.class* files. That's not even trying to
  resolve references between the files, just handling an order of magnitude more files.

- Different versions of the same product are produced from the same source code.

- More products are produced using the same source code in different ways.

One purpose of the results in this appendix is to encourage toolsmiths to measure the tools
that they support. Writing small project generators is an interesting challenge of making
sure that the generated projects resemble real projects. I'm not aware of any public project

that generates skeletons of projects' source code, but I think this would be an excellent tool to create. It could also be used to demonstrate best practices for creating build files for different build tools and to demonstrate how different SCM tools scale.

Scaling of Compilers

To investigate some of the issues of how a compiler scales, I wrote a small generator program to generate C source code files. This made it easy to vary the number of source files, the number of functions per source file, and the number of included files. Two separate compile scripts were also generated: one that used static libraries (one library per source file) and one that used a single (large) command line with all the object files explicitly named in the command.

The source files that were created were named *source_0.c* through *source_<N>.c*, where *<N>* was the number of files created. Each *.c* file contained a variable number of functions and looked like the following:

```
void file_0_fn_0() { }
 .
 .
 .
void file_0_fn_9() { }
```

Source files that were used for testing scaling with the number of included files looked like:

```
#include "file_0_include_0.h"
 .
 .
 .
#include "file_0_include_9.h"

void file_0_fn_0() { }
 .
 .
 .
void file_0_fn_9() { }
```

and each header file contained the appropriately numbered copy of this:

```
#ifndef FILE_0_INCLUDE_0_HDR_GUARD
#define FILE_0_INCLUDE_0_HDR_GUARD

#define DEFINITION_0_0 "ABC"

#endif
```

A single *main.c* file contained extern references to all of the defined functions and a call to each function. Durations were measured using the GNU *time* tool.

How the Compiler gcc Scales

This section describes some simple measurements of the generated projects that were made using a laptop named *matt-laptop*, with a 300MHz Pentium II CPU and 192MB RAM, lightly loaded, running Red Hat Linux 8.0, and using *gcc* 3.2.

In summary, as the number of files being compiled increases, the time taken also increases linearly. As the size of the files being compiled increases, and all else is equal, the time taken also increases linearly. Link times also increase linearly as the number of object files or library files being linked together increases. To study how the *gcc* preprocessor scales by itself, "Number of included files," later in this appendix, shows what happens when the number of #include lines in each source file is increased (each header file was a different file). This change seems to have a smaller effect on the relative compilation times.

NOTE

The purpose of these figures is to compare how the time taken by a well-known compiler changes with different arguments, not to compare *gcc* to other compilers.

Number of source files

With 10 uniquely named functions per source code file, the time to compile and link a single executable from different numbers of source files is shown in Figure A-1.

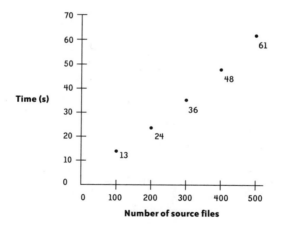

FIGURE A-1. Compiler time versus number of source files

Number of functions

For a project with 100 source files, the time was measured for compiling and linking a single executable with a varying number of functions in each source file. The results are shown in Figure A-2.

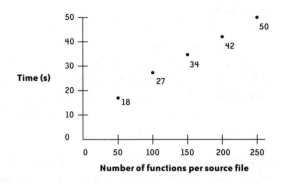

FIGURE A-2. Compiler time versus number of functions per source file

Number of libraries

For a project with 10 functions per source file, and with one library file per source file, the time to link a single executable is shown in Figure A-3.

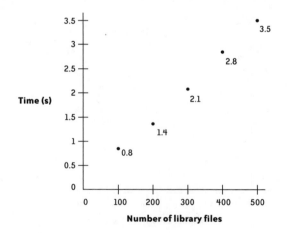

FIGURE A-3. Linker time versus number of library files

Number of included files

A project with a large number of included files was generated. Each included file was unique, and all the included files were guarded with unique guard strings, as is common with C header files. For 10 functions per source file and 100 source files, Figure A-4 shows the effect of the number of included files on the overall compiler time. Disk access and whether a file is already cached in memory probably have more effect than processor speed does in this case.

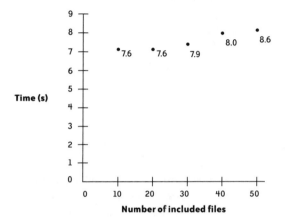

FIGURE A-4. Compiler time versus number of included files

Most compilers are collections of fairly complicated separate tools such as preprocessors, compilers, and linkers. Each of these applications has its own performance characteristics. So the simple analyses of this section should be taken only as a rough indicator of how a build process will scale. Before deciding on a build tool, it is good practice to generate some large projects that resemble your application and to test the performance of potential build tools with these projects.

Scaling of Build Tools

Comparing Recursive and Included make

There are two different ways that projects using *make* generally set up their makefiles. The first way, known as *recursive make*, is probably still the more common of the two ways. With recursive *make*, a top-level makefile contains a list of subdirectories, each of which has its own makefile. During a build, *make* recursively descends into each subdirectory and executes the instructions in the makefile there.

The other model, called *included* or *nonrecursive make*, was popularized by Peter Miller's classic paper "Recursive Make Considered Harmful," which suggests that the overhead of the time spent starting *make* with all the different makefiles becomes substantial as the project grows. A different idea is to create one large makefile before you start the build that includes all the makefiles that exist in each subdirectory. Debate over the two approaches still continues, and their results for a simple project are compared in Table A-1. The build state names are the ones that were defined in Chapter 5.

TABLE A-1. Recursive make and included make

Build state	Recursive duration (seconds)	Included duration (seconds)
Virgin	10.2	10.1
Changed	1.1	0.4
Up-to-date	1.1	0.3
Clean	2.5	1.5

These results were obtained on *matt-laptop*, the same machine that was used for the results in "How the Compiler gcc Scales," earlier in this appendix. In each case a virgin version of the same generated project with 10 subdirectories, each of which had 10 *leaf* subdirectories (i.e., subdirectories that have no subdirectories), was used. In each leaf subdirectory, there was one C source file with just one function defined in it. The recursive makefiles each had calls to each subdirectory's makefile with $(MAKE) -C *dirname*. The included top-level makefile had 100 include statements, one per leaf subdirectory. Each of the leaf source files was compiled into a static library, producing 100 such libraries in total. At the top level, a C source file used each of the 100 functions, and thus was linked with all 100 libraries. The changed build involved changing the modification time of the leaf file that was built last in a virgin build.

Table A-1 shows that virgin builds take about the same time with either scheme, since compile time is the dominant factor, but all other kinds of builds take approximately half the time if you use the included makefile approach.

There are other, similar results by Boris Kolpackov, available from *http://kolpackov.net/projects/build/benchmark.xhtml*.

Resources

THIS APPENDIX LISTS SOME SOURCES OF INFORMATION about software tools and development environments. Many of these sources are the ones I found most useful while researching this book. The actual steps involved in choosing and then changing to a new tool are described in "Steps When Changing Tools" in Chapter 3.

Online

The online resources are divided, somewhat arbitrarily, into places with content and places that focus more on discussion. For instance, an article on one author's web site may be discussed somewhere else such as on Slashdot or in a weblog.

Content

The web sites in this section contain original articles with generally useful content and less ranting than some of the discussion sites listed in "Discussions," later in this appendix:

IBM Developer Works (http://www.ibm.com/developerworks)
　　Lots of good, short articles from a variety of authors.

Advogato (http://www.advogato.org)
　　A wide range of articles on all aspects of software, with some thoughtful comments.

Freshmeat (http://freshmeat.net/articles)

Lively editorial articles, some of which cover tools and development environments.

Testing Foundations (http://www.testing.com)

Contains the work of Brian Marick, author of *The Craft of Software Testing* (Prentice Hall). A new book, *Scripting for Testers* (Pragmatic Bookshelf), is apparently in progress.

David A. Wheeler's Personal Home Page (http://dwheeler.com)

Lots of good articles, especially on security and SCM.

Brad Appleton's Home Page (http://www.cmcrossroads.com/bradapp)

Many SCM-related articles.

Artima (http://www.artima.com)

Regularly has wide-ranging software-related articles. Run by Bill Venners.

Jeffreys Copeland & Haemer's "Work" Columns (http://alumnus.caltech.edu/~copeland/work)

A wonderful series of articles written by two guys named Jeffrey, originally published in the now-defunct magazines *RS/Magazine* and *SunExpert*, that cover many different aspects of tools. In my opinion, these well-written articles deserve a far wider audience.

Steve McConnell (http://www.stevemcconnell.com)

Many articles and presentations from the author of *Code Complete* and other books about the process of writing software.

Ian Sommerville—Software Engineering (http://www.comp.lancs.ac.uk/computing/resources/IanS)

Articles by the author of the textbook *Software Engineering,* who has taken a leading role in computer science education.

Discussions

The web sites in this section generally contain links to articles and contain discussions about the articles:

Slashdot (http://www.slashdot.org)

Current news of a technical or geeky nature, with links to developer-related articles and lots of comments, some of which are even on-topic. Well-established, widely read and quoted, with plenty of strong opinions. Many of the comments show a bias toward Unix and Linux.

Joel on Software (http://joelonsoftware.com)

A weblog and also numerous questions each day in the "Business of Software" and "Design of Software" sections. Lots of tools-related discussion, but fewer comments than on Slashdot.

StickyMinds.com (http://www.stickyminds.com)

Articles related to tools and some recommendations for books. Also publishes the magazine *Better Software.*

Newsgroups

> *comp.software.testing* and *comp.software.config-mgmt* sometimes have interesting discussions on tools for testing and SCM. Their FAQs have some tool lists but tend to feel dated, perhaps due to the general move away from newsgroups.

Tool-specific mailing lists

> One sign of a good tool is the tone of community around it. Every tool is different, but if there is a mailing list for users or developers, subscribe to it. The archives of these mailing lists can be the best place to look for bug fixes, workarounds, and ideas for customizing the tool. Some developers write weblogs that include information about the tool, or they record IM sessions for later use.

Directories

Directories are web sites organized by topic into categories. When you want to make sure that you haven't forgotten about some tool or other when considering your options, a directory of available tools is useful.

Open Directory (http://dmoz.org)

> The Open Directory Project claims to be the largest human-edited directory of the Web. Just as Yahoo! created its own categories for the Web, the Open Directory Project has created categories, but in a nonproprietary fashion. Most tools appear in some category or other here.

Google Directory (http://directory.google.com)

> The Google Directory uses the Open Directory hierarchy as the basis for its own directory. The Computers category at *http://directory.google.com/Top/Computers* is a good place to start when searching for information about development environments. The Programming and Software categories contain many links to different tools.

CM Crossroads (http://www.cmcrossroads.com)

> This is a site focused on configuration management in a broad sense, with numerous SCM-related articles, polls, forums, and job postings.

Wikipedia (http://wikipedia.org)

> The Wikipedia is a multilingual Wiki with unusually helpful, though brief, articles about everything anyone has bothered to write about, which turns out to include lots of software development tools. Since it is a Wiki, content changes faster than on most other web sites.

Epinions (http://epinions.com)

> Epinions is a shopping comparison web site, but its Programming Tools section has reviews on many software tools—at least, the ones people have paid money for. Some of these reviews are quite insightful.

Magazines

All the magazines in this section have web sites where you may be able to pick up a free trial subscription, since their income is mostly based upon advertising in the magazines:

ACM Queue (http://www.acmqueue.org)
  A collection of general programming articles each month, with a useful number of ones about tools and different development environments.

Software Development (http://www.sdmagazine.com)
  Lots of articles about different tools, and the annual Jolt awards for tools. Part of CMP's Developer Network, which includes *Dr. Dobb's Journal, BYTE.com, C/C++ Users Journal*, and *The Perl Journal*.

Better Software (http://www.stickyminds.com/BetterSoftware/magazine.asp)
  Mostly articles about general software development, but some tool-specific articles.

Java Developers Journal (http://jdj.sys-con.com)
  One of a number of language-specific magazines from Sys-Con Media; often has articles about tools for projects written in Java.

Books

The books listed in this appendix cover each of the named topics in a general sense. Books that cover just one specific tool are listed in the chapter that discusses such tools. For instance, books that are just about CVS are referred to in the section "CVS" in Chapter 4.

Automation and General Tools

Pragmatic Project Automation. Mike Clark. Pragmatic Bookshelf. 2004.
  This book describes good automation practices using CruiseControl (see "CruiseControl" in Chapter 3).

Essential Open Source Toolset: Programming with Eclipse, JUnit, CVS, Bugzilla, Ant, Tcl/Tk, and More. Andreas Zeller and Jens Krinke. Wiley. 2005.

Software Configuration Management

Open Soure Development with CVS, Third Edition. Karl Fogel and Moshe Bar. Paraglyph Press. 2003.
  Also available online at *http://cvsbook.red-bean.com/OSDevWithCVS_3E.pdf*. This book covers much more than just CVS; SCM best practices and different approaches to open source development are also discussed. The names of the authors alternate on different editions.

Pragmatic Version Control with CVS. Dave Thomas and Andy Hunt. Pragmatic Bookshelf. 2003.
  This book and the next one in this list are from the same series; they discuss using SCM tools in the context of an automated development environment.

Pragmatic Version Control with Subversion. Mike Mason. Pragmatic Bookshelf. 2005.

Software Configuration Management Patterns. Stephen P. Berczuk and Brad Appleton. Addison-Wesley. 2002.

Building Software

Managing Projects with GNU make, Third Edition. Robert Mecklenburg. O'Reilly. 2004.
As the title suggests, this book is mainly about *make*, but the third edition has useful discussions of how build tools scale, performance, portability, and debugging build files, all of which have relevance beyond *make*.

Multi-Platform Code Management. Kevin Jameson. O'Reilly. 1994.
One of the earliest books to describe a complete build environment in detail.

Testing Software

This section includes books that refer to testing environments, not just books about how to test software.

Pragmatic Unit Testing in Java with JUnit. Andy Hunt and Dave Thomas. Pragmatic Bookshelf. 2003.

Pragmatic Unit Testing in C# with NUnit. Andy Hunt and Dave Thomas. Pragmatic Bookshelf. 2004.

Test Driven Development: By Example. Kent Beck. Addison-Wesley. 2002.

Managing the Testing Process, Second Edition. Rex Black. Wiley. 2002.

Testing Computer Software, Second Edition. Cem Kaner, Jack Falk, and Hung Nguyen. Wiley. 1999.

Effective Software Testing—50 Specific Ways to Improve Your Testing. Elfriede Dustin. Addison-Wesley. 2003.

Tracking Bugs

Are there any books about what you want in a bug tracking system? I've never seen one.

Documentation Environments

Word Hacks. Andrew Savikas. O'Reilly. 2004.

LaTeX: A Document Preparation System (User's Guide and Reference Manual). Leslie Lamport. Addison-Wesley. 1986.
This book is also a good example of how to describe using a documentation tool.

Releasing Products

Ship it! A Practical Guide to Successful Software Projects. Jared Richardson and Will Gwaltney. Pragmatic Bookshelf. 2005.

Maintenance

Working Effectively with Legacy Code. Michael Feathers. Prentice Hall. 2004.

Refactoring: Improving the Design of Existing Code. Martin Fowler, Kent Beck, John Brant, William Opdyke, and Don Roberts. Addison-Wesley. 1999.

Software Exorcism: A Handbook for Debugging and Optimizing Legacy Code. Reverend Bill Blunden. APress. 2003.

Politics and People

The Mythical Man Month. Frederick P. Brooks. Addison-Wesley. 1975.
  Though it describes the way your father wrote code, most of it still rings true. Much of what is written in this book is now assumed knowledge in the software industry.

Facts and Fallacies of Software Engineering. Robert L. Glass. Addison-Wesley. 2003.
  Lots of opinions, with good justifications and rebuttals.

Great Software Debates. Alan M. Davis. Wiley. 2004.
  A series of short essays on different topics, ranging from academia to industry and back. Not really debates, but thought-provoking writing anyway.

Developing Software

Some of these books are specific to languages or methodologies, but I have found them all useful at one time or another.

The Practice of Programming. Brian Kernighan and Rob Pike. Addison-Wesley. 1999.
  The related web site is at *http://cm.bell-labs.com/cm/cs/tpop*.

The Art of Unix Programming. Eric S. Raymond. Addison-Wesley. 2003.
  Also available online at *http://www.catb.org/~esr/writings/taoup*. Contains many examples of the ideas in this book, with a Unix bias.

Mastering Regular Expressions, Second Edition. Jeffrey E. F. Friedl. O'Reilly. 2002.
  This is *the* book to build your confidence in what you can do with all of your text-based tools.

Code Complete, Second Edition. Steve McConnell. Microsoft Press. 2004.
  The second edition has a related web site at *http://cc2e.com*.

The Pragmatic Programmer: From Journeyman to Master. Andrew Hunt and David Thomas. Addison-Wesley. 1999.

Expert C Programming. Peter van der Linden. Prentice Hall. 1994.
  If only for the terrible puns, this is my favorite advanced C book.

Programming Pearls. Jon Bentley. Addison-Wesley. 1986.
  A strongly pragmatic approach to programming, with lots of references to development environments.

General Design

Much of what makes a product or tool useful is a good design. Listed below are two books that, while not directly related to software design, will encourage deeper thought about the issues behind designing things.

Notes on the Synthesis of Form. Christopher Alexander. Harvard University Press. 1964.
  The basic idea is simple: make your categories fit how you work, not the other way around. This building architect's books helped inspire the various books about software patterns.

How Buildings Learn. Stewart Brand. Penguin. 1995.

A fascinating book describing how buildings change, with lots of photographs and drawings showing the same buildings changing over time. The different aspects of a building such as internal layout and services change at different rates, just as software products change their different parts at differing rates. No answers, but plenty of ideas to consider about how to design things that can change gracefully over time.

Conferences

SDExpo (http://www.sdexpo.com)

Lots of software tool vendors. Organized by the same company that produces the magazine *Software Development.*

Emerging Tech (http://conferences.oreillynet.com/etcon)

A general technology conference, but with some good presentations on different tools and their technologies.

LinuxWorld Expo (http://www.linuxworldexpo.com)

Obviously specific to one operating system, but with lots of speakers who are experienced software developers and toolsmiths.

ICSE (http://www.icse-conferences.org)

International Conference on Software Engineering, organized by the ACM and IEEE. Mostly papers from academia, but useful for seeing what ideas other people have already investigated.

University and College Courses

Computer Science is no more about computers than astronomy is about telescopes.

—E. Dijkstra

The above epigraph may explain why no universities or colleges appear to have courses that discuss software development environments in any detail. Programming courses will usually have some documentation about their local development environment, but no discussion of why it was chosen. Some adult education courses may cover some of the tools discussed here, but usually without very much context.

If you do know of any academic courses that discuss how to create a practical software development environment, I'd be very interested to know about them. Maybe you're interested in teaching others what you know about this subject? Such a course would probably discuss SCM tools, build tools, testing tools, bug tracking systems, documentation, and releasing software. My contact details can be found at *http://www.pobox.com/~doar.*

INDEX

A

AAA (authentication, authorization, and accounting), 38
access, SCM, 54
accessibility, bug tracking, 154
accounting, 38
ACL (access control list), 42
  CVS and, 60
administration, PDEs, 18
Ant, 15, 105
  build files, 105
  Davidson, James Duncan, 106
  dependency and, 110
  Maven, 112
  parallel builds, 110
  platform dependency, 111
  properties and, 110
  slow startup, 110
  tasks, JDiff and, 109
  weaknesses, 110
  XML and, 105
    limitations, 110
Anthill, 31
APIs (application programming interfaces), 13
Appleton, Brad (SCM), 280
Arch, 16, 67
  ArX, 68
  changesets, 68
  CVS and, 58
  documentation, 68
  history of, 68
  Lord, Tom, 68
  merged files, 52
  SCM and, 67
    tools, 16
atomic operations, Subversion, 65
attachments, bug tracking and, 155
Austin, Chad (SCons), 116
authentication, 38
authorization, 38
Autoconf, 99
Automake, 100
automated releases, 213
  automated release information, 214

automation, 24
  consequences, 25
  debugging and, 25
  discipline, 269
  documentation, 193
  installation tools, 219
  output and, 25
  problems with, 25
  resources and, 25
  testing automation, reasons for, 128
automation environments, 26–32
  Anthill, 31
  batch files, 30
  CI and, 26
  CruiseControl, 32
  shell scripts, 30
  Tinderbox, 31
Autotools (see GNU Autotools)
awkward people, 265

B

backups
  CVS, 57
  PDEs, 19
  SCM, 56
    corruption detection, 56
    disaster recovery and, 56
    intrusion detection, 56
batch files
  automation environments, 30
  build tools and, 93
  testing environment, 135
  watchdog timers, 30
Berliner, Brian (CVS), 59
BerliOS, 22
binary files
  CVS, 61
  Subversion, 66
  Unix installation tools, 221
BitKeeper, 16, 70
  McVoy, Larry, 71
  Torvalds, Linus, 71
Blandy, Jim (Subversion), 65
BoostJam, 116
boundary conditions, testing and, 131

installation (*continued*)
testing, 225
third-party products, 226
tools, 218–225
automation, 219
debugging, 219
flexibility, 220
installer automation, 226
installers, 220
language, 219
media support, 220
portability, 219
requirements, 219
size, 219
stability, 220
Unix, 221–223
update installers, 220
Windows, 223–225
uninstallers, 226
InstallShield installation tool, 224
integration, 22
BPM and, 24
bug tracking and SCM tools, 175
CI, 26
email and, 23
middleware and, 24
PDEs and, 18, 22
URLs and, 23
internal project documentation, 197
internationalization (i18n), 37
interoperability tests, 127
interpreters, 78
interrupted build state, 82
intrusion detection, 56

J

Jam, 112
BoostJam, 116
build files, 105
grist, 115
header files, 116
language, 115
phases, 116
Seiwald, Christopher, 112
weaknesses, 115
Jamfiles, 105, 113
Java
CVS clients, 61
source code, import lines, 88
Javadoc, internal documentation, 197
JDiff
Ant tasks, 109
API stability and, 143
JIRA bug tracker, 15, 163

K

Kehoe, Brendan (GNATS), 160
Kernighan, Brian, 125

Kingdon, Jim (CVS), 59
Knight, Steven (SCons), 116
Knuth, Donald (TeX), 144, 192
release numbering, 205

L

L10n (localization), 37
labeling builds, 32
labels, 42
languages, installation tools and, 219
LaTeX, 192
Leblanc, Steve (SCons), 116
legal licenses, release preparation and, 208
Libtool, 100
license keys, release preparation and, 209
localization (L10n), 37
locking models, 42
logs
change logs, 42
cleanup, automation and, 25
Lord, Tom (Arch), 68

M

machines, names for, 34
MacKenzie, David (GNU Autotools), 99
maintenance, 14
cleanup, 239–242
code rot, 230
introduction, 3, 229
migration and, 232
product maintenance, 232
bug tracking, 238
build reproduction, 235
builds, 238
code, 234
company name changes, 236
copyright date changes, 236
documentation, 239
people and, 239
politics and, 239
product name changes, 235
SCM and, 237
testing and, 238
tool rot, 230
tools life span, 231
make, 15, 94
Automake, 100
cake, 95
clock, 97
cook, 95
debugging, 97
dependency analysis and, 96
documentation, 95
Feldman, Stuart, 94
gmake, 95
history of, 94
included, 96

ABOUT THE AUTHOR

MATTHEW B. DOAR began writing code as a child with his father in Yorkshire in the late 1970s, studied engineering and then computer science at the University of Cambridge, and finished up with a PhD in computer networking. He has been a professional software developer for over 10 years at a number of different companies, writing C, C++, and Java code for large projects and tools. He also wrote JDiff (*http://jdiff.org*), an open source tool for comparing the Java APIs of different versions of large projects. Matt currently works near San Jose, California, as a toolsmith by day. During the writing of this book, he changed companies, learned to play the clarinet, and accidentally delivered his own son. More technical information and contact details are available at *http://www.pobox.com/~doar*.

COLOPHON

OUR LOOK IS THE RESULT of reader comments, our own experimentation, and feedback from distribution channels. Distinctive covers complement our distinctive approach to technical topics, breathing personality and life into potentially dry subjects.

Abby Fox was the production editor and copyeditor for *Practical Development Environments*. Matt Hutchinson proofread the book. Sanders Kleinfeld and Claire Cloutier provided quality control. Johnna VanHoose Dinse wrote the index.

MendeDesign designed and created the cover artwork of this book. Karen Montgomery produced the cover layout with Adobe InDesign CS using the Akzidenz Grotesk and Orator fonts.

The animals on the cover of *Practical Development Environments* are goldfish (*Carassius auratus*). Goldfish can in fact be gold, orange, white, black, blue, brown, silver, bronze, and red. Moderately hardy, goldfish have an average life span of around 10 years. The oldest goldfish on record lived for over 43 years.

The early history of the cultivation of goldfish is unclear, but it is generally accepted that by the time of the Sung dynasty (960–1280), goldfish were being bred in China. However, it was not until around 1500 that goldfish first appeared in Japan, and they did not find their way into Europe until the seventeenth century.

Marcia Friedman designed the interior layout. Melanie Wang and Phyllis McKee designed the interior template. This book was converted by Keith Fahlgren to FrameMaker 5.5.6 with a format conversion tool created by Erik Ray, Jason McIntosh, Neil Walls, and Mike Sierra that uses Perl and XML technologies. The text font is Adobe's Meridien; the heading font is ITC Bailey; and the code font is LucasFont's TheSans Mono Condensed. The illustrations that appear in the book were produced by Robert Romano, Jessamyn Read, and Lesley Borash using Macromedia FreeHand MX and Adobe Photoshop CS.

The ichthyographic portion of this colophon was written by the book's author. The word *colophon* is derived from the Greek *kolophōn*, meaning "summit" or "finishing touch."

Better than e-books

Buy *Practical Development Environments* and access
the digital edition FREE on Safari for 45 days.

Go to www.oreilly.com/go/safarienabled
and type in coupon code CIIF-GSKH-UI66-ZYH6-PGJL

Search
thousands of
top tech books

Download
whole chapters

Cut and Paste
code examples

Find
answers fast

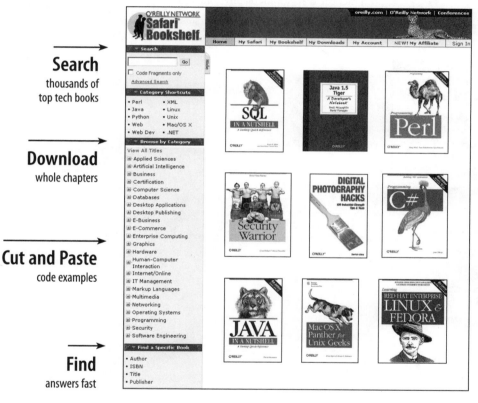

Search Safari! The premier electronic reference
library for programmers and IT professionals.

Related Titles from O'Reilly

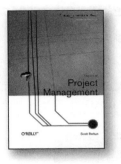

Software Development

The Art of Project Management

Head First Design Patterns

Head First Design Patterns Poster

Essential Business Process Modeling

Essential Service Bus

Practical Development Environments

Prefactoring

UML 2.0 in a Nutshell

O'REILLY®

Our books are available at most retail and online bookstores.

To order direct: 1-800-998-9938 • *order@oreilly.com* • *www.oreilly.com*

Online editions of most O'Reilly titles are available by subscription at *safari.oreilly.com*

Keep in touch with O'Reilly

Download examples from our books

To find example files from a book, go to: *www.oreilly.com/catalog* select the book, and follow the "Examples" link.

Register your O'Reilly books

Register your book at *register.oreilly.com* Why register your books? Once you've registered your O'Reilly books you can:

- Win O'Reilly books, T-shirts or discount coupons in our monthly drawing.
- Get special offers available only to registered O'Reilly customers.
- Get catalogs announcing new books (US and UK only).
- Get email notification of new editions of the O'Reilly books you own.

Join our email lists

Sign up to get topic-specific email announcements of new books and conferences, special offers, and O'Reilly Network technology newsletters at:

elists.oreilly.com

It's easy to customize your free elists subscription so you'll get exactly the O'Reilly news you want.

Get the latest news, tips, and tools

www.oreilly.com

- "Top 100 Sites on the Web"—PC Magazine
- CIO Magazine's Web Business 50 Awards

Our web site contains a library of comprehensive product information (including book excerpts and tables of contents), downloadable software, background articles, interviews with technology leaders, links to relevant sites, book cover art, and more.

Work for O'Reilly

Check out our web site for current employment opportunities:

jobs.oreilly.com

Contact us

O'Reilly Media, Inc.
1005 Gravenstein Hwy North
Sebastopol, CA 95472 USA
Tel: 707-827-7000 or 800-998-9938
 (6am to 5pm PST)
Fax: 707-829-0104

Contact us by email

For answers to problems regarding your order or our products:
order@oreilly.com

To request a copy of our latest catalog:
catalog@oreilly.com

For book content technical questions or corrections: **booktech@oreilly.com**

For educational, library, government, and corporate sales: **corporate@oreilly.com**

To submit new book proposals to our editors and product managers:
proposals@oreilly.com

For information about our international distributors or translation queries:
international@oreilly.com

For information about academic use of O'Reilly books:
adoption@oreilly.com
or visit:
academic.oreilly.com

For a list of our distributors outside of North America check out:
international.oreilly.com/distributors.html

Order a book online

www.oreilly.com/order_new

 **O'REILLY®**

Our books are available at most retail and online bookstores.
To order direct: 1-800-998-9938 • *order@oreilly.com* • *www.oreilly.com*
Online editions of most O'Reilly titles are available by subscription at *safari.oreilly.com*